Soul Barnacles

POETS ON POETRY

David Lehman, General Editor
Donald Hall, Founding Editor

New titles

Tess Gallagher, *Soul Barnacles*
Rachel Hadas, *Merrill, Cavafy, Poems, and Dreams*
Larry Levis, *The Gazer Within*
Ron Padgett, *The Straight Line*
Charles Simic, *A Fly in the Soup*

Recently published

Edward Hirsch, *Responsive Reading*
John Koethe, *Poetry at One Remove*
Yusef Komunyakaa, *Blue Notes*
Philip Larkin, *Required Writing*
Alicia Suskin Ostriker, *Dancing at the Devil's Party*
James Tate, *The Route as Briefed*

Also available are collections by

A. R. Ammons, Robert Bly, Philip Booth, Marianne Boruch,
Hayden Carruth, Fred Chappell, Amy Clampitt, Tom Clark,
Douglas Crase, Robert Creeley, Donald Davie, Peter Davison,
Tess Gallagher, Suzanne Gardinier, Allen Grossman, Thom Gunn,
John Haines, Donald Hall, Joy Harjo, Robert Hayden,
Daniel Hoffman, Jonathan Holden, John Hollander,
Andrew Hudgins, Josephine Jacobsen, Weldon Kees,
Galway Kinnell, Mary Kinzie, Kenneth Koch, Richard Kostelanetz,
Maxine Kumin, Martin Lammon (editor), David Lehman,
Philip Levine, John Logan, William Logan, William Matthews,
William Meredith, Jane Miller, Carol Muske, John Frederick Nims,
Geoffrey O'Brien, Gregory Orr, Marge Piercy, Anne Sexton,
Charles Simic, Louis Simpson, William Stafford, Anne Stevenson,
May Swenson, Richard Tillinghast, Diane Wakoski, C. K. Williams,
Alan Williamson, Charles Wright, and James Wright

Tess Gallagher

Soul Barnacles

TEN MORE YEARS
WITH RAY

Edited by
Greg Simon

Ann Arbor

THE UNIVERSITY OF MICHIGAN PRESS

Copyright © by Tess Gallagher 2000
All rights reserved
Published in the United States of America by
The University of Michigan Press
Manufactured in the United States of America
⊚ Printed on acid-free paper
2003 2002 2001 2000   4 3 2 1

A CIP catalog record for this book is available from the British Library.

Library of Congress Cataloging-in-Publication Data

Gallagher, Tess.
    Soul barnacles : ten more years with Ray /Tess Gallagher;
edited by Greg Simon.
        p.   cm.
    ISBN 0-472-11105-1 (cloth : alk. paper)
    1. Gallagher, Tess—Marriage.   2. Authors, American—
20th century—Biography.   3. Married people—United
States—Biography.   4. Carver, Raymond—Marriage.
I. Simon, Greg.   II. Title.
PS3557 .A41156 Z47   2000
811′.54—dc21
[B]   00-47942

"That's not who we are to each other," I said, as he tried to explain who I was to him now, in terms of earlier. We were walking to the Deux Magots to meet Maya. Then the expression I was searching for came: "We're soul barnacles," I said, and we looked at each other as we walked, and he laughed a laugh which had a little island of *uh-huh* in its middle.

In the high violet light of that summer evening, it seemed I was covered with soul barnacles—anchored to the ones I loved by what we'd written and said, bound to each other, invisibly and forever.

—T.G.

Contents

Preface

Because we have chosen them,
those who have no reason to be braided
in moonlight
are bound together.

—T.G.

It was a relationship that could not have begun under more inauspicious circumstances. Between them, as Tess Gallagher recalls in her eulogy from *Granta*, she and Raymond Carver had "left behind something like thirty years of failed marriage." The late hours of their first night out together were spent in a Texas emergency room among doctors and nurses who suspected that her ripped pierced earlobe was not an accident. (It was.) And she mentions the wicked gleam in the eyes of her twice-bankrupt peer the first time she took out her Visa card.

But luck, as the rest of their story soon demonstrates, is less a matter of chance than instinct. Holding fast to Raymond Carver—one of his friends once described him as "the most unhappy man I'd ever met"—was something of a gamble. When she's gambling, Gallagher relies on her instinct: "Finally the number twenty-four occurs to me with such freshness and surety," she writes about a successful night in a Wiesbaden casino, "that I feel I *must* bet on it. Dostoevsky is with me!" This fearless single woman, at thirty-four, had more resources when they met—in modern literature, family and friends, and in the Pacific Northwest—than Carver had ever dreamed. With her usual forbearance, she slowly but surely helped him "build and rebuild on [his] capacity for joy."

Soul Barnacles is an attempt to make a record of that capacity for joy that Tess Gallagher shared with Raymond Carver, which she also refers to as "that cushion of hope we count on to extend life past the provisional." Although the individual pieces of writing are posthumous to Carver, Gallagher moves with breathtaking ease between the past and the present. She tackles each new project with the same relentless honesty that she poured into *Moon Crossing Bridge,* the book of poems, posthumous to the *them* of her relationship, in which she silvered and sealed in grief the terms of their endearment. Familiarity with *Moon Crossing Bridge* will lend resonance to the prose in *Soul Barnacles,* but nothing forecasts or will ever supersede its tender intimacies, the sense of loss it engenders, and her tremendous will to shape some kind of future from that. "No-choice-but-to-go-ahead," Gallagher says, and at that point the timeless depth of her twinning with Carver begins to emerge as she struggles to define and resolve his absence to the world and in her own world.

The calm she was achieving, the resolution she was shoring up while coping with Carver's absence was quickly put to the test when Hollywood came calling. In order to bring to the screen, as she later put it, "the sense of strangeness and compulsiveness inherent in human behavior" that permeates Carver's work, a director had to come forward who wasn't afraid to tackle Carver's other dominant theme, dislocation. On the rebound from misadventure on a film project in Italy, Robert Altman devoured Carver's stories on the flight home to America and moved thereafter to have them scripted as the basis for one of his next films. When *Short Cuts* came out, the film was lauded for its unyielding eye on American life, but also attacked for being unfaithful to the literature that had inspired it. Although Gallagher admitted that she "missed a certain *interiority* of the characters," her admiration for the film's artistry also led her to quickly point out to detractors that Altman's aim, indeed that of most directors, is necessarily more societal than literary. The two letters she wrote privately in March and November 1993, one to Altman after she had seen the finished film, and the other to Robert Coles after his review of the film had appeared in the *New York Times,* are wonderful examples of the power of sustained thought, eloquence, and devotion, all of it enhancing a wished-for rapprochement.

Each of Carver's major book projects that Gallagher saw through since his untimely death from cancer in the summer of 1988—his last book of poems, his *Collected Poems,* a collection of unpublished prose including five newly discovered stories, various editions of his short fiction in translation, books of tribute to him, and the Altman-Barhydt filmscript—drew from her a serious, evolving restatement of their separate and mutual presences. Although poetry had spiritually sustained her prior to Carver's death, it is prose that ultimately served her, as it now can serve us, as an act of centering or grounding. It is prose that leaves us enriched by her fortitude and openness to loss and remaking.

As Gallagher resumed the reading of her poetry in public, she also found, I think, that trying to enter and reenter the sudden loss of a man of words required additional words, a torrent of words that at times surprised and confounded her. Although considerations of space did not permit including all of them here, there is an incredible array of Gallagher interviews that circle and swoop around her life with and without Carver. To the best of my knowledge, no American writer now living has ever been interviewed as often and as intensely as Gallagher was in the years immediately after Carver's death. She became an absolute master of this difficult terrain, learning to subtly push or pull questions (and questioners) into more profitable areas of discussion, and to deftly manage a bloodless parry to the thoughtless intrusiveness that sometimes accompanies this form. Because they are both hand and heart driven, Gallagher's interviews reveal the breadth of her daily interests and concerns (painting, gardening, family, music, film, theater, and travel), but also her willful bonding with truthfulness and revelation in a world that is often chaotic, sorrowful.

Gallagher has at times mentioned the fact that she would often read Carver's poems and stories in draft, and in the intensity of her reading and with his encouragement, would *finish* the new writing by adding or cutting passages or phrases. To anyone not familiar with Gallagher's ferocious manner of reading work in progress—*anything within reach,* when she is in the mood for it—this might seem presumptuous. But on the few occasions when she has applied herself to my work, the lines that came to Tess were so astonishingly good—enlarging poems or adding depth charges to prose—that I had a difficult time believing she would give them to me. (She did.)

It was a significant editorial task to cut this explosion of words down to manageable size. In the face of an embarrassment of riches, it seemed wise to choose the best single way she described many of the things she was driven to consider more than once. Tess and I *winnowed,* a beautiful Old English word that I allow myself to think Tess and Ray might have spent some breakfast time mulling over in the cooperative, resonant way they would have sifted such a bountiful manuscript themselves, had his health not cut short the life they shared.

The writing in this book—introduction, essay, interview, letter, or journal—is that rare kind of record that tracks the existence of equals, written by one of those equals. Now that I have read all of it, I feel I understand and appreciate at least some of the pleasure Raymond Carver took in his daily life with Tess Gallagher, those times he saw close up what his work inspired in her, how it climbed so quickly and fully into another's poetic mind and expanded there into something that amazed and lifted them both. I am also grateful in ways I cannot fully express for the opportunity to companion them, at Tess's invitation, in the creation of this book.

Greg Simon
Portland, Oregon

Two Darings

William L. Stull and Maureen P. Carroll

*They do not apprehend how being at variance it
agrees with itself: there is a connection working in
both directions, as in the bow and the lyre.*
—Heraclitus, Fragment 45

Well before his death at age fifty in August 1988, Raymond
Carver spoke of having lived two lives. As Carver saw it, his first
life had all but ended before his fortieth birthday. After a child-
hood on the poverty line, a too-early marriage, and ten years of
"crap jobs" and "ferocious" parenting, in his thirties he had
taken to the bottle with a vengeance. "I was completely out of
control and in a very grave place," he told an interviewer in
1983. Between October 1976 and January 1977 Carver under-
went four hospitalizations for acute alcoholism. "I was dying
from it, plain and simple, and I'm not exaggerating."

Miraculously, on June 2, 1977, estranged from his dysfunc-
tional family and making a last-ditch effort at sobriety, Carver
vowed never again to take a drink. "I'm prouder of that, that
I've stopped drinking," he said later, "than I am of anything in
my life." For the eleven years remaining to him he counted
June 2 his second birthday, "the line of demarcation" separat-
ing his new life from his old. "There were good times back
there, of course," he allowed. "But I'd take poison before I'd
go through that time again." Moreover, less than six months
after this turning point Carver met Tess Gallagher, the poet,
short-story writer, and essayist who was to be his collaborator
and companion for the next ten years. They began living

Published in *Philosophy and Literature* 2, no. 22 (1998). Reprinted by
permission of William Stull and Maureen Carroll.

together on New Year's Day 1979, and what followed is literary history. Carver, who had all but consigned himself to the grave, lived to write the books that made him the most respected and influential short-story writer of his generation. As his former student Jay McInerney observes, "Look at all the short-story writers younger than Ray, and there's hardly one that, you might say, didn't come out of Carver's overcoat."

Even after learning of the cancer that would cut short his second life, Carver counted his remaining days a gift, a miracle, and a blessing. "My life was a mess domestically, my health was a shambles," he told Gail Caldwell a few weeks before his death; "this, in a way, is like a picnic, compared to that." From beyond the grave he expressed his astonishment and gratitude in a posthumously published poem aptly titled "Gravy":

> Gravy, these past ten years.
> Alive, sober, working, loving and
> being loved by a good woman.

"Don't weep for me," he urged his friends. "I've had ten years longer than I or anyone / expected. Pure gravy. And don't forget it."

It is sobering indeed to think how little we would have of Raymond Carver's work had he not lived his gravy years. Before he stopped drinking, Carver had published only one book with a major press. This was *Will You Please Be Quiet, Please?* (1976), a collection of twenty-two stories eked out over fifteen years. The book received a National Book Award nomination in 1977, but at a time when the short story still languished in the shadow of the novel, the collection marked at most an auspicious debut. To date, most of Carver's work had appeared in the small-circulation "little" magazines his early mentor John Gardner had championed as "where the best fiction in the country and just about all of the poetry was appearing." Carver had also published three slim books of poetry with small presses: *Near Klamath* (1968), *Winter Insomnia* (1970), and *At Night the Salmon Move* (1976). In November 1977, the same month he met Gallagher, a second volume of fiction from his first life appeared. Published by Noel Young's small but respected Capra Press, *Furious Seasons* contained only eight stories. The book had a print run of one hundred hardbacks and twelve hundred paperbacks, making it more a collector's item than a public confirmation of Carver's early promise.

What do we have today of Raymond Carver's work in addition to these bright but scattered gleanings? Thanks to his stable and productive second life, the harvest is substantial. Most prominently there are three landmark books of short fiction, each of which received a glowing front-page notice in the *New York Times Book Review: What We Talk about When We Talk about Love* (1981), *Cathedral* (1983), and *Where I'm Calling From: New and Selected Stories* (1988). There are also half a dozen small-press books, the most notable of which was quickly given national distribution: *Fires: Essays, Poems, Stories* (1983). Add to these something unimaginable to John Gardner, four major-press books of poetry (the last sadly posthumous): *Where Water Comes Together with Other Water* (1985), *Ultramarine* (1986), *In a Marine Light: Selected Poems* (1987), and *A New Path to the Waterfall* (1989). There is as well *Dostoevsky: A Screenplay* (1985), coauthored with Tess Gallagher, and a string of influential anthologies: *The Best American Short Stories 1986, American Short Story Masterpieces* (1987), and *American Fiction 88.*

What's more, the tragedy of Carver's early death has, if anything, hastened the translation of his writings into more than twenty languages and the publication of works uncollected in his lifetime. Among these works, many of them introduced by Tess Gallagher, are *Carver Country: The World of Raymond Carver* (1990, with photographs by Bob Adelman), *Conversations with Raymond Carver* (1990), *No Heroics, Please: Uncollected Writings* (1991), *Carnations: A Play in One Act* (1992), *Short Cuts: Selected Stories* (1993, issued in tandem with the film by Robert Altman), *All of Us: The Collected Poems* (1996), and *Call If You Need Me: The Uncollected Fiction and Prose* (2000).

Having once come back from the dead, Raymond Carver would surely be delighted by his afterlife in art. "Beats all I saw or heard of, this life," he crowed to his publisher, the distinguished editor Gary Fisketjon, in the early 1980s. Modest as he was, Carver knew his finest work was built to last.

"We're out there in history now, Babe," he told Tess Gallagher in his final days, and even in the hospital he quipped, "Well, I'm on to the next new life."

Clearly, in terms of prolificacy, range, and resonance, the Raymond Carver we celebrate today is the Carver of the gravy years. During those years Carver's voice and vision steadily expanded. The process of enlargement is best evidenced by a comparison of his so-called "minimalist" masterpiece, *What We Talk about When We Talk about Love* (1981), with its "more generous" successor, *Cathedral* (1983). What crystallized the change for Carver was the title story of the latter book:

> When I wrote "Cathedral" I experienced this rush and I felt, "This is what it's all about, this is the reason we do this." It was different than the stories that had come before. There was an opening up when I wrote the story. I knew I'd gone as far the other way as I could or wanted to go, cutting everything down to the marrow, not just to the bone. Any farther in that direction and I'd be at a dead end—writing stuff and publishing stuff I wouldn't want to read myself, and that's the truth.

Reviewers acknowledged Carver's increasing amplitude, as did the American Academy and Institute of Arts and Letters. In 1983 the academy awarded him one of its first Strauss "Livings," a fellowship bringing him five years' support for full-time writing.

In a happy irony, the award took Carver, both the writer and the man, far afield. In 1984 he left the East Coast for the Pacific Northwest, and for the next year he forsook fiction for poetry. This about-face surprised his agent and his audience— and no one more than Raymond Carver. "I've never had a period in which I've taken so much joy in the act of writing," he later said. "I felt *on fire.*" Almost as abruptly, Carver returned to fiction in 1985, and over the next two years he wrote the seven new stories that are collected in *Where I'm Calling From* (1988). His work of this period is generally longer, looser, and more openly reflective than his previous fiction. The capstone of the series is "Errand," a retelling of the dying days of Carver's literary inspiration and "companion-soul," Anton Chekhov. In a *tour de force* of fact and fiction unlike anything else in Carver's work or anyone else's, the writer dissolves the barriers dividing life and art in order to transcend a devastating loss.

Not long after the appearance of this groundbreaking story Carver received word of the lung cancer that was to claim his life within a year. Yet even as his health declined, he continued writing work that blurred the boundaries of mode and genre. Completed in the last weeks of his life, Carver's final book, *A New Path to the Waterfall* (1989), fuses poetry and prose, original composition and allusive quotation, into a life-affirming dialogue between the living and the dead.

What was the wellspring of the waterfall of confidence and creativity that flowed through Raymond Carver's second life? In dedications, essays, and interviews, and above all in his poetry, Carver left no doubts. It was his intimate partnership with Tess Gallagher, their overlapping lives as lovers, as comrades, and—most important—as writers. "I can't imagine living with somebody who's not a writer," Carver said in 1988. "You share a set of common goals and assumptions, you understand each writer's need for privacy and solitude." For these reasons, although he and Gallagher spent most of their time together, they maintained two houses. This unique working/living arrangement made for what Gallagher calls "luminous reciprocity," a mixture of independence and interdependence that enlarged each other's work. "Our lives were just on fire with activity and there was no time to be wasted," she recalled in 1989. "We were making choices long ago as if we were in a terminal situation."

Terminal situations were well familiar to both Raymond Carver and Tess Gallagher. Like Carver, Gallagher is the oldest child of working-class parents who migrated from the middle South to the Pacific Northwest in the wake of the Great Depression. Both Carver and Gallagher grew up in homes disrupted by alcoholic fathers, and both knew firsthand what Gallagher calls "the tyranny of family." Before they met, each had experienced the collapse of a marriage—in Gallagher's case two marriages. Romantics by temperament, they had both become realists. Geographically, culturally, and economically, Gallagher and Carver come from the same place. Indeed, it is fair to say that the physical and mental state known as "Carver Country" is equally Gallagher Country. The two writers share an abiding subject—the vicissitudes of working-class family life—and the foundation of a style: Chekhovian attention to detail.

By 1979, when Gallagher and Carver began living together, she had already earned her literary spurs. She had published two books of poetry with Graywolf, a prestigious small press: *Instructions to the Double* (1976) and *Under Stars* (1978). Using a phrase that applies with equal force to Carver, the critic Harold Schweizer writes of Gallagher, "She is the acute observer of the large in ordinary occasions." When Schweizer turns to Gallagher's sensibility, however, he reveals a wider tonal range than can be found in Carver's early writings. "Her work is a combination of metaphysical wit and lyric grief, ranging from the profane to the metaphysical, from cabbage to the dreams of the dead." If metaphysical wit and lyric grief increasingly figure in Raymond Carver's work of the 1980s, one need not look far for their source.

Where Carver and Gallagher strikingly differed when they met was in self-confidence. "When we first got together back in 1978, she was writing and I wasn't writing," he said. "I was in the process of recovering my life." Having published nearly all the work of his alcoholic years, Carver faced a blank. "And in this new life, it wasn't all that important if I never wrote again," he added. "But Tess was writing, and that was a good example for me." The list of Carver's publications over the next ten years reveals how well he followed Gallagher's example. First, surveying the emotional wreckage of his first life with a newly sober eye, Carver wrote the seventeen spare but unsparing stories that became *What We Talk about When We Talk about Love* (1981). Next, having cut his writing to the quick, he restored and expanded it in the twelve new stories in *Cathedral* (1983). "There is more of a fullness as a result of Tess's good eye and encouragement," he said in 1986, comparing the work of his two lives. "Not only the internal circumstances of my life changed but the external circumstances changed as well. I suppose I became more hopeful, somewhat more positive in my thinking." As the books that follow *Cathedral* amply demonstrate, Carver's personal and artistic upswing continued through his gravy years.

Clearly, by the early 1980s Tess Gallagher had replaced the

literary mentors of Carver's first life, John Gardner and Gordon Lish. "I show her everything I write except letters, and I've shown her a few of those," Carver said in 1983, adding, "She has a wonderful eye and a way of feeling herself into what I write." His typist, Dorothy Catlett, recalls a telling development of this period, one his manuscripts confirm. "As the revision process continued, a different hard-to-read handwriting would be threaded into the typing along with Ray's. That handwriting, I was to learn, belonged to Tess. Ray explained to me that he and Tess were each other's best critic." Supportive as she was, Gallagher did not hesitate to challenge Carver. She insisted he take his writing "all the way to Coleman's," the Irish-American pub in Syracuse, New York, that became their shorthand for a work's true destination. Rough drafts in hand, the two writers sat down on the couch in the room they called the library. "First I'd tell him all the happy, glad news," Gallagher recalls, "then I'd get down into the mean business." Carver never flinched. "She cuts me no slack at all," he said, "and that's the best way."

Constructive criticism flowed in both directions, especially once Gallagher began writing the stories that comprise her first book of short fiction, *The Lover of Horses* (1986). "He'd go over my stories very closely," she recalls. "I have the drafts of these among my papers." Comparing their approaches, she says, "He was better at cutting things out and at generalizing." Carver's influence extended to her poetry as well. Looking back at the poems in *Willingly* (1984) and *Amplitude* (1987), Gallagher says, "I think with Ray I got more and more narrative and linear, while trying to marry that to lyrical bursts inside the narrative." Much the same can be said of Carver's late stories and the genre-bending work he and Gallagher assembled into *A New Path to the Waterfall* (1989). "It was a wondeful gift, that sharing," Gallagher concludes, "a kind of extraordinary collaboration of hearts and imaginations."

This introduction is not the place for a full-scale study of his intertextual dialogue with Tess Gallagher. Such a study is overdue, however, and a single example will suggest its directions. Few would dispute that the quintessential Raymond Carver story is "Cathedral," Carver's humorous and moving tale of a blind guest who helps his spiritually blinkered host

The mortician took the vase of roses. Only once while the young man had been speaking did he betray the least flicker of interest, or indicate that he'd heard anything out of the ordinary. But the one time the young man mentioned the name of the deceased, the mortician's eyebrows had raised just a little. Chekhov, you say? Just a minute, and I'll be with you.

Do you understand what I'm saying? Olga said to the young man. Leave the glasses. Don't worry about them. Forget about crystal wine glasses and such as that. Leave the room as it is. Everything is ready now. We're ready. Will you go?

But, *at that moment,* the young man was thinking of the cork that still rested near the toe of his shoe. He could feel his knees bending, felt himself lean down, still gripping the vase, to retrieve *it.*

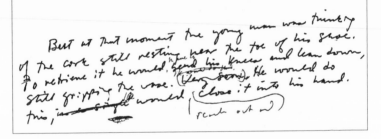

But at that moment the young man was thinking of the cork still resting near the toe of his shoe. To retrieve it he would bend his knees and lean down, still gripping the vase. (He would) (close it into his hand.) (reach out and) this,

A draft page from "Errand," Raymond Carver's last story, with hand notations by both Carver and Tess Gallagher. Most of the handwriting here is Gallagher's suggestion of the ending action of the waiter to which Carver adds the words "reach out and." The hand additions in the typescript are Carver's. Copyright © Tess Gallagher.

expand his vision of himself, his home, and his community. "Cathedral" is the title story of Carver's best-known book, a much-reprinted anthology piece, and the story that, in his words, marked the "opening up" of his work. It is also one of the richest examples of his creative collaboration with Tess Gallagher.

The extratextual roots of "Cathedral," the raw materials of

the story, lie not in Carver's background but in Gallagher's. As she explains, " 'Cathedral' was based on a blind friend of mine from Seattle. This man and I worked for the police department designing a fingerprint retrieval system." Gallagher drew fingerprints on a special tablet, and her colleague, Jerry Carriveau, ran his sensitive fingers over the outlines, classifying their features. A visit by Carriveau to the Carver-Gallagher household in Syracuse in 1981 was the catalyst for both writers to draft versions of the story. Ironically, much of the initial writing took place on what was to have been a pleasure trip to New York City: "Instead of going out on the town," Gallagher writes, "we both fell with a vengeance to our work and didn't venture out except in the evenings."

Carver's version became "Cathedral," but it was only with Gallagher's prodding that it made it all the way to Coleman's. As was often the case, she helped him with the ending:

> When Ray showed me the last draft I suggested that his character close his eyes. So Ray wrote, "My eyes were still closed. I was in my house. I knew that." I think, by closing *my* eyes on that line, I got the feeling of being inside of something also. And then this is the line that came out of what I hand-drafted there: "But I didn't feel like I was inside anything." That recognition just took the top off the whole story. I could feel it physically, as if the roof had lifted off that imaginary house. I had the same sensation as when I've finished a poem and I've written exactly the right line. Then Ray added this: " 'It's really something,' I said." It's a perfect last moment, so offhanded and emotionally undercut and true.

Gallagher's counterversion of the story was initially titled "The Harvest." This sassy, saucy metafiction was published in the *Ontario Review* in 1983, and its pyrotechnics will dazzle anyone familiar with "Cathedral." Of the two versions she now says, "My story became its own story, but it was also in dialogue with his. Literature isn't a closed circuit. It's a universe full of intersecting dialogues." Recently, continuing her dialogue with Carver, Gallagher revised and expanded "The Harvest" under the title "Rain Flooding Your Campfire." This version appeared in the *Sycamore Review,* and it is collected in her second book of stories, *At the Owl Woman Saloon* (1997).

Raymond Carver more than once wrote poems and stories that alternately approach a single situation. Examples of this include the story "Why Don't You Dance?" and the poem "Distress Sale"; the story "Blackbird Pie" and the poem "Late Night with Fog and Horses." Carver did not do any genre doubling with "Cathedral," but Gallagher did. Her poem "Reading Aloud" in *Willingly* (1984) casts a lyrical sidelight on the story as it reenters that time she spent writing to Jerry Carriveau, learning to think blind:

> Long days I read aloud to your friend
> the words that are the fountain sounds of the mind
> causing light to fall inside itself over
> the missing shapes of the world. "What do you think
> when I say 'wings'?" I asked once. "Angels,
> birds," he said, and I saw he could fly
> with either. Once, about diamonds,
> "Their light—a hiss in the rain
> when the cars pass."

As further evidenced by "The Hands of the Blindman" in *Amplitude* (1987), blindness and sight, Carver's focal symbols in "Cathedral," prove to be leitmotifs in Gallagher's work.

Literature and love were the forces that drew Raymond Carver and Tess Gallagher together more than twenty years ago. These forces bind them still in Carver's posthumously published works with introductions by Gallagher, including most recently his collected poems, *All of Us* (American edition, Knopf, 1998). Literature and love link them too in Gallagher's prolific writings since Carver's death, most wrenchingly in her poems of mourning, *Moon Crossing Bridge* (1992), but also in the life-affirming sensuality of *Portable Kisses* (expanded edition, 1994) and the pointed reflections of *My Black Horse* (1995). Fresh evidence of their creative collaboration can be found in *Can I Get You Anything?* and *The Favor,* two one-act plays Carver and Gallagher coauthored in 1983. Still more is available in this volume.

"Couples are wholes and not wholes," says Heraclitus. This paradox is richly resolved in the dialogue between Raymond Carver and Tess Gallagher. The dynamism of their partnership is best captured by a single image beloved of both writers. The title of one of Raymond Carver's last poems in *A New Path to the Waterfall* is "Hummingbird," and its subtitle is "*for Tess*":

> Suppose I say *summer,*
> write the word "hummingbird,"
> put it in an envelope,
> take it down the hill
> to the box. When you open
> my letter you will recall
> those days and how much,
> just how much, I love you.

In a recent letter reflecting on her life and work with Raymond Carver, Tess Gallagher writes:

> This morning an image came to me—that it was like the overlapping hum of two hummingbirds when we worked. You couldn't tell where one began and the other ended. Only afterwards, stepping away, can things be said about the contribution of each and, as you'll understand from my image of hummingbirds, such speaking is a kind of violation of the process and result.

It may at first seem paradoxical for two poets to choose as their emblem a bird known not for its song but for its audacity. This paradox is resolved in Tess Gallagher's poem "Bonfire," which is subtitled "*for Ray*":

> It wasn't for music
>   you came to me, but
>   for daring—mine
> and yours.
>
> When they have to, they will write in the Book
>   of Welcome:
>   *Two darings, two darlings.*

Part 1

Excursions

April 22 — Visited Joyce's grave. It must be
the 3rd time we've done so. Again I left a
daffodil in his open book. There are no flowers
blooming there near the statue of Joyce cross-
legged, wearing his monacle and staring wryly
out. But there was a fan-shaped bush which
was beginning to bud. We remarked to each other
that his daughter was still living in the sanitarium
for the insane. A light rain was falling.
    We began to walk down other rows of graves
to admire and read other grave stones.
"My Time Stays in your hands": a sundial on
the stone. Also a pillar of birds. An
owl with moss on it's back. Some very Japanese
like (Nagochi) shapes, simple and beautiful as a
full ~~pitcher~~ pitcher. Ray admires two
ducks welded together in flight.

The owl
with moss
on its back

I buy flower seeds + bulbs for mom in a
shop downtown. We get lost in the rain +
a very kind woman understands my German
+ offers to drive us back near the hotel.
Harold and Lynne come at
        8 p.m. to take us to the

A page from a journal with a drawing of a gravestone owl in Flutern Cemetery near James Joyce's grave. Photo copyright © Tess Gallagher.

European Journal,
April 5–June 26, 1987

Paris, April 5

Loss of raincoat now seems loss of armor—compounded now by the loss of the expensive watch Ray gave me. Lost or stolen? I didn't hear it fall. We had been walking much of the day, so impossible to retrace our steps.

Incident at Café Bonaparte where a couple in sunny chairs gets up to allow us to take their places and a man sitting in shadow leaps into the seats before we can sit down. He has no compunctions at all about this. We sit in shadow then. A man next to us helps Ray order a carafe of water.

Our hotel is small but comfortable. There's a place for Ray to smoke, so we need only one room. The area of Paris where we've located is on the Left Bank. Many bookstores nearby.

Published in *Antaeus* 61 (autumn 1988). Copyright © Tess Gallagher.

Note: I kept two ledger-style journals during travels that Ray and I made to Europe in 1987. We took two separate trips that year so as to rest in between and to attend to mail at home. At the time I began these journals, I had been contemplating the idea of beginning to write a novel, but decided to go to Europe with Ray in order to enjoy that time with him, and to help promote his books abroad. I proposed to keep a journal in which I recorded the names of those we met and what we did, something Ray might have called a "rough record." The form the journals took was rather scrapbooklike since I taped in theater programs, news clippings, postcards, and Polaroid photos I took. I also occasionally sketched, within the handwritten text, things I couldn't describe.

Ray goes into one to see if they have his book. They don't. At the Café Bonaparte I say: "Well it doesn't look like you're going to be mobbed here." Ray: "Well, it's only Sunday."

Loss of watch puts me outside time. A very odd sensation to be in while in a strange place—my watch which had been such a good companion all this while. Why *now* to lose it? I tell Ray it seems as if my poem in which I wish to travel light as Gandhi has been answered! Each day I lose some treasure. He laughs and says maybe I should stay in tomorrow as he doesn't want to lose *me!*

Back at the hotel, ads on French TV very seductive—even how coffee is stirred. There really is another idea of the sexual—it contains the sensual here as it does not in America.

Journal number 1 begins on March 26, 1987, and covers travel from Seattle to Syracuse to New York City to Paris to Saint Quentin, France, to Wiesbaden, Germany, to Zürich, and ends with our getting on a plane for Rome. It was written in a pastel, clothbound ledger with unlined pages, in black ink—a ledger that I had already begun as a poetry-drafting notebook.

Journal number 2 is black with red spine and corner tips. It continues the trip begun in journal number 1 and resumes on April 23, 1987, in Rome and covers travel to Milan, Zürich, and home to Port Angeles. The journal also accompanies us on a second trip: Seattle to London; then Ray goes to Scotland with Christopher MacLehose and Richard Ford; meanwhile I go to Dublin and on to Belfast alone. We each return to London where we live in a flat for a month, rented from Leslie Bonham Carter. During this time we meet Salman Rushdie and Marianne Wiggins. Ray had met Marianne that winter in Australia on a reading tour on which he also met Doris Lessing, who gives a garden party for us during our London stay. We met Drago Štambek, a Croatian medical doctor and poet, at the party. Next we travel to Paris from London with Richard and Kristina Ford, Jonathan Raban and Ray's Collins-Harvill editor, Christopher MacLahose.

In Paris we meet Ray's publisher, Olivier Cohen, and Ray's French translator, François Lasquin. We travel with François to Saint Quentin and a festival where Ray is honored as one of the leading practitioners of the short story in the world.

In 1988 the journals were originally edited by Ray, and then by Daniel Halpern for publication in *Antaeus 61*. I have substantially enlarged that offering here and reedited slightly. [T.G.]

Ray and Tess, Paris, April 1987. Photo copyright © Tess Gallagher.

Paris, April 6

Slept very little. Ray had taken a sleeping pill. I began to doze near morning—up and down, coughing. No watch so no idea of time. A call wakes us at 10 A.M.—photographers downstairs for Ray. Things aren't arranged here—they just happen.

Another item missing now—my hairbrush! Last I remember seeing it was in NYC at the airport, braiding my hair then. But when I took my hair down here I should have missed it. Hopefully it will reappear.

Lunch with Edmund White who says he'll *take* being pegged as a "gay writer"—he's waited so long to be acknowledged. Makes the remark that he wouldn't take up smoking or drinking again even if he discovered he was dying of AIDS. He's just written a book on the death of a number of friends by AIDS. Death of David Kalstone a surprise—from AIDS. I recall reading his books at the U. of Washington in 1969. Edmund very kind spirited and lively. Ray and I both like him very much.

Gilles Barbedette—a critic, also at lunch. He liked my jokes because I am sardonic. Realizing now, as I write, that Ray and I had to come a long, unexpected way to sit at that table. Clear this Frenchman has had every advantage. Later Ray says to me he's sorry not to have his essays to show Gilles—I say, no, it's better as it is: the minute one of these French critics *thinks* they understand you they're finished with you. Better he's puzzled/curious.

Some talk about deconstructionist theories. Barthes, Foucault, etc., who aren't read anymore in France, Gilles says. Passé. Reduced to a fad. But a joke, G. says, how Americans have taken it all up in the most serious way. (Rather like the Russians of Dostoevsky's era, snapping up anything French out of a sense of inferiority.)

Ray is appreciated in the same way as Marguerite Duras—for his style, the particularity of that—not because he's a realistic writer or a minimalist, this last a term he rejects, and rightly so.

White tells us he wants to go back to America so he can write about things there. America—his workshop. *Our* workshop. How things are almost *too* perfect here in Paris for him. He needs the abrasiveness of American life. He's originally from Texas. Describes a grave-tending occasion that reminds me of Missouri and my mother's family, my murdered uncle. He also retells a story by Willa Cather, which makes us want to reread her.

White walks us over to the Orangerie des Tuileries after lunch and we see Monet's *Water Lilies.* I remember seeing them from my time before in Paris in 1968. The idea of Monet's *growing* the flowers he would later paint—lovely. The idea of painting the unseen, because he was painting light in water. The way an approximation becomes all one needs, can bear of the real at certain times.

"I didn't have anybody on my side for years except that dog. She defended me." My telling Ray of Satin—my childhood dog. Reminded of her by the Parisian taxicab driver with her dog beside her on the seat. Her covering it tenderly with a small cotton blanket to protect it from the sun. A block later she was swearing viciously at another driver.

Paris, April 7

Lunch with the son of a street sweeper who was born in Brittany. He works as a journalist for a publishing house and wants to write. Has two kids and a wife. Very frank discussion about how the French think they *do* have everything worth having, but that in fact their novels are bad, their poetry all but dead. People publish "books," he says, as "things"—not to make something live. The best-sellers come from America, and they are read like science fiction. He says the French like to discover their own writers from abroad—why people who aren't regarded much in America are taken up here.

Ray isn't feeling well. Hardly touches his food. A photographer is waiting when we get back to the hotel and takes him away to the Eiffel Tower to be photographed. I lie down and sleep an hour—the wine, I suppose. Then Ray comes and we both sleep.

Paris, April 8

A very late evening after Ray's reading at the English Language Bookstore, The Village Voice. Ray reads "Collectors" and "The Father" to a packed upstairs room. People are even standing on the stairs. C. K. (Charlie) Williams is there (living in Paris with French wife). Also Peter Taylor who has just received the Hemingway prize for *A Summons to Memphis*. Williams (elegantly tall!) says he gets writer's block when he finishes a book of poems. Is thinking of starting up a poetry-writing group in Paris.

I meet Ray's French translator, François Lasquin—and he says he's had to do this translation too quickly. He would have liked to have gone over it five more times, he says. He makes a meager living as a translator. Not an easy life. He'll be with us at the short-story festival at Saint Quentin. None of his translation was read at the bookstore because it was an English-speaking audience. Two women came up to me after Ray's reading and said how much they enjoy my poems, and asked when will I have a new book? The proprietress of the bookstore, Odile Hellier, is very lovely, apologizes for not having my books, says there have been several requests.

Paris, April 9

Lunch with Elizabeth [Ray's publicity representative at Mazarine]. She takes us to a deli run by a Jewish man who's lost his voice. Our waiter tells how the owner shot his wife, was sent to prison, and became gay. This story out of the blue. Elizabeth laughs . . . as if it's theater—which it may be. People seem to be able to be exactly who they are here. We see Olivier Cohen, Ray's publisher, at lunch too, with his sister who writes about architecture. Elizabeth says it's easier to promote a book by a foreign author than one by a French writer. Cohen talks about Richard Ford—says *The Sportswriter* probably moves too slowly for French readers, but that *A Piece of My Heart* is very good and that he wants to publish it.

We take a short rest at our hotel. Then Brigitte, my young poet friend from Syracuse, calls. We agree to meet and go to the Musée d'Orsay. Ray will join us after his rest. We begin on the fifth floor which we've been advised to do. It's crowded. Good and bad painters are thrown together. Periods are not respected. The bad pointillists next to Monet. Seeing van Gogh's painting of his room and his self-portraits—this most amazing. His intention so firmly impressed into his strokes. *Not* a man of doubt in his painting. The Degas *manqué* of horses in bronze. His ballet dancers so awkwardly balanced in those paintings that it reminds me of what I was saying about "singing it rough" in my essay. Things come alive when they are seen in more than their balanced presentation. The pastels were in such a dark alcove we couldn't see them well. Ray joining us and we see the Gauguins together—*The Blue Horse* my favorite.

Ray and I go for dinner at the Moulin Rouge and take in the "spectacle"—really beautiful girls in elaborate costumes, very fast-paced, but because I've danced the cancan in Texas in the *Merry Widow* in 1966, I can tell how the girls are sparing themselves. I remember being so sore after dance practice that I could hardly climb the stairs to my bedroom.

The dancers smile a lot and, as Ray says, seem to be enjoying themselves and in the "seeming," they do. There are acrobats and also a ventriloquist who makes people from the audience come up on stage with him. Then he causes odd, embarrassing noises to come out of their mouths. Next he brings a white dog on stage and allows it to "talk." The audience loves this, of course. There are a lot of Japanese people in the audience. Everyone well-dressed. Ray may have been the only one *not* in a suit. But he'd worn a tie. Rare. He and I danced two or three times, really enjoying ourselves, and then he bought me a pink rose to take back to the hotel in memory of our night.

Coming out, a taxicab driver tries to scalp us. He wants one hundred francs (about eighteen dollars) to take us back to the hotel. Ray tells him to forget it. He finds a cab for fifty francs, which was probably still about five francs too much.

Once we are safely back near our hotel we sit outside at the Brasserie Lipp and I have tea and Ray has coffee—just to sit and watch what's going on out in the street—a pleasure. Mostly young people, very playful with each other. Some short dresses, but jeans mostly. Strikingly handsome gay men. Not many gay women.

We come back to the hotel and eat chocolate. I smoke Ray's pipe. He smokes French cigarettes he doesn't like. I read Cocteau's diaries out loud for us.

We go with Jean Vautrin [French novelist, television and short story writer] and his wife, Anne, and the person in charge of the cover of Ray's book (a Hopper painting) to see "Buffo"— a one-hour performance of Jean's and Anne's friend, Howard Buten, an American who has invented a character (clown) based on his work with autistic children. Very funny but also moving performance. He uses musical instruments, plays a harmonium with his nostril, takes a baby violin out of a cello and plays, gets his tongue stuck on his trumpet, makes a drum set from some buckets. A certain pathos in the face, the face of the child-dream. Of delight in objects we scorn: the wad of paper which becomes a flower. Kissing the bow of the cello so tenderly it becomes like an arm. The obsession of the spot of contamination which he moves everywhere trying to rid himself of it—then gives it to a man he brings on stage.

Howard joins us for dinner. A man who fell in love with a French woman and stayed here seven years ago. Jean and Anne know him because of their autistic child who is fifteen and whom they go to see every fortnight. The child is now in an institution since they can't manage him at home anymore. Howard has helped them cope with their grief and made it possible for them to go on. Jean is a lovely man—stocky. Vautrin is a name he's taken to write screenplays under. He is also a director. His "real" name is Jean Herman. Anne was an actress before this child was born, but then had to give up acting. Jean gives no details as to his son's condition, just seems genuinely challenged by it all, loving and sad. He says later that such children are regarded as in the Middle Ages in France. He is given no help with the care by the government. I tell him Reagan has allowed many of the funds to be withdrawn for the disabled in America: survival of the fittest . . . the new morality! He doesn't like Reagan either.

Buten is a writer of novels. He is going to leave one for Ray to read. Laurence, the blonde book cover editor, doesn't speak much English but it would be worth learning French just to know what is in that beautiful head.

Ray to Tess: (Paris, Thursday, 9 April 1987) handwritten extemporaneous promissory note,

I'll be glad to get home!
R.C.
Hotel des Saints-Pères
I promise (intend) to go walking every day, just about, with Tess on the beach in Port Angeles.
R.C.

Saint Quentin, France, April 11

Yesterday was a day of travel to this town one hour by train from Paris. We traveled with François. The night before leaving we spent with Maya [Maya Nahum, a novelist] and Olivier. Maya is Tunisian. She's writing a novel. Has children. Very beautiful woman. She likes to fish so we invite them to Port Angeles.

During the train ride we learn about François. He was born to his mother when she was forty-seven. She was supposed to be sterile but he slipped through. His mother died last year. He said it was like being raised by a grandmother. His father would have liked him to take a doctor's degree, but he quit or was kicked out of schools because he didn't attend. He also had TB twice and had to go to sanatoriums. He has lived in America—in NYC and also was in Tucson. Today he told me a story about getting lost in the black part of Tucson and how a black prostitute took him home. In the morning he waited for her to dress so she could give him a lift into town eight miles away. He didn't recognize the woman when she returned. She was wearing a beehive wig. Meanwhile, the woman's daughters came and went from the room. The woman's son had died and she kept saying, he, François, looked like her son. This amazed François.

This morning I went with François to a museum and he knew a lot about the porcelain and the furniture and paintings. Then we went to a farmer's market and bought socks for him (cotton) and soap made with honey. We bought licorice sticks to suck on—a kind of bark he said he had chewed as a child. It was raining and he loaned me his neck scarf, says he will give me his mother's raincoat which is silk. I am very moved by this, as I know it is a sign of friendship.

Saint Quentin, April 12

The one time I don't carry my camera a spectacle happens. We arrive fashionably late to the award ceremony at which the woman who looks like a model, Noëlle Châtelet, will receive a medal for her short stories. We hear Ray's name mentioned. Noëlle says a few things in receiving the award—very simple, elegant, sincere. She's given a huge bouquet of flowers and a green velvet case with a silver medal: the Prix Goncourt, which she lets me hold later. Then a man comes for Ray and he's taken onto the stage lit with TV lights. He is presented with a painting of the town. We shake hands with Noëlle. Her hands are icy and she tells us she was very moved by the award speech because they mentioned her husband who died last year (of lung cancer, Olivier has told me . . . so young, at fifty-one years).

In her own speech Noëlle has spoken of how her husband encouraged her. She was writing during the time he was dying. "She has a great need to be elegant," Olivier says, "because of the hardship of her husband's death." She is very pale and uses brown makeup on her eyelids so they seem recessed into her head, sculpted almost. Her look is dreamy and removed, sad and as if she is trying to forgive life, even for its joys. Her father was born in this town, so it is a big occasion for her to accept the award here, presented by the mayor and the Prix Goncourt judges.

Then follows a cocktail session. Glasses of a green drink in two shades—one has mint liqueur and the other grapefruit, little pieces of apple cut up into them. A woman keeps trying to get Ray to drink some: "Does it have alcohol?" "Only a little," the woman says. He refuses. She persists. He says no. He's sure. Platters of sweet cookies are served with the drinks. Nothing done halfway. Lavish. Through the glass doors of the dining room we can see a banquet table that runs the length of the room. It is an amazement—as in some time of kings and queens. The photographer promises to give us photos of it. We go in and gaze with wonder like two spectacle-starved children.

There is food arranged in the shape of animals. An alligator, a hedgehog, a turkey's tail made from smoked fish. Over the table is the stuffed head of a wild boar with its red tongue arched in its half-opened mouth and its black eyes glittering down over the feast. There are ducks next to baby ducks—the heads made of chicken necks. Jean Vautrin leads everyone in a dive toward the lobster. There are vats of wine, red wine, and small beakers placed on the table. The cold meats and pâtés and salads are just the beginning. Next we go to huge copper pans and are served meat in a wonderful sauce. Ray has an au gratin dish. Bottles of red wine are brought to the table. Not much is finally drunk. The custom with drinking, at least in Paris we are told, is for drinking to begin with the meal and end when the meal is finished—leaving even expensive bottles of wine unfinished.

(Ray has just come in as I write. He's been out trying unsuccessfully to find eggs and bacon! on a Sunday morning in Saint Quentin. Failure. He sits down and eats a stale croissant I saved from yesterday's breakfast, for an emergency. He opens a Coke. Coke and croissant. "I have a whole new respect for Vance" [Ray's son who lives in Wiesbaden], he says, "living for a year in a country where English isn't spoken. I'll be glad to hear English again.")

At the banquet a jazz band begins to play. We eat desserts—a strawberry tart on a custard base, also lingonberry mousse—very light. Jean Vautrin and a woman with red hair fringed with white lead the dancing. Ray and I also go to dance.

Just as we're preparing to leave—having said good night to everyone, the lights dim in the huge hall under the enormous chandeliers. The music, a blare of horns, signals a time of heraldry. Into the hall march cooks in tall white hats, carrying a cake so big it takes three people to bear it. They carry it to Noëlle who stands and bows slightly to them, admires the cake. It is fizzling with sparklers. Behind the cake come other servers with platters of cream puffs and pastries. The cake is placed on the buffet table and the lights go up at either end of the buffet. A man begins to pour into the top glass of a pyramid of champagne glasses and pink champagne begins to cascade into the other glasses like a fountain. A woman pours into the pyramid at the other side. We hear glass falling, breaking? and see two servers rush to support the pyramid near the cake. Once the fountain has cascaded, individual glasses are filled. Then the careful reaching for each glass so as not to upset the pyramid.

I drink champagne and Ray gets two cream puffs for us which we eat. Then François walks us back to the hotel.

During dinner I sit next to François. He tells me a bit more about his mother. She had wanted to be an architect and she

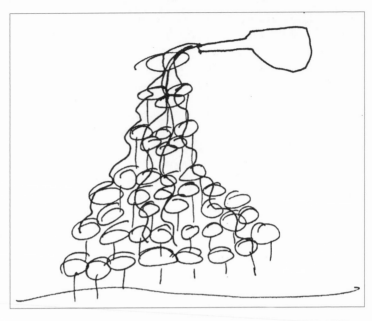

Champagne pyramid at Saint Quentin celebration, April 12, 1987, drawing by Tess Gallagher. Copyright © Tess Gallagher.

told her father. But her father didn't think much of this idea. He said no. So next she wanted to be a singer and a cabaret dancer. She even got a job after an audition. But she locked herself in her room for three weeks and wouldn't come out. Earlier she had thrown her schoolbooks into the river because she was bored with school. She finally married his father in order to get away from home. But she was always a thwarted talent. "She raised a garden and was a very good cook. We were very good friends. I loved her," he said. When he finishes eating there are stains on his Salvation Army suit, but he doesn't mind. The great thing with him is that nothing fazes him. Once in awhile he checks the zipper in his pants, which has been malfunctioning, slipping down, but he's not in any real worry . . . it's only *if* he can catch it, he will. I'll see him again. When we come in June. I nearly cry saying good-bye. I realize we understand each other at some deep level and are loyal beyond reason—very rare, very tender. The Hungarian side of him—the Irish side of me—the hinge of this.

Saint Quentin, April 13

After good-byes to our French friends Ray goes to talk to Jean V. about his stories, one of which we like—the other too cluttered and going in too many directions. The hardest thing is for Ray to tell him. But he does and when I come down they seem good with each other. I take Polaroids to give Jean and one for us. Martine Grelle, the organizer of the festival, comes to drive us to the train. She's been up until 3 A.M., looks ravished. She had a dream as a child of writers and people coming together to talk and hear writing. She hasn't any ambitions to write herself—"Nothing here," she says, and pats her chest. She's found what she can do and does it with humility yet with confidence, and as if her dream is all the "right" she needs. She's utterly charming.

Remembering on the train to Paris something François said about translating: "The writer only has to take what is coming from himself and put it into words, but the translator has to take on the foreign world; he must go so deeply into *what is not his* that he forgets himself. He can get lost." Then he explained how, when he first began to translate Ray's stories he thought Ray looked ironically upon his characters. Then he saw a clear photo of Ray and realized he was wrong, that Ray would never condescend to his characters. He had to go back and correct his beginning efforts.

Our flight to Frankfurt goes well and we are glad to find Vance waiting for us after we come through customs. Enormous energy. He picked up our heavy bags like they were nothing. Then we took a train to Wiesbaden and the Penta Hotel.

Wiesbaden, Germany, April 15

Yesterday we rented a Mercedes so as to have a comfortable drive and took a trip along the Rhine—Inge [Ray's daughter-in-law] with me in the back seat, Vance up front. After problems figuring out how to get into reverse we leave the hotel and go for a scrambled eggs breakfast at Vance and Inge's. The apartment is very cozy but small for the three of them and on a busy corner. Vance says he can't work there at the desk and they sleep with ear plugs in. We look at scrapbooks of their travels to Peru, to an isolated place in North Africa, small places whose names don't stay with me. Photos of them on beaches and in small boats. There is a huge map of the world in the living room with red flags on it where Inge has flown in her job as a flight attendant.

We take Buggy [Ray's granddaughter] to the baby-sitter's, then head out. We see vineyards on the steep slope to our right. No vineyards much on the other side because the sun doesn't hit there. I'm lulled by the car and don't talk much, just look. There are barges on the river carrying goods. Inge and I get a short chance to talk when Vance and Ray talk. She says she hasn't any close friends and that once when she was needing to confide in someone she wrote me a letter which she finally didn't mail. She said it helped just to write the letter.

We stop at the rocks where the Lorelei is said to have bewitched the sailors by sitting there combing her long blonde hair. Vance and Inge seem affectionate with each other. We take a few photos. Then we find a restaurant at a village near the Rhine where the proprietor agrees to fix us a meal of pork and spaetzel. He doesn't want to give us any bread for fear we won't eat all our food.

Later, Ray and I nap at the hotel in the early evening after our drive along the Rhine, then have coffee before going to the casino in Wiesbaden. This is the Spielbank Casino where Dostoevsky won, then lost a fortune. There is even a room in the casino named after him, the Dostoevsky Room! I get fifty marks' worth of five-mark chips. We begin to play roulette at table 5. I bet on red with Ray and win a couple of times, then on "even" and win. I watch a black man who is betting on the numbers by putting chips on the lines between numbers. This gives him more chances but lowers the payoff. I watch for a while, finding it hard to maintain a spot near the table because bettors crowd past me, sometimes gouging me. I know I'm going to have bruises tomorrow, but there's no way to take care. I hadn't realized how physically aggressive one has to be to play roulette!

Finally the number twenty-four occurs to me with such freshness and surety that I feel I *must* bet on it. Dostoevsky is with me! I don't even persuade myself of this. *I know it.* It is the first bet I've placed on a number. The odds are thirty-five to one. After the roll my chip (five marks) is the only one left as the others are scooped away. "That's mine!" I tell Ray. There is a sort of sigh that comes from around the table as the croupier says 175 marks and makes a stack of chips (all blue with one red one-hundred-mark chip) and asks me to come around to gather my chips. I don't want to lose my place so I motion for him to shift them around to me and smile, but he again wants me to come to him. He's afraid the stack will topple. I start there. But by then he's swiftly pushed them across the table. He starts to retrieve them but by then I've returned to my place near Ray. I'm afraid I won't get to take my winnings up myself—which seems foolishly important. So, once again, the croupier shoves the chips over in my direction. I give a five-mark tip to the croupier who says, "Congratulations," and I understand how rare such a win is. After this I bet on three more numbers but don't win. Then on red and black and win. But I feel exhausted by having won earlier. As if, by connecting up with that strange current of clairvoyance, I've used up my "normal" energy too. It is 10:30 P.M. and we have agreed to gamble exactly one hour, and then eat.

We go into the luxurious adjoining dining room: marble pillars, huge chandeliers, candles and flowers on each table, elaborate gold designs on ceiling. At one corner a flashing display board shows the numbers coming up at the various tables. We get interested in table 3 because many reds have come up in sequence. We watch it all through dinner. A light meal with lobster salad—just the cheeks of the lobster slightly warmed. I have quail soup which is mostly broth with bits of meat. Quail? Carrots and other vegetables cut into marble-sized bits in soup. For dessert Ray has fruit with sorbet and liqueur. And I have a cake in liqueur with strawberries and kiwi, mint leaves for decoration. Then coffee with cookies. Our waiter is very nice and the place is a real class operation, but the portions are skimpy enough to make us recall our working-class roots. No, it wouldn't satisfy someone who'd put in a day logging!

On the train to Zürich, April 16

Writing on the train which will take four hours to get to Zürich. Anxious to see Harold.* Yesterday the big event was Wolfram Thieman† coming, a German friend of my youth. I stayed at the hotel to wait for him as I suspected he would be there exactly at 5 P.M. (Six hours from Bremen where he lives.) He came exactly at five. I had just woken up from a two-hour nap. I seem to need a lot of sleep because of my cold.

Ray is back in Smoking. There are five in my first-class compartment. The man to my left uses Mont Blanc pens and lets me try them out. He tells me one can obtain one of these in solid gold for one thousand marks. Passing villages with comforters and rugs hanging out the windows. Reminding me of how the air cleans and freshens.

Remembering what a welcome addition Wolf was to the evening yesterday. He and I had a coffee and talked politics at the hotel. He gave me a gift from his wife Isa—a lovely tea mug. Very thoughtful of her. Wolf had given rides to several university students on the way—one of them a woman who works with the Greens on women's issues.

His good humor is infectious. Much energy. Brightness. Industry. Curiosity. Delight. All those things one loves in a man. And his affection for me is deep and good and loyal. What a miracle friendship is! I am amazed at its intricate circuitry. How many places we've met—he and Isa meeting me in NYC off the train from Syracuse in the middle of a snowstorm that time.

Wolf and I drive to Meinz and get lost on Vance's direc-

---

*Harold Schweizer, our Swiss friend in Zürich who is a poet and literary critic, scholar, and assistant to the chairman of the English department at University of Zürich. [This and subsequent notes to the journal are by T.G.]

†A German friend of mine from my days traveling in Ireland in 1968, now a scientist in Bremen.

tions, end up having to retrace our way twice. Finally we arrive at the Bahnhof in Meinz and find Vance and Ray. We have a coffee and I introduce them. I realize how important it is to me that Ray like Wolf. Ray is exhausted, I see. He seems like someone who's been stunned. The enormous energy it takes just being a father. But Wolf is fresh air and Ray tries to rally, excuses himself and goes to the men's. Comes back in another gear and the talk is political again. Ray loves how Wolf knows his history and also how he thinks about various questions. Wolf admits he's a bit of a chauvinist for his country in the matter of American military installations which don't share their decisions with Germany. They can push the button and send missiles without consulting the German government. He says this keeps Germany an occupied country—as it does.

Wolf and Ray do like each other very much and Wolf invites us to Bremen. We drive Wolf back to his car and let him out at a stoplight. He walks with such energy and gaiety! I love seeing him—he waves and smiles and waves as we drive away.

Zürich, April 17

Harold meets us in Zürich. He seems the same as I remember him*—boyish, a wry sense of humor that crops up delightfully. But he tells us he isn't sleeping. He has to take a special herbal tea Lynne [Harold's American wife] has found, and this seems to work. "It's your upcoming move,"† I tell him. And he says "Yes" as if it hadn't quite occurred to him—it was so obvious.

The hotel is exactly right. They have chosen it with care. Very homey. The furniture antique, flowered draperies, chandelier over the two beds which are fitted out with the plump down comforters typical for here . . . though many hotels, Harold says, don't use them now. Our breakfast is included in the fee.

---

*From our previous trip in 1981, when I'd been a guest of the University of Zürich.

†Harold had just accepted a teaching position at Bucknell University.

We eat lunch with Harold (he takes a glass of wine with me—red because white keeps him awake) in the old section of the city. He tells us how Lynne is taking on doing translations at the university. He has read my poetry manuscript for my book *Amplitude: New and Selected,* and says, "We're going to fight tomorrow!"—he wants to take out three poems and put in two others. Also to revise endings on a couple of others.

Ray and I walk together down the narrow streets and stare in windows, then come back for an hour-and-a-half nap. Then a light supper of smoked salmon and eggs poached in sauce with shrimp—also asparagus soup, a great summer favorite here. Ray is having a gigantic bowl—goblet!—of fresh raspberries and cream when Lynne and Harold arrive. They have come to see us at the hotel after church. We order some local red wine—a light rosé. There is so much to tell—the rough time with L. last summer and with Ray's mother at Christmas. My own mother's bad back. Harold tells the happy story of his job search. For his lecture at Bucknell University he presented Kierkegaard as a contemporary poet! He is a gambler—to come to America with all his eggs in one basket for the one job interview. Of course he didn't let *them* know this at Bucknell, or even me, though I guessed.

Zürich, April 18

Worked with Harold on my poems. Going carefully poem by poem. He wants some rather overpopular poems out: "The Hug" and "Beginning to Say No" and "Shirts" among them. We also take out "Crossing" and completely rewrite "Time Lapse with Tulips." We run out of time. Ray disagrees and wants "The Hug" back in.

Ray and I take a boat ride on the lake. "See"—Zürich See. It's very sunny and many people are strolling along the promenade—a holiday feeling. The Easter holidays are here, so the shops are all shut except for some near the lake—the Café Odeon where Ray and I stop for a while after the boat ride: Pound, Joyce, Lenin, Tristan Tzara (who started dadaism)—all came here. Last time we were in Zürich the café seemed to be frequented mostly by gays. Harold tells us, "It's changed." Ray goes inside, comes out, and says the men are lined up at the bar—as before. One strangely overdressed man at a table across the sidewalk from us who strains to watch every woman as she goes by—he's wearing a thin tie— looks Italian, like out of one of Fellini's films.

We come back to the hotel and I read Cocteau aloud. Dinner sent to the room. I order up pots of hot water so I can take cups of the medicinal tea Lynne has sent to help with my sinus infection. I fear I'm going to lose my voice.

Ray makes a try at getting some good videos to watch at the hotel desk, but they're awful. We finally watch a Wim Wenders film on the TV about a director who's dying of lung cancer while they make the film of Nicholas Ray, or "Nick," as the director is called throughout the film. He is cadaverous, reminds me of my father near the end . . . especially the episodes of coughing, and how those sleeping in the house cover their ears. The sound is painful. At the end Nick says, "Cut," and that's the end of his life and of the film, except for an epilogue in which the crew is out on a Chinese "junk" with black sails carrying Nick's ashes in an urn. They are talking about him, drinking sake. One guy says, "Nick would have burned the boat"—no one else wants to burn it. Maybe the guy's drunk but that's the best thought in Nick's terms: "Nick would have burned the boat." Fine film. Lucky to see it. Took guts to make it, for sure. Ray likes it, too; no thoughts expressed about his own smoking, but of course that fear is with me as we watch.

Harold calls while we are looking at the bad videos earlier: he wants to tell me he's reread the new poems and loves them—I'm "getting better"—these are "the best." "They are just so moving!" he tells me. This means a lot since these are so fresh not many people have seen them. He says there's one he wants to take out. I say, "I wonder if it's the same one I want to take out." We'll see. Tomorrow we'll visit the Thomas Mann archives at the university.

Zürich, April 19

Ray needs to eat at noon—his hypoglycemia—so sandwiches of ham and cheese are brought to the room. Arrangements are made for our travel to Rome. I call Nancy Watkins* in Rome and she will arrange first-class train seats for us from Rome to Milan. It has been eight years since she and Gian sat in my little house in Tucson and ate sweet rolls for breakfast with me and Michael Cuddihy, editor of *Ironwood!* She says Riccardo [Riccardo Duranti, poet and translator] hasn't finished his introduction to my poems yet and that summer is a bad time to bring out a book. So maybe they'll wait.

Ray buys me daffodils which are open today on my desk. Harold arrives with chocolate and huge bouquets! One for each room. Beautiful cut-glass vases are sent up from the desk.

We find the guard at the Thomas Mann archives "unusually friendly," as Harold tells us later. He lets us go into areas forbidden to others. Harold picks books off the shelves of Mann's collection looking for handwritten notes. We see much underlining, but *Joseph and His Brothers*—the book he wants—he can't find. Extensive notes in there, he says. The Eastern influence of objects on Mann's desk. A bust of an Indian Buddha. Some horn knives, a photo of his wife. His actual study, which has been reassembled here, was on the other side of the lake. Goethe actually visited the man who owned this particular house. "They haven't vacuumed these carpets since Goethe walked here," Harold jokes. We see an illegible letter from Freud to Mann on the wall. Also on a small page in neat script, the first page of *Death in Venice*. Harold says he regrets he didn't do scholarly work on Mann,† since all these materials were here. He takes us into a lovely study room for those who come from around the world to study Mann—many Japanese, Harold says. We've left the Mann archives and are sitting at a garden café, but I'm still back at the archives in my mind—seeing Harold open a walking stick of Mann's to show us and the guard a cylindrical flask inside it for liquor.

---

*Artist and publisher (with her husband Gian Franco Palmeri, the poet) of *Arsenale,* a literary journal, and of Labirinto (the publishing house that proposed to publish twenty of my poems in translation).

†He worked instead on Theodore Roethke, another of our fated connections, since I was Roethke's student in his last class at University of Washington in 1963.

Ray and Harold Schweizer, Zurich. Harold is showing Ray a bar on the threshold for cleaning one's boots. Photo copyright © Tess Gallagher.

Ray goes to nap and Harold and I to the Restaurant Kunsthaus to work on my *New and Selected*. Harold's help is invaluable and we quickly work through *Under Stars, Willingly,* and the new poems—which Harold says are "uneven" but whose unevenness contributes to the wealth of the best poems, which come in the middle of the section—from "If Blood

Were Not as Powerful as It Is" through "Present," then including "Bonfire," and "Amplitude," which he thinks is very good. He says in reading "If Poetry Were Not a Morality" he thought I was writing very badly as he read it, that I could never pull it all together, and then I did! He's moved by my intellect—not the emotions, he says, in this poem. I need to hear more on "The Story of a Citizen," which he says he'll reread. We work on "In Macio"—change the ending. Long discussions on "Eating the Sparrows," which Harold wants out because of the ending. He likes to clip the poem off early and resents what he sees as the "message" aspect of poems—as intrusion, thinks I overvalue my "singing" and lack humility at end. But I say, "After all, Harold, it's not a nightingale. It's only a sparrow. One of the lowliest singers." Inconsequential. Not to be missed except as God says; not a sparrow shall fall but that He knows it. Also I remind him of the fate of poets in China, where the poem is set—their singing silenced during the Cultural Revolution. We agree that my ending style is more that of the hypnotist who has a way in *and* a way out—does not clap her hands to wake the patient up. My rhythmic equilibrium is just quite different from his.

Disastrous dinner out at a restaurant. Ray is starving and we pass up a quiet restaurant near the hotel. I tell him later he must tell me these things. I can't always gauge his hunger condition which is more demanding than mine because he gets anxious if he doesn't get food. We wait for a table at the bar and watch the owner toss a bottle of liquor at his barman to catch. He *just* does! Then he calls the man's name and throws one champagne glass, then another. Each of them clashes to the floor. It's theater. They laugh and the barman sweeps the glass out from under his feet.

When we're finally able to get a table my meal (grilled shrimp) comes before Ray's so I share it. I also get bread for him. But he is the last to be served in the entire restaurant and I finally have to inquire. The owner is very sorry, yes the food is coming—duck breast in date sauce. He comes over and apologizes to Ray. He even has the barman bring shots of liquor to me and the two strangers near our table. He knows Ray doesn't drink. "I'll drink yours for you," he says, and we click glasses and drink in one swallow. None of it mollifies how Ray feels.

The meal is still a disaster for him. We walk back to the hotel and watch Irish ballet on TV and eat Swiss chocolates.

Wappenswil, Switzerland, April 20

Easter Sunday and we go to Wappenswil (about twenty miles from Zürich in the mountains, really foothills) where Harold and Lynne live with their two children, Micah and Phoebe. Lynne has prepared a traditional Swiss meal—pork inside puff pastry. We catch up to each other's lives while the dinner is cooking, look at photos of their visit to us in Syracuse. After dinner the children search for eggs Lynne has colored with natural dyes, using a nylon stocking and flowers for the patterns.

Phoebe and I pull up grass and tempt one adult black sheep grazing nearby to eat out of our hands. We can't approach the lambs, however. Ray goes in for a nap and Harold, Lynne, and Micah and I go for a short walk with rain threatening.

Talking with Harold while he cleans up the kitchen about his having trouble writing poems. He says he's afraid his poems fall short of the truth he wants to tell. Or maybe he scorns his efforts because he doesn't want to write ungenerously. I recall Milosz who says one should write reluctantly and hope good angels attend instead of demons.

Lynne stays with the children and Harold takes us to Martin and Maryann's for wine and cheese pies. Afterwards Martin drives us back and tells us how the "Midas touch" has made it impossible to buy houses in Zürich. Only by inheriting can young people afford such things. I take "sleeping tea" for Ray. It seems the Swiss are deeply involved with "natural" medicines. Even the children take them.

Zürich, April 21

Some loud machine awakens us—trees being cut down, Ray says. I thought drilling. It's 8 A.M. but we don't get up. Luxuriate in the Swiss being back at work after the holiday and us still on holiday. Harold's teaching today so we'll go about on our own. The daffodils Ray got me are beautifully open on the desk now. The yellow roses in Harold's bouquet are wide too. Read Harold's new poems and found five or six I like a lot. He's getting better, more confident—though the question of just how much or little to tamper with his somewhat foreign syntax is still with me.

Yesterday Harold took us into a nearby town (Winterthur) to visit the Römerholz Museum, intimate and full of impressionist and preimpressionist paintings I won't forget. Harold has been there many times so he had his favorites which he likes to revisit. I buy a poster of *A Girl Reading*, which is a joint favorite of Harold's and mine. Next we visit Kyburg Castle where Ray gets down on his knees and puts his head on the chopping block to see what it would feel like. I can't resist chopping my hand down on his neck to complete his imagination . . . or maybe to make light of a moment, which was anything but that. Later we learn that the iron maiden—an iron woman-shaped device full of spikes that gouged into a person once *she* was shut—wasn't used in this particular castle, although it was on display. There was a Christ high on the wall near the chopping block with gouts of blood caught to His feet and beading His hands like grapes. Also impressive for their silence and cruelty were the prison rooms in the tower. No light—except a slit—and gouges on the wall made with fingernails? where prisoners must have marked the days.

In the armaments room of the knights Harold points out the famous Swiss halberd. An instrument which made the Swiss much feared in Europe. Until the invention of guns, Harold tells us, they had vanquished every enemy. The armor shows them to have been small men. Their halberds were extremely long.

(Outside the window of our hotel room I hear the tree fall as I write this. Then a bird scream.)

After going through the castle we find a country inn and have a rest and a bit to eat. Ray has ice cream with hot blueberries and Harold and I have hot potato salad with sausage and wine. Then we drive past the bakery. "There's where I stood and stuffed myself," Harold says.

Ray and I eat a meal at the Mövenpick, upstairs—walking there in the rain. Ray has lamb. I eat asparagus soup. I read the last of *Cocteau* when we get back to our suite. Enjoying the extravagance and accuracy of R. Howard's claim that the greatness of French literature springs from the homosexual response to "The Possession of the Mothers." In Ireland the possessiveness of mothers just short-circuits male sexuality into drink and literature, without the French insistence on a sexual life. As Medbh McGuckian [Belfast poet] said, "It's awful to think of how many men in Ireland suffer from the 'Guiness Droop.' " So in Ireland, whatever the sexual orientation, neither sex is offered much, and literature, music, drinking, and gambling get it all.

Zürich, April 22

We visit Joyce's grave. It must be the third time we've done so. Again I leave a daffodil in his open book. There are no flowers blooming near the statue of Joyce, cross-legged, wearing his monocle and staring wryly out. But there is a fan-shaped bush beginning to bud. We remark to each other that his daughter is still living in the sanitarium for the insane. A light rain is falling.

We walk down other rows of graves to admire and read other gravestones. "My time stays in your hands": a sundial on the stone. Also a pillar of birds. An owl with moss on its back. Some very Japanese (Noguchi-like) shapes, simple and beautiful as a full pitcher. Ray admires two ducks welded together in flight.

Afterwards, I buy flower seeds and bulbs for Mom in a shop downtown. We get lost on the train and a very kind woman understands my German and offers to drive us back near the hotel. Harold and Lynne come at 8 P.M. to take us to the Kronenhalle where James Joyce ate often. We pass Joyce's table on our way upstairs. There is a small watercolor there. He would drink at the Odeon, then come over to eat at the Kronenhalle. It was owned by a wealthy woman who loved art and artists. She used to dress up in a blue wig and her jewels and come down to meet her guests and ask if they had enjoyed their meals.

A huge Chagall painting is at one end of the room. Behind

us is a Bonnard sketch of fruit. In the corridor on the way to the toilette are more Chagalls which I remember from our visit before. At the table near us is an Indian-looking man with green coat and gray fedora. He bows with his hands under his chin. Makes elaborate gestures when we glance in his direction. Has a long graying beard. When we ask who he is later, the waiter doesn't know but thinks he's an artist. At one point the man buys a rose and after an elaborate conversation with the waiter who speaks French with him, he writes a note and the waiter leaves with rose and note to deliver them downstairs. Later the man begins to sing to himself rather loudly.

I eat calf's liver. For dessert, ice cream with caramel sauce, and Ray has strawberries. Lynne and Harold have chocolate mousse. Harold tells a travel-in-America story about a huge man on a bus whom Harold knows is smoking pot, "Mary-je-wana" as H. calls it. Harold deplores this aloud and the man ultimately pulls a penknife and seems ready to stab Harold. But he abruptly turns and dashes up to the driver who's driving and knocks him in the head. The driver passes out on the emergency brake. The bus halts in the center of the freeway. Cars go around. The driver comes to and leaves, "flees," as H. says. A short while later a police car arrives and two policemen get out and come onto the bus for the man. He is huge and just pushes them aside. Another cop car comes and the two downed officers revive and help the fresh cops subdue the man. A new bus driver appears and the bus continues.

Our evening together is warm and memorable. We "laugh a lot," as Ray puts it. We go for drinks at the hotel. We tell Harold how much we admire his poems. I give him my favorites on which I've made a few notes.

Zürich, April 23

Harold takes us into the old quarter to have a sweet, then drives us to the airport: I give him his essay on me with a few marks to help. We aren't sad saying good-bye. He'll take a boat to America in July. Lynne will go ahead to buy a house. We thank him once again for the wonderful visit.

I'm flying over the Alps as I write this. Houses visible on even the sharp snowy slopes. A valley, a few houses clutched together. The Alps go on FOREVER! Astounding. Not like my Olympics—to be flown over in a short time. I see a jet below us, flying through the Alps.

Rome, April 26

No time to write in Rome. Too much to see, to do! One of the important meetings has been with Fernanda Pivano who knew Hemingway and was his Italian translator beginning with *For Whom the Bell Tolls*. She shows us photos of herself as a young woman with her husband and Hemingway. We learn she's written an afterword to Ray's book, which is just coming out in Italian: *What We Talk about When We Talk about Love*. This will be of great help in securing Ray a good readership in Italy, she tells us, a bit too proudly, I think. Formerly she had only been writing on "the Beats," but recently she began to follow contemporary American fiction and sees Ray as the "Papa" of an entire present younger American generation. Ray is naturally flattered, though he doesn't think of himself in such terms. He enjoys being in touch with anyone who knew Hemingway and enjoys looking at the photos.

Rome, April 27

Friday—we meet Nancy and Gian at the "Cemetery for Foreigners," as we understand the local name for the cemetery in which Keats, Severn, and the ashes of Shelley are buried. It doesn't open until 3:20 P.M., so we go for a sandwich (pizza bread) and Cokes and tea. Nancy and Gian order a fruit drink. A kind of frappé. Gian uncharacteristically allows his photograph to be taken at the outdoor tables with Ray and Nancy, then with me and Ray.

Once inside the cemetery we're led into an office where several people at desks look up. A man who speaks English gives us a "rule sheet" which cautions us with twelve rules—one of them is "don't pet the cats . . . they might have rabies."

Ray and Tess outside the "Cemetery for Foreigners," in Rome, waiting for it to open. Photo copyright © Nancy Watkins.

There is a black cat near Keats's grave. "There's always a cat here," Gian says. He also wonders where the other cats are—"There used to be many cats here." Nancy says there are about three hundred cats at "the pyramid" nearby.

The grave of Shelley is on a kind of shelf. E. J. Trelawny is

Gianfranco Palmery, Tess and Ray, Rome, near Cemetery for Foreigners. Photo copyright © Nancy Watkins.

next to Shelley. Purple iris stand tall on the graves around. I tell Nancy I've bought bulbs of purple iris for my mother in Switzerland. She says I won't be allowed to take them through customs. I admit I've hidden them. She says her mother gave her some chives that had bugs in them, that the rules are made for a reason. She's right, yet I understand how the desire for the strange, the exotic, causes infractions of such rules. The time at the graves is too short since we have to go to the university.

The session goes well—most of the questions are asked by Americans, though one Italian in the back says that although European literature has traditionally scorned U.S. writing, there's a change he sees now—as if Europeans are now looking *toward* the U.S. A university professor denies that *this* (scorn for U.S. writing) has been the perception of "Europeans." "Why do you think there is such underestimation of American literature?" Ray asks the man. No real answer evolves. The man is a writer. Only two people raise their hands when Ray asks how many want to be writers. Quite different from the States where more than half might have responded.

Before the university session we are beset with photographers. I sit with Ray for a couple of shots.

The room is packed. Some students standing. Afterward a young woman comes up to me and says she doesn't know my work but that she just admires me as a woman; where can she get my poems? She wants to read in English, her boyfriend is English. She says she used to write but became blocked. I say I'll send her a book. She seems astounded, offers money. No, I say, it's for the hospitality of your country. I take her address.

Finally Riccardo Duranti breaks up the interviews and we go for dinner at a restaurant within walking distance. There are so many "starters" that I'm full when the main course of lamb comes. Sitting next to me is a very interesting woman who has translated Tillie Olsen and Grace Paley—"to know them," she says. She tells me that translating is terribly undervalued. A lot of work and it doesn't pay. You have to do it because you just have to do it, she says. She has two daughters, is divorced, has been evicted from her house of many years. Now lives in the same building as Kathleen Fraser.* We agree to meet next morning at 10:00 A.M.

Fernanda Pavano sits across from Ray and me at the dinner. She doesn't eat. Is there just long enough to talk a little, putting in an appearance. There is so much happening I only remember her lime-green outfit—very cool and comfortable-looking in the heat.

Milan, April 29

Dinner with Mr. Bondechini, editor for Mondadori. He has arranged this meal so as to preempt our meeting with the Garzanti† staff. He is feeling sheepish about having allowed Garzanti to "pick up" Ray's books previous to *Cathedral* (a book which Mondadori brought out but which didn't sell). Now Ray's work has "caught on" and Mr. B. is sharking around us to see what he can "pick up" himself, to get back into the

---

*A poet from San Francisco whom Ray and I know.

†Garzanti publishing house brought out *What We Talk about When We Talk about Love* while we were there. Mondadori was their competitor.

Riccardo Duranti, our Italian translator, with Ray, Rome, April 29, 1987. Photo copyright © Tess Gallagher.

action. He wants to scalp *Fires* of its stories, drop the poems and essay, and put them together with new stories. (Ray and I just listen, don't say much.) He seems to value Ray because of the literary buzz. My uneasiness causes me to go overly much in an agreeable direction to hide my mistrust of him. My feeling is visceral and I don't seem to have a choice. He is anxious to find out who is *in* in American writing. It's clear he decides what to honor from what other people "think" and not by reading himself.

Garzanti publicity representative phones at 10:00 A.M. and

Piero Gelli, Ray's editor at Garzanti, with Ray and Tess in Milan.
Photo copyright © Tess Gallagher.

at 10:30 is at the hotel. Anna Drugman—one of the top publicity people for the press . . . if not the top. And Piero Gelli—editor-in-chief. They are very welcoming and we immediately like them. Gelli is dark, frosty-headed, trim. His English has a few bumps but he's sharp in a sincere way which comes through. He's scheduled to the minute and doesn't stay long. Anna D. wastes no time in letting us know in a nice way that since we went to Rome first, there is no way for her now to make a "big splash" with the media in Milano. She wishes we'd come to Milano first. But . . . she has still managed to get a full schedule of interviews and photo sessions on for Ray. I hardly see him for the next two days—until evening. We apologize to Ms. D. about Rome, perhaps insincerely, since we wanted to go there first because of our friends, Riccardo and Nancy and Gian—media be damned.

London, June 1

We're met by Mark Crean, Christopher MacLahose's [Ray's editor at Collins-Harvill] assistant. He's shy, driving Christo-

*Rare photo of Ray in tuxedo, prior to our attending
British-American Arts Society dinner, London, 1987.
Photo copyright © Tess Gallagher.*

pher's Jaguar because his own is "in the shop in a com*er*"
(coma). Ray is very impressed with the leather-seated Jaguar
with wooden console. Mark drops us at our rented flat at 13A
Clarendon Rd., which is off Bayswater Rd. near the Holland
tube station. We've taken it for a month. The flat has a narrow

but bright kitchen area, dining area, little study, bedroom, and living room with electric fireplace. We don't locate central heating until after a visit from the maid who lives nearby. The furnishings are a few modest antiques, wicker, and unfinished wood. Living room is lemon yellow. A huge bouquet of flowers has been arranged on the dining-room table, compliments of Collins-Harvill. The apartment provides a good base for interviews, meeting photographers, an Australian filmmaker, and going out to dinners in Soho and for theater elsewhere. We'll also travel back to Paris between events in London.

Dublin, June 5

In Dublin on my way to Belfast while Ray finishes out the book appearance trip in Scotland with Christopher and Richard. Heard old-time jazz outside my hotel. Taken back to musician's union by the musicians for more jazz, jazz like out of the twenties or thirties. Very pure. The men very kind and with a real love of what they do. Also saw *Say Cheese*—a humorous play at the Abbey. I was so tired I kept nodding off at the start. It was mostly silly, about marriage in Ireland, the actors all really fine, though. Play itself seeming a bit sitcom. The idea of the promotional and the romanticization of marriage in Ireland, the hotel keepers who serve unmarrieds without batting an eye.

Walked around St. Stephens Green—my old haunt. Went to Easson's bookstore. Found Ray's collected stories, but his poems haven't reached Ireland yet. Good just to be on my own in Dublin again—anonymously so too, as I was in 1968 during the Vietnam War when I first came to Ireland.

June 9

I was only able to reach Ciaran* through the Northern Arts Council at the last minute before taking the train to Belfast.

---

*Ciaran Carson, musician and poet, then head of Traditional Music for the Northern Ireland Arts Council; *Under Stars* is also dedicated to him.

The trip was lovely, tracks running along the sea, sharing a compartment with a man whose English was impossible to understand. I finally just gave up and read in Edna Longley's book on war and poetry which is pretty good. At least it helps me to place everyone.

That night to a music session near the Belfast docks. Music so-so, dominated by a young fiddle player who likes to play tunes so difficult no one can accompany him. Deirdre [Deirdre Shannon, fiddle player, Carson's wife] and Ciaran have a discussion about this when we get home—Ciaran forgiving him, saying he's young, but also the idea that, maybe they should have told him. Their child, Manus, was the main event of the day. Really a beautiful child. I'd brought him a stuffed horse music box which he seemed to love. He took to me and wanted to be on my lap much of the time that first day, and for the entire visit.

June 10

Party at Michael Longley's.* His friend Lester from Philadelphia visiting. Brian and his wife from the Arts Council. Medbh McGuckian and her husband, John, there too. Prior to coming to the party, Ciaran had gone for a jar with an old friend. Seems he'd given the fellow the proofs for his book and the criticism had been severe. I talked film with Brian, chatted some with John and Medbh and Lester. Some talk about how a particular friend had been saved from drink by marrying "the right woman."

After eveyone left except Lester and Ciaran and I (Michael very tired on the couch) Ciaran began to talk about my poem "If Poetry Were Not a Morality." He said I needed the "I" too much—how could I write "I'm the kind of woman who . . ."??? What kind of woman writes this? Calls too much attention to the writer. And how do I know what kind of woman I am anyway? Michael Longley began defending the

---

*Belfast poet and then head of the Northern Ireland Arts Council Literature Programs.

Edna Longley, Tess, Ray, and Paul Muldoon, Belfast, 1985.
Photo copyright © Tess Gallagher.

"I" as both personal and an extension beyond self, but Ciaran was having none of it.

Belfast, June 11

Day spent mostly with Medbh at her house. She makes tea and we talk. I decide not to stay over for a party the next night as I'm missing Ray. We make new plane plans for me to get back to London the next day. I read Medbh's poems and she reads mine. I find her poems much more clear, yet holding their mysteries so beautifully—and not "clear" in the usual narrative ways. Spiritual reserves, sensual and evocative. Full of undertow. Strong calm presence.

I visit quickly with Edna Longley and then go to a pub to join Deirdre and Ciaran. Edna presents the view that drinking may be a needful spur to the darker realms of the psyche for some artists. And she may be right. But I still don't really buy it, the necessity of it, and tell her so. I like her so much but do feel way outside the way things go in Ireland, now that I've been with Ray these years with drink a kind of poison and trouble we don't want. She says she's just come from a session in Dublin with Seamus Deane—how they sat in the car and argued until all hours. Drinking in Ireland seen as a medium for "creative" encounter. This is a moment when I see how far I've come from those early days in Ireland.

Also remembering Ray's being with me at Michael and Edna's in 1985 and our staying at Muldoon's flat, the musicians coming out to entertain us there because Ray didn't want to be in the pubs or to find it awkward to leave when he wanted. His suddenly deciding he'd had enough of the music and needed to rest, just excusing himself and going up the stairs, turning at the top and saying to me: "Come along soon now." Then the hard time I had of getting everyone to really leave when they hadn't finished their drinks. Feeling a bit inhospitable, but managing to get the place quiet. That quicksand of music and drink—how many Irish artists and writers perish from it. I wonder if Ray's example will strike any of them at some later moment.

Leaving London, June 23

Written enroute to Glasgow. Accompanied by Mark Crean and Stephen Williams who has been hired by Collins-Harvill to attend to promotion of the reading tour by Richard Ford, Ray, and Jonathan Raban.

Awakened at 8:15 A.M. in our rented flat by the arrival of a washing machine repairman. The repairman manages to burn out the motor in the machine and replace it in the course of the morning. The next day it still won't work. Ray and I have been up until 3:00 A.M. after a lovely dinner at Salman Rushdie's, where we met his new girlfriend, Marianne Wiggins. She is a novelist and short-story writer published by Collins in England. Marianne is in her late thirties (Salman just turned forty on Saturday). She begins to smoke when Salman starts to tell a story Ray and I are enjoying, even though it was the third time (had heard it twice at parties two years ago). In the story a woman who speaks French very well calls Salman and pretends to be a French reporter for a French magazine arranging to interview him. On the second call she says: "What if I'm not working for this magazine and just want to meet you?"

"Well then I should be very angry because it will mean you've been wasting my time," Salman says. She admits she just wants to meet him. He explains that he's married and that he isn't up for anything. She still wants to meet him, so he agrees to meet her in a particular bar. If she hasn't turned up in ten minutes within the time set, he tells her he plans to leave. She comes fifteen minutes *after* the agreed-upon time and finds him still there. He recognizes her as a very beautiful Indian woman with whom he's spoken briefly in the lounge of his publishing house. They talked for half an hour and have a drink and that's that. Later I mention to Ray how upset Marianne was—at having to hear/imagine this scene again. Then Ray recalls Salman saying to her: "That's the third cigarette you've smoked tonight."

There was a long discussion about Salman's wanting to go to Columbia in NYC to teach for a term. He wants to go in order to be able to write American characters in American settings. Bob Towers has made the invitation and we encourage him to accept it, once he's finished his novel.

At one point, Salman remarks that if he were to be arrested he would at least have plenty of time to write (perhaps the idea of being arrested had to do with his visit to Nicaragua?).

Anyhow, Marianne says—in reply? comment?—"That sounds like the remark of an unhappy man." It's a kind of remark that demands that Salman reassure her, which he vaguely but unconvincingly does.

Salman shows us around the house. Lots of Indian prints— he has a taste for the surreal. He also shows us a painting by Günter Grass (two hands with stones) and says he and Grass became acquainted during his visit to Germany. He also tells us how hungry the media was—without success—to get him to say something mean about Grass.

Story of their New York agent who came for weekend as a houseguest and they each gave him their work to read. He was very much in deference to Salman but treated Marianne less well. I felt for her, understood how she had suffered from it, and was glad to see how supportive Salman was of her.

Meal was chicken and ginger cooked in a wok so it smoked up kitchen where we were to eat, but the smell was delicious. Salman took me outside to show me the garden. He had planted some of the flowers himself. The white primroses were in bloom and deep purple clematis. Going into his son's playhouse with Salman, musty damp smell.

Salman mentioned their plans to go to Kashmir next year in August, but Marianne didn't seem to have accepted these plans. Her face seemed full of doubt, concern, worry looking for a focus. Tossing her hair. Both of them dressed very casually—she in sweatshirt cut low, revealing neck and shoulder. He in light cotton pants and shirt. Ray and I had "dressed" for dinner, not knowing what sort of occasion it was, whether other people would be there. Very nice to find just the four of us since on all the other occasions we'd seen Salman before it had been a mob scene.

Paris, June 26

Reading at French Center for Writers: Maison des Ecrivains (rue de Verneuil) was the main activity of the day because it meant a reunion with François (Ray's French translator) and also Laurence, both of whom we'd met on our earlier Paris trip.

After the reading and reception we walk to the house of Beverly Gordey whose husband, Michel, was once married to Chagall's daughter. They remained friends even after the end of the marriage. Chagall used to give them little drawings as presents, until they had children. Then he gave them chocolates. Many paintings no one has ever seen are there. Michel is a retired journalist, one of the first allowed to visit USSR when journalists began to be allowed in again. Beverly told a story about arriving in France, newly married from America, with Michel's luggage and trunks. In one was a tuxedo shirt with a drawing on it. "What a shame," she thought, "someone has ruined this perfectly good shirt." So she threw it out. (She

Kristina and Richard Ford, Jonathan Raban and Ray, Paris.
Photo copyright © Tess Gallagher.

knew nothing about Chagall: "It's an awful story to tell on myself," she said.) She is a rather elegant American, tall and well-dressed. Michel is many years older. He told me he was rereading John Dos Passos and really loving it.

Story Olivier [Olivier Cohen, Ray's editor at Mazarine] told of his father taking him to Deux Magots and pointing out Albert Camus: "You see that man over there? That's Albert Camus. You don't know who he is now, but you will later. He is a writer, and someday he'll be recognized as a great man and a great writer and everyone will know his name." And Olivier has remembered, and because his father was right about Camus there is a sense of literary history being, in some sense, aware

Ray and Tess at Deux Magots, Paris, 1987.
Photo copyright © Tess Gallagher.

of itself *as* it happens, but also as if it is a wonderful secret waiting, always waiting to be told later.

And there we are at the Deux Magots, Ray wearing what I call his "Camus jacket," the leather flight jacket I gave him for his birthday. We are in love and holding hands. Famous to each other, the way lovers are. A stranger asks if we'd like our photo taken because my Polaroid is on the table. We say, "Okay," and he snaps the photo, not knowing or caring who we are. Just doing a favor to two strangers, then slipping away into the streets of Paris.

Raymond Carver, 1938 to 1988

Even though I don't choose to express the loss in this way, I understand Leonard Bernstein's having gone to bed and stayed there for six months after his wife died of cancer. But in my family no one would be so indulged. You have to get up, make an effort at normalcy, do your share, and how you feel doesn't come into it . . . part of the working-class ethic, I suppose. But that's where both Ray and I come from. Ray once said to me, speaking about the days before we met, "I never had *time* to have a nervous breakdown." The "iron will" which he says in one of his poems is necessary for making art, must, I think, have been forged during just such times when there was "no-choice-but-to-go-ahead."

Yet Ray and I learned somehow to do more than just go ahead; we learned how to go ahead with hope. When we joined lives nearly eleven years ago in El Paso, Texas, we were both recovering from an erosion of trust and hope. Between us I think we'd left behind something like thirty years of failed marriage. We more than rebuilt trust. We got to a place where trust was second nature. But along the way, we had a saying that helped us. We used to say: "Don't get weird on me, Babe. Don't get weird." And believe me, by then we'd both lived enough to know what weird was.

Published in *Granta* (Autumn 1988). Copyright © Tess Gallagher. I delivered these remarks at Legends, a nightclub in London, where a memorial was arranged for Ray by his British editor, Christopher MacLahose, in November 1988. Attending were many of Ray's European editors, as well as many writers, including Edmund White, Richard Ford, Joy Williams, Drago Stambuk, Salman Rushdie, and Sir and Mrs. V. S. Pritchett. [T.G.]

Tess at Ray's gravesite, Ocean View Cemetery, Port Angeles,
Washington, August 1988. Photo copyright © Betty Udesen,
Seattle Times.

You probably know the story. Ray'd been off alcohol about a
year when we began to live together. He was shaky. He didn't
know if he'd ever write again. He literally ran from the phone
when it rang. He'd been twice bankrupt. I can still remember
how his eyes lit up when he saw my Visa card.

I think now we built and rebuilt on Ray's capacity for joy,
which extended even to the ability to take immense pleasure
in someone else's pleasure, and this capacity continued into
his last days. But it hadn't always been this way. Since his death
I've become the repository for many people's memories and
stories about Ray. I've read letters from friends he knew dur-
ing what he called his "Bad Raymond" days that he was, ac-
cording to one writer, "the most unhappy man I'd ever met."
Twenty years later the two met again and the friend was aston-
ished at the transformation.

Theodore Roethke wrote, "The right thing happens to the

happy man," and I was privileged to witness as Ray became that happy man. I'm often remembering how glad he was to be alive, and because he was happy to be alive Ray grieved to be leaving his life so early. I won't hide that from you. If will alone could have prevailed, he'd be alive today and with us.

Still, at each turn during his illness he asked: What can I do with the life that's left? He chose to work, to write his poems, in spite of the terror of a brain tumor and later, in June, of the recurrence of cancer in his lungs. His response to that blow was to think of something important to celebrate, and on June 17 we were married in Reno, Nevada. It was a very Carveresque affair, held in the little Heart of Reno Chapel across from the courthouse. Afterwards we went gambling at Harrah's Club and with every turn of the wheel I won. I couldn't stop winning.

Near the end Ray knew, he was sure, that his stories were going to last: "We're out there in history now, Babe," he said, and he felt lucky to know it. He had a period of clear celebration when his book of stories, *Where I'm Calling From,* came out that spring. There was a brief interlude when we were free from the mental suffering that accompanied his disease and during which he accepted joyously and gratefully the wonderful reviews, induction into the American Academy and Institute of Arts and Letters, a doctorate of letters from the University of Hartford, and the Brandeis Medal for Excellence.

I'm in mourning and celebration for the artist and the man, and also for that special entity which was our particular relationship which allowed such a beautiful alchemy in our lives, a kind of luminous reciprocity. There is a scientific term which suits: *mutuality.* We helped, nurtured, and protected each other, and what's more, in the Rilkean sense, we guarded and respected each other's solitude. In our days we were always asking: *What really matters?*

Ray gave me encouragement to write stories and I gave him encouragement to write his stories and his poems, poems through which he worked out his own spiritual equanimity; for he was, I think, at his death, one of those rare, purified beings for whom, as Tolstoy says, the only response is love. He lived every day with the assurance and comfort that I cherished him. As Simone de Beauvoir said, when challenged by feminists for her devotion to Sartre and his work: "But I *like* to work in the garden next to mine." I'll miss working in that strange, real garden—Ray's garden. Everything I ever gave there I got back in his gifts of attention to my own work. It has sustained me since his death to be putting his last book in order. I'll miss his delight and laughter in the house and his unfailing kindness, for he was, before anything, my great friend.

All those qualities you sensed about Raymond Carver, that he was a man who would do the decent, the right and generous thing—that was how he was. I can tell you from inside the story. He was like that. And he managed this in a rather complicated life. For his hardships didn't all end back there in the bad old days, and the nature of those hardships is recorded in his stories and poems.

In the last book he completed, one of the epigraphs is a quote from Robert Lowell which reads: "Yet why not say what happened?" I see this as central to Ray's attitude toward his art and its relation to his life. He carried some burdens of guilt about "what had happened," and he worked out his redemption and consequently some of ours in his art.

A few days after Ray's death I went into his study in Port Angeles—the study he'd always dreamed of, with a fireplace and a view of valley and mountains, then water beyond. I sat at the desk awhile. Just sat. Then I reached down and pulled open a drawer. Inside I found a dozen folders full of ideas for stories that would have carried him well into the year 2015. I'm sad we won't be reading those stories. But I can't stay in that sadness long. I keep feeling how much, in such a short time, how incredibly much he gave! We have to accept the blessing of that, and Ray believed that he had been graced and blessed, and that he had done his utmost to return that blessing to the world. As he has.

I was standing with a friend at Ray's graveside overlooking the Strait of Juan de Fuca a week after his death, and the friend remembered a line from Rilke and said it aloud. It seemed to express the transformation Ray has come to now: "And he was everywhere, like the evening hour." To conclude I'd like to present the last poem in his final manuscript.

Late Fragment

And did you get what
you wanted from this life, even so?
I did.
And what did you want?
To call myself beloved, to feel myself
beloved on the earth.

Soul-Making

Last things, we learn, have rights of their own. They don't need us, but in our need of them we commemorate and make more real that finality which encircles, and draws us again into that central question of any death: What is life for? Raymond Carver lived and wrote his answers: "I've always squandered," he told an interviewer, steering a hard course away from the lofty and noble. It was Carver's Law not to save up for some longed-for future, but to use up the best in him each day and to trust more would come. Even the packaging of the cigarettes he smoked carried the imprint of his oath in the imperative: NOW.

This injunction would bear down on us with increasing intensity in the final months of his life. In an episode eerily like that preceding the death of Chekhov, to whom he had paid tribute in his story "Errand," Ray had been diagnosed with lung cancer after spitting up blood in September 1987. There would follow several months of struggle after which the cancer would reoccur as a brain tumor in early March 1988. After twice swerving off recommendations for brain surgery by several doctors, he would undergo seven weeks of intense, full-brain radiation. The respite was short, however, for by early June tumors would again be found in his lungs.

These are the facts of that time, enough to have made realists of us if we hadn't been realists already. Nonetheless, much as Chekhov had kept reading the train schedules *away* from the town in which he would die, Ray kept working, planning, believing in the importance of the time he had left, and also believing that he might, through some loop in

An earlier version of this essay introduced Raymond Carver's *A New Path to the Waterfall* (Atlantic Monthly Press, 1989).

fate, even get out of it. An errand list I found in a shirt pocket after his death read "eggs, peanut butter, hot choc" and then, after a space, "Australia? Antarctica??" Ray's insistent belief in his own capacity to recover from reversals during the course of his illness gave us both strength. In his journal he wrote: "When hope is gone, the ultimate sanity is to grasp at straws." In this way he lived hope as a function of gesture, a reaching *for* or *toward,* while the object of promise stayed rightly illusory. The alternative was acceptance of death, which at age fifty was, for him, impossible. Another journal entry revealed his anguish as the pace of the disease quickened: "I wish I had a while. Not five years—or even three years—I couldn't ask for that long, but if I had even a year. If I knew I had a year."

In January 1988 Ray began keeping a journal under the inspiration of Stephen Spender's *Journals/1939–1983,* but with the discovery of his brain tumor it broke off suddenly in March, though he would start again later in another notebook. Our attentions turned instead to the drafting of a short essay to appear in the commencement booklet for the University of Hartford, where Ray was to accept a doctorate of letters in May.

During much of this time I had been clinging to the stories of Chekhov, reading one after the other of the Ecco Press volumes, and now I offered two passages to Ray from "Ward No. 6" to illustrate the epigraph from Saint Teresa ("Words lead to deeds . . . they prepare the soul, make it ready, and move it to tenderness"), which he'd taken from my book of poems, *Amplitude,* to begin his essay. Ray incorporated the passages from Chekhov into his piece, and this was the beginning of an important spiritual accompaniment which began to run through our days, and which eventually would play an important part in the writing of *A New Path to the Waterfall,* his last book.

The fervor with which we both seized on these particular moments in "Ward No. 6" came, I think, directly out of the ordeal we were undergoing with Ray's health, and this was particularly true of the second passage in which two characters, a disaffected doctor and an imperious postmaster, his elder, suddenly find themselves discussing the human soul.

"And you do not believe in the immortality of the soul?"

"No, honored Mihail Averyanitch; I do not believe it, and, have no grounds for believing it."

"I must own I doubt it too," Mihail Averyanitch admits. "And yet I have a feeling as though I should never die myself: 'Old fogey, it's time you were dead!' but there is a little voice in my soul that says: 'Don't believe it; you won't die.' "

In his framing of the passage Ray underscored the power of "words which linger as deeds" and out of which "a little voice in the soul" is born. He seemed almost grateful to observe how, in the Chekhov story, "the way we have dismissed certain concepts about life, about death, suddenly gives over unexpectedly to belief of an admittedly fragile but insistent nature."

I continued to bring Chekhov into our days, reading a story first thing in the morning, then telling it to Ray when I came down for breakfast. I would give the story in as true a fashion as I could, and Ray would inevitably become engaged by it and have to read it for himself that afternoon. By evening we could discuss it.

Another of Ray's influences came from one of the books he'd been reading early in the year, Czeslaw Milosz's *Unattainable Earth*. In the interest of what he called "a more spacious form," Milosz had incorporated prose quotes from Casanova's *Memoirs,* snippets from Baudelaire, from his uncle Oscar Milosz, Pascal, Goethe, and other thinkers and writers who'd affected him as he was writing his poems. He also includes his own musings, which take the form of confessions, questionings, and insights. Ray was attracted to the inclusiveness of Milosz's approach. His own reading at the time included Federico García Lorca, Jaroslav Seifert, Tomas Tranströmer, Robert Lowell, *The Selected Poems* of Milosz, and a rereading of Tolstoy's *The Death of Ivan Ilych.*

In early June, when we were given the devastating news that tumors had again shown up on x rays of his lungs, it was to Chekhov, our literary companion, to whom we instinctively turned in order to restore our steadfastness. One night I looked at certain passages I had bracketed in the stories and realized that they seemed to be speaking toward poems of Ray's I'd been helping revise. On impulse I went to the computer, shaped some of these excerpts into lines, and gave them titles. When I showed the results to Ray, it was as if we'd discovered another Chekhov inside Chekhov. But because I'd been looking at the passages with Ray's poems in mind, there was the sense that Chekhov had stepped toward us, and that while he remained in his own time, he seemed also to have become our contemporary. The world of headlong carriage races through snowstorms, of herring-head soup, of a dish made of bulls' eyes, of cooks picking sorrel for vegetable soup, of peasant children raised not to flinch at the crude language of their drunken parents—his world was at home with the world of Raymond Carver.

It was a bewildering time for us, but instead of giving over to visitors and a parade of sorrowful good-byes, we made the decision not to tell anyone about the cancer's recurrence in Ray's lungs. This allowed us to keep our attention on the things we wanted and needed to do. One important thing we decided was to celebrate our eleven years together by getting married in Reno, Nevada, on June 17. The wedding was what Ray called a "high tacky affair" and it took place across from the courthouse in the Heart of Reno Chapel, which had a huge heart in the window spiked with small golden lightbulbs and a sign that read *Se habla español*. Afterwards we went gambling in the casinos and I headed into a phenomenal three-day winning streak at roulette.

When we returned home Ray wrote "Proposal," which carries the urgency of that time, the raw sense of life lived without guile, or that cushion of hope we count on to extend life past the provisional.

> Back home we held on to each other and, without
> embarrassment or caginess, let it all reach full
>   meaning. This
> was it, so any holding back had to be stupid, had to be
> insane and meager. How many ever get to this? I thought
> at the time. It's not far from here to needing
> a celebration, a joining, a bringing of friends into it,
> a handing out of champagne and
> Perrier. "Reno," I said. "Let's go to Reno and get
>   married."
> (From "Proposal," *A New Path to the Waterfall*, 116)

Our having married anchored us in a new way and it seemed we had knowingly saved this occasion to give ourselves solace, and perhaps also to allow us to toss back our heads once more in a rippling cosmic laugh, as from that "gay and empty journey" of which Kafka writes.

This was also the time during which Ray wrote "Gravy." The idea for the poem had come from a conversation we'd had while sitting on the deck at Sky House, facing the Strait of Juan de Fuca, taking stock. "You remember telling me how you almost died before you met me?" I asked him. "It could've ended back then and we'd never even have met. None of this would have happened." We sat there quietly, just marveling at what we'd been allowed.

> No other word will do. For that's what it was. Gravy.
> Gravy, these past ten years.
> Alive, sober, working, loving and
> being loved by a good woman. Eleven years
> ago he was told he had six months to live
> at the rate he was going. And he was going
> nowhere but down. So he changed his ways
> somehow. He quit drinking! And the rest?
> After that it was *all* gravy, every minute
> of it, up to and including when he was told about,
> well, some things that were breaking down and
> building up inside his head. "Don't weep for me,"
> he said to his friends. "I'm a lucky man.
> I've had ten years longer than I or anyone
> expected. Pure gravy. And don't forget it."
>
> ("Gravy," *A New Path to the Waterfall*, 118)

Here Ray displaces the devastating significance of impending death by memory of a death narrowly avoided, when in 1976 he nearly died of alcoholism. In effect, he used his oncoming death as proof of a former escape; and death, he realized, once displaced by such an excess of living during the ten productive years he'd been allowed, could never be quite as unrelenting. For Ray, of course, in facing his death, there was the question of whether the memory of his life would persist importantly through the survival of his writings. At the same time, his poems suggest that an artist's obsessions and signs, fragmentary and intermittent as they may be, belong to a world of necessity that transcends anyone else's need of them.

Shortly after our wedding, we had been given a gift. Our painter friend Alfredo Arreguin had been working on a large canvas about which mysterious, tantalizing hints had been leaked at intervals to us by his wife, Susan Lytle, also a painter. The day before our wedding reception, Alfredo and Susan arrived at Ridge House with the painting strapped to the top of their car. The painting, once hung in our living room, proved to be of several salmon leaping midair toward a stylized waterfall. In the sky, what Ray would call "the ghost fish" were patterned into clouds heading in the opposite direction. The rocks in the background were inhabited as well, studded with prehistoric eyes.

Each morning we took our coffee in front of the painting where Ray could sometimes be seen sitting alone during the day, meditating. When I look at it now, Ray's vitality seems embedded in the pageantry of a cycle we had seen played out year after year in the river below our house. In the painting the salmon are heading upstream, bowed eternally to the light in a fierce, determined leap above water, and above them the ghost fish float back unimpeded in an opposing current, relieved of their struggle.

Three weeks after Ray's death, as I entered into the computer the last corrections Ray had made to his poems, I realized I had perfectly, though unwittingly, enacted the instructions of his poem "No Need" the night before his death.

> I see an empty place at the table.
> Whose? Who else's? Who am I kidding?
> The boat's waiting. No need for oars
> or a wind. I've left the key
> in the same place. You know where.
> Remember me and all we did together.
> Now, hold me tight. That's it. Kiss me
> hard on the lips. There. Now
> let me go, my dearest. Let me go.
> We shall not meet again in this life,
> so kiss me goodbye now. Here, kiss me again.
> Once more. There. That's enough.

> Now, my dearest, let me go.
> It's time to be on the way.
> ("No Need," *A New Path to the Waterfall,* 119)

The three kisses which had been meant as "Good night" had, at the time, carried the possibility that Ray would not wake again. "Don't be afraid," I'd said. "Just go into your sleep now" and, finally, "I love you"—to which he had answered. "I love you too. You get some sleep now." He never opened his eyes again, and at 6:20 the next morning he stopped breathing.

In "Late Fragment," the final poem of his last book, his voice has earned its coda.

> And did you get what
> you wanted from this life, even so?
> I did.
> And what did you want?
> To call myself beloved, to feel myself
> beloved on the earth.
> —("Late Fragment," *A New Path to the Waterfall,* 122)

There is the sense that the need to be beloved has been central to the effort of the life and, therefore, to the writing, and that one's own willingness to award that to the self—to "call myself beloved" and, beyond that, to "feel myself beloved on the earth"—has somehow been achieved. When I was thinking of what poem to put on his gravestone, this one claimed the right. And many who visit that windblown bluff, I've come to know, carry the poem away with them to use for a wedding ceremony or to honor one of their own dead.

For a recovering alcoholic, the self-recognition Ray expresses in this poem, and the more generalized feeling of love he was allowing himself, was no small accomplishment. He knew he had been graced and blessed and that his writing had enabled him to reach far beyond the often mean circumstances from which he and those he wrote about had come, and also that through his writing those working-class lives had become a part of literature. On a piece of scrap paper near his typewriter he had written: "Forgive me if I'm thrilled with the idea, but just now I thought that every poem I write ought to be called 'Happiness.' " And he was happy, in spite of facing up to a much too early death. During those last, long summer evenings, we were both in the keeping of a grateful equanimity as we talked of our life together as writers, lovers, and helpmates.

In Alaska, on one last fishing trip, we raised glasses of Perrier to toast the finishing of Ray's book, and to pay tribute to ourselves, for managing to complete it against so many odds. In the crucial last days of our work, guests had arrived for an extended stay and Ray's son had come from Germany. We'd kept working, parceling out the day. "Don't tell them we've finished," Ray said to me—"them" meaning the guests. "I need you here." So the book as pretext allowed us a few more precious mornings with each other before what would be the final onset of his illness.

After our guests had left, we began making calls, trying desperately to arrange a trip to Russia to see Chekhov's grave and to visit the houses of Dostoevsky and Tolstoy. I wanted to find certain places associated with Akhmatova. Even though this wasn't to be, our planning in those last days was, in itself, a kind of dream-visit that lifted our spirits. Later, when Ray entered the hospital, we talked about what a great trip it would have been. "I'll go there," I said, "I'll go for us." "I'll get there before you," he said, and grinned. "I'm traveling faster."

After Ray's death, at home in Port Angeles on August 2, 1988, the mail was heaped for weeks with letters and cards from people all over the world mourning his passing. Many sent moving accounts of their having met Ray even briefly, things he'd said, acts of kindness performed, stories of his life before I had known him. Copies of obituaries began to arrive from papers around the country, and one day I opened a packet from London with the obituary from the *Sunday Times*. The headline above the photograph of Ray with his hands in the pockets of his leather jacket reads simply: "The American Chekhov." From the *Guardian* there was the possessive "America's Chekhov." I seemed to be reading these *with* Ray, and to be carrying his knowing of it. Either headline would have been accolade enough to have made him humbly and deeply grateful.

To the end, Ray's poetry was a spiritual necessity. The truths Ray came to through his poems involved a dismantling of artifice to a degree not even William Carlos Williams, his early inspiration, might have anticipated. Ray had read Milosz's lines in "*Ars Poetica?*" and they'd confirmed his own poetics:

> I have always aspired to a more spacious form
> that would be free from the claims of poetry or prose
> and would let us understand each other without exposing
> the author or reader to sublime agonies.

> In the very essence of poetry there is something indecent:
> a thing is brought forth which we didn't know we had in us,
> so we blink our eyes, as if a tiger had sprung out
> and stood in the light, lashing his tail.

Ray used his poetry to flush the tiger from hiding. He did not look on his writing as the offering of commodities to a readership. He was purposefully disobedient when pressures were put on him to write stories because that's where his reputation was centered and where the largest reward in terms of publication and audience lay. He didn't care. He was not "building a career." He was living a vocation, and this meant that his writing, whether poetry or prose, was tied to inner mandates. These insisted more and more on an unmediated apprehension of his subjects, and poetry was the form that best allowed this.

In his own fashion, Ray did as much to challenge the idea of what poetry can be as he did to reinvigorate the short story. He wrote and lived his last ten years by his own design, and as his companion in that life, I'm glad to have helped him keep his poetry alive during the journey. I'm grateful for the comfort and soul-making he drew from it, and for the gifts he left us all, despite his own too-early going.

Foreword to *No Heroics, Please,* by Raymond Carver

There is a particularly intimate feeling, as if one were joining a secret, when we are given the chance to see the work of an artist or writer before they have discovered themselves or been discovered by their public. This book, beginning as it does with some of the first stories written and published by Raymond Carver, includes the reader in those early, formative moments of his fiction and poetry.

Ray, in a poem on Anna Akhmatova and Modigliani, recalled their exuberance in a time before their talents had come to bear on the world, sitting in the Luxembourg Gardens, "reciting Verlaine to each other. Both of them / 'as yet untouched by their futures.'" Although Ray would become one of the world's most acclaimed practitioners of the short story, he was to be "untouched" by his own future until well into his forties. After more than twenty years of writing he enjoyed five years of gradual acknowledgment, then died suddenly of lung cancer at fifty.

This collection allows us to make that arc with Raymond Carver from prediscovery days to the unfilled ambitions for the next work indicated in his late essay "On Longer Short Stories." His death came at a time when he'd felt he was on the verge of a new way of writing. His stories had deepened, become longer and more intricate psychologically and spiritually, nonetheless maintaining what he would hold to from

No Heroics, Please: Uncollected Writings of Raymond Carver, edited by William Stull (Vintage Books, 1992). Originally published by Harvill, London, in 1991. Copyright © Tess Gallagher.

Pound to the end: "Fundamental accuracy of statement is the ONE sole morality of writing."

Throughout the book, much of it occasional prose from his last ten years, we experience a man immersed in his art and life. The final essay, written as the cancer advanced, concludes with a meditation on a line from Saint Teresa* which could serve well to indicate where Carver arrived: "Words lead to deeds. . . . they prepare the soul, make it ready, and move it to tenderness."

Saint Teresa's verb "move" was a word central to Ray's ambitions as a writer. We meet it often in his reviews and introductions to various short-story anthologies. He wanted readers to be "*moved,* and maybe even a little haunted." But he also wanted to "shrive" his readers—a beautiful old biblical word meaning to "be at scribe," "to hear the confession of," but also to "give absolution to" a person, to "purge." Ray was making his art, but it involved him in the methods of absolution—hearing and telling. He trusted that if he managed this sequence truly enough, the dividends would carry into the lives of his readers.

I have a real respect and affection for the writings collected in this book, not only for their immediate biographical and scholarly value, but because they reflect so truly the passion and clarity of the spirit behind them. I feel greatly indebted to William Stull, who initiated the idea for this book. He did the often tedious work of actually collecting these pieces from newspapers and periodicals. But more than this, he cherished them, arranged them, and made important editorial decisions about them. His special attention is a direct gift toward an understanding of Ray's genesis and the amazement we can now more completely feel for Raymond Carver's extraordinary journey. I am also grateful to our British editor, Bill Swainson, who helped immensely in shaping and directing our work.

This book begins with "Furious Seasons," Ray's first published story, for which Faulkner and Joyce are evident mentors.

---

*Taken from the epigraph of *Amplitude: New and Selected Poems,* Graywolf Press, 1987.

It represents perhaps the path not taken, since the borrowed devices—flashbacks and stream of consciousness—will seldom appear in his future work. Richard Day, one of Ray's first teachers in the short story, recognized the young writer's skill in avoiding an obvious pitfall: "He tells the 'now' in past tense and the past events in the 'now,' breaking up the surface in such a way that he disguised what would otherwise have been simple melodrama."

It was a particularly interesting story for me to reread since it shows that Ray hadn't yet adopted two principles of short fiction which later became his laws: clarity and purposefulness of expression. But the movement in this story is seamless, held together by that hum of tension he later mastered.

A rough gem of a story, "The Hair," seems antecedent to the later story "Careful." A hair stuck between the character's teeth in this story causes life to seem untenable. We also witness the first moments of that honed *dis-ease* for which Carver became famous. "The Aficionados," also written at this time, is one of only two parodies Ray wrote and published. At twenty-four he'd never attended a bullfight except in Hemingway's fiction, so it's no wonder he swerves off stylistic vestiges of Hemingway's iceberg theory, to a raucously dramatic meltdown in the final scene. He took his jabs at his literary mentor under the pseudonym "John Vale," but Hemingway was an important literary model who would later give way to Chekhov.

The reviews, introductions, and essays collected here are valuable for regenerating the current of Ray's enthusiasms, his love of a pure "good read," for vagaries of character, for the turns and twists of plot, but always with that ultimate mandate of something important at stake. As Ray said in a statement he attributed to Bill Kittredge: 'What you do matters. What you do, right or wrong, has consequences, brother."

Prior to our meeting in 1977, Ray had written no serious essays or reviews. Over the preceding four years he had essentially stopped writing altogether, but the invitation to appraise the work of his peers, as well as other changes in his life such as a steady teaching income, allowed him slowly to regain confidence in himself after ten deeply debilitating years of alcoholism.

As we read what he says about teaching writing or the reasons behind his choices for an anthology, we draw instruction from his noticing, his respect for "vivid depiction of place," "demonic intensity," and his awareness of "what counts": "Love, death, dreams, ambition, growing up, coming to terms with your own and other people's limitations."

Ray's sorties into the public arena of reviewing had variously humorous and chastening results. I still recall how depressed he was after reading the Hemingway biography by Jeffrey Meyers. Ray felt that a prerequisite for writing a biography should be a love of one's subject, and he was scathingly acute about this as a failing of Meyers's biography in his review of the book. Meyers attempted to defend himself with a letter in the *New York Times Book Review*, but he achieved his ultimate comeback in person.

Ray had made a trip to Stanford to read his stories. There'd been a luncheon at which he'd been asked to shake hands with the man about to be seated to his left. It was an awkward moment, the man staring into his shoelaces, the handshaking between them. Ray, not having caught the man's name, mumbled an overcongenial "Happy to meet you!" The hosts, assuming an affinity for Hemingway, had seated Ray and Meyers next to each other. "I kept wondering why this man was eating with his back to me," Ray said.

America may be a big country, but its literary circles can draw a noose at any spot on the map. On another occasion we'd flown to Dallas for an event only to discover Donald Barthelme among the cocktail guests. He seems, to my memory, to have been like a Cheshire cat puzzling the koan of whether or not to eat me. Ray had just published a review of a recent collection of Barthelme's stories, toward which he'd been mildly inclined, while still genuinely admiring him as an original, a master in his own right.

At the party, Ray was within earshot but keeping a healthy distance. I, however, in the odd luck of such gatherings, had been shuffled into close range. Barthelme twinkled kindly at me and said, in a louder-than-necessary voice: "When I don't like something I find it sufficient to surround it with a generous amount of silence." Ray, of course, heard this in ricochet. Back at our hotel we laughed uproariously and I demanded hazardous duty pay. The next time we saw Barthelme was at the celebration of Ray's having been awarded the Harold and Mildred Strauss Living Award, which provided a five-year stipend allowing Ray to write full time. Barthelme, one of the judges, had become his benefactor.

In my relation to Ray's work I've tried to avoid taking the position of guarding the keep. I do bear a special relationship to his writing, having companioned his life and work during his last eleven years, having suggested and reviewed line by line the revisions he speaks of in his wonderful essay "On Rewriting." We discovered how each poem or story could evolve, for we understood writing as a process of revelation.

Given this relationship to the later work, it was not second nature for me to stand aside for a story like "Bright Red Apples," which doesn't seem to know what it's about, or for a couple of the poems I might have quietly put back into the drawer. But I think Ray, in his ultimate humility about origins and talent, would have been guilelessly forthright even toward work written a quarter of a century before he would hit his stride. I loved his honest regard for his poems, not simply as aesthetic success stories or failures, but as moments of aliveness which had held the fabric of his life together during dire times. I'm grateful to every one of them. Those I particularly prize are "Soda Crackers," "Forever," "Adultery," "Prosser," "For Tess," and "A Summer in Sacramento."

In one of her essays Kay Boyle speaks of writers who were stunted because they never found "their people," those for whom they could speak. Raymond Carver's good fortune was not only that he came from his people, but that he was able to bring their mostly unattainable dreams to bear on the world's literature. When Ray writes the words "Forever . . . Forever" in the introduction to the Franklin Library edition of *Where I'm Calling From* (his last book of stories published in America), I hear the iron will it took to get there, and the hard double ring of live words spoken only as we can think them for him now, quietly in our reading.

I believe Ray would be glad if some young or even middle-aged writer, reading his beginning efforts or his advice in the essays, felt they could do as well or better, or certainly no worse. There's something here for the teacher and those who simply love being inside the story of a particularly American writer, one who brought about a renaissance in the short story that has its impact even at this remove. Beyond this, Ray would be pleased if a reader or scholar found something to amplify the work he meant to last, yes, forever.

Introduction to *All of Us: The Collected Poems of Raymond Carver*

"Without hope and without despair"—this quiet banner of determination from Isak Dinesen flew over the last ten years of Raymond Carver's life. Most of these poems were written during that time, some in a great lunge of reception, almost two hundred drafted between October 1983 and August 1985.

Ray had written poetry and fiction in tandem, beginning in 1957. This collection, which spans more than thirty years, allows us to see that his poetry was not something he wrote between stories. Rather, it was the spiritual current out of which he moved to write the short stories for which, after his death, he would be called by the *Guardian* newspaper (London), "America's Chekhov." Now that the entirety of his poetry has been collected, its full mass and density can at last be appreciated.

It is said of Lao-tzu, the great Chinese author of the *Tao Te Ching*, that people became attached to his style because it had a "gem-like lucidity," was "radiant with humor and grace and large-heartedness and deep wisdom" (Stephen Mitchell). In looking for a way to characterize what endears Ray's poems to me, these remarks seem appropriate.

With the poetry we come to love, and with Ray's in particular, at some point we surrender, and the consciousness of the speaker in the poems is taken into the bloodstream to be recirculated through our lives. We are grateful when a poet gives us new ways of thinking and feeling on trampled ground, and for radiance itself as that new way. What we also find in these poems is an extraordinary sensibility that stays approachable, even companionable.

Ray's presence in the poems, as with the man himself in life, continually disarms through some paradoxical capacity both for knowing and innocence. His self-humor steadily redeems him, along with his amazement and curiosity about the complexities of human life and its connection to animal life. I think of a moment in "Prosser," when he wants to find out what geese like about green wheat. He writes: "I ate some of it once too, to see." As in his fiction, he demonstrates often that he knows how to pace himself and knows too, with Isaac Babel, that a period in the right place can stop the heart: "Geese love this shattered wheat also. / They will die for it."

I recall a commentary on the life and work of Emily Dickinson in which Dickinson's poems were described as having arrived so directly out of the necessities of the soul that they violated even the notion of poetry as a formed artifact of language. They were instead the soul incarnate in its most vital appearance. The meaning was perhaps that language and the poet's nature were so in accord that the interlocutor of voice was wholly absorbed by what it was saying. In a similar way, Ray's artlessness burned so fiercely it consumed all trace of process. Once in a while we get a writer like this, a comet without a tail, yet whose arrival and impact are undeniable.

Anyone who has ever felt befriended by a person at a crucial moment will recognize the place from which I prefer to regard this lifetime in poetry. For eleven years I was Ray's companion and literary collaborator, and finally his wife. I saw the poems in draft and, from *Fires* onward had the great pleasure of arranging them in books. Because of this I experienced the poems as intimates. Sojourners. The sinew of a shared life. And this intimacy embraces even those poems written before we met in 1977. Often in revised versions, they form an integral part of the story. Since this book is essentially the tracing of a passage from one shore to another, inception is as important as arrival.

I am stricken to the core by an early poem, "Morning, Thinking of Empire," where a mundane act becomes the chilling image for a marriage's inevitable interior dissolution: "I coolly crack the egg of a fine Leghorn chicken." The moment seems unsurvivable, the collapse of a shared universe rendered unflinchingly. In the context of the entire poem we experience it action by action, as a series of spiritually irretrievable moments which cut the partners off from each other and obliterate all hope for the regeneration of the marriage:

> We press our lips to the enameled rim of the cups
> and know this grease that floats
> over the coffee will one day stop our hearts.
> . . . .
> I coolly crack the egg of a fine Leghorn chicken.
> Your eyes film. You turn from me and look across
> the rooftops at the sea. Even the flies are still.
> I crack the other egg.
> Surely we have diminished one another.

The word "surely" here is a cliff and an avalanche, accompanied by the steel-eyed gaze and barely containable assessment of the speaker.

The poems, throughout, are keenly attentive to life as it is being lived, but from 1979 on they also make retrospective safaris into the jungle of old harms, renegotiated from safer, saner ground. Ray had gradually absorbed some attitudes I held toward time in poetry—for one thing, that it was more than lived time, and might therefore enlarge one's spiritual reach. My feeling that all time—past, present, and future—exists within reach at the moment the poem is being written was helpful to him. He allowed himself to reenter older work with the present moment as definitive and regenerative.

From early to late, the poems *are* beautifully clear, and this clarity, like the sweet clang of spring water to the mouth, needs no apology. Time spent reading Ray's poems becomes quickly fruitful, for the poems give themselves as easily and unself-consciously as breath. Who wouldn't be disarmed by poetry which requires so much less of us than it unstintingly gives?

I am aware of those honed minds that find Ray's transparency somehow an insult to intelligence. They would have applied an editor like a tourniquet. I might have served as such, had I thought it true to his gift. I didn't. If Ray hadn't given and published in the ample way he did, I believe we would not receive his guileless offering with the same credulity and gratitude. Certainly poems like "My Boat," "The Old Days," "Woolworth's, 1954," "My Car," "Earwigs," "You Don't Know What Love Is," "Happiness," and any number of poems I love might have been omitted. Overreach was natural and necessary to him, and to fault him for it would be like spanking a cat for swallowing the goldfish.

The narrative directness of his poems, as well as the precision of phrase and image, amplifies access until we push through into yet another chamber of astonishing, unadorned truth. Suddenly, like deer caught at night in headlights, blind mystery stares back at us with equal force. We are pinioned—"flimsy as / balsa wood" ("Balsa Wood")—or told "the mind can't sleep, can only lie awake and / gorge" ("Winter Insomnia"), or birds arrive as omens, "the clacking of their bills / like iron on iron" ("The News Carried to Macedonia"). We glimpse the extravagant yet matter-of-fact sensuality, of the world around us: "lean haunches" of deer "flicker / under an assault of white butterflies" ("Rhodes"). Wonder in everyday forms appears in a shirt on a clothesline filling out to "near human shape" ("Louise"), or a hand reaches through to touch the sleeve of a suit inside a garment bag, a burial suit, and this "reaching through" ("Another Mystery") becomes an entrance to another world which is also the same world.

Many of the later poems have the daybook quality of nature and life observed moment to moment. We feel befriended and accompanied by the spirit in these. Ray's often third-person fictionalized stance places him alongside the reader, watching with conflicting feelings as events unfold. He is a poet of great suppleness of being, and his ability to hold contraries in balance while sorting out their ramifications, not oversubscribing to either side, amounts to courage for us all.

We are often with the poems as we are with our neighbors and loved ones, taking them for granted, failing deeply to assess their comings and goings—we are that used to them. Then one day something happens. A father's wallet, an ordinary familiar object, comes into our hands, suddenly luminous with the power of the dead. In the final moments of Ray's "My Dad's Wallet"—perhaps a working-class version of Rilke's "Washing the Corpse"—it is "our breath coming and going" which signals death's communal arrival. Readers of his fiction will recognize that this phrase overlaps the ending of his story "What We Talk about When We Talk about Love." Sometimes, without embarrassment, Ray used the same events or recognitions in both poems and stories. The poems often clarify emotional or biographical ground left obscure in the stories. "Use it up," he used to say. "Don't save anything for later."

In the last lines of "The Caucasus: A Romance" the speaker calls his effort to represent what took place "but a rough record of the actual and the passing." This line might be a talisman for what Ray aimed at throughout—the felicitous hazard of rough record. While we may locate his pulse with this phrase, we must also understand that he revised tirelessly and that "rough" indicates truth unbeguiled, not carelessness. Ray meant to graft language onto experience in all its tenacious vitality, its rawness. To that end he gave us "yellow jackets and near / frostbite" ("Trying to Sleep Late on a Saturday Morning in November"), the "large dark bullethole / through the slender, delicate-looking / right hand" ("Wes Hardin: From a Photograph"), a heart "on the table" that is "a parody of affection" ("Poem for Dr. Pratt, a Lady Pathologist"), the young man "who keeps on drinking / and getting spit on for years" ("Reading"). His brilliant intuition for moments of consequence can wield a scythe across a lifetime—"The dying body is a clumsy partner" ("The Garden")—or discover "violets cut just an hour before lunch" ("The Pipe").

There is the feeling that all Ray's poems are in some sense escapes into the act of self-witness, as in "The Poem I Didn't Write." Each one bears the scarred patina of words gotten down on the page however the writer could, something wrestled from the torrent, using only that language which came readily, even haphazardly. Artifice gives way to velocity, to daring—"But the soul is also a smooth son of a bitch" ("Radio Waves")—to improvisation and exactitude of the moment: "At night, a moon broad and deep as a serving dish / sallies out" ("The Caucasus: A Romance"). Clichés go by like underbrush: "my hair stood on end" ("Wenas Ridge"). Then suddenly we are ambushed by memory "like a blow to the calf" (also "Wenas Ridge"). Clichés in Carver cajole the actual, until his attentiveness brings the next nuance of miracle into focus: "Suddenly as a signal, the birds / pass silently back into pine trees" ("With a Telescope Rod on Cowiche Creek"). His diction and syntax are American and find their antecedents in William Carlos Williams and Allen Ginsberg, Emily Dickinson and Louise Bogan. He also absorbed poets I brought close, including Rainer Maria Rilke, Theodore Roethke, Paul Celan, William Heyen, Seamus Heaney, Federico García Lorca, Robert Lowell, Czeslaw Milosz, Marianne Moore, Derek Mahon, W. B. Yeats, and Anna Akhmatova.

From the vantage of his poetry, Ray's life took on pattern and reason and gratitude—"my whole life, in switchbacks, ahead of me" ("Wenas Ridge"). Poetry, helicopter-like, gave him maneuverability over rugged, hostile terrain, a place where he could admit such things as ambivalence about Jesus while he continued to pray to "snake" ("Wenas Ridge"). Perhaps in the blunt-nosed zigzag of poems, he could attain elevation without the sleek evasions of elegance, irony, or even the easy exit of transcendence—all of which he would have chosen to forgo had they not, for the most part, been outside his nature and his aesthetic.

We don't love his poetry for its biographical peaks and valleys alone—though who wouldn't marvel at a man who walks away from near death by alcohol, and who keeps writing with a brain tumor and two-thirds of a lung gone to cancer? Rather, it's the intensity of down-to-earth searching that holds us throughout, the poet's willingness to revisit extremities, the sites of loss. We admire his ability to embody experience in fresh language and actions which occur not as a biography, but in moments created for and by those very poems: "I bashed that beautiful window. / And stepped back in" ("Locking Yourself Out, Then Trying to Get Back In").

Many American poetic voices of the past thirty years have traveled far, too far, on sincerity. Still more have proffered the sad and ofttimes dire contents of their lives as their main currency. Their sincerity often involves a subtle kind of salesmanship, an attempt to convince by forthrightness, by emptying a kit bag at the listener's feet, hoping for the reward of attention at any cost. Such writers assume themselves to be somehow bold and courageous for having torn the door off the confessional.

Ray's poetry escapes the pitfalls of the merely sincere by forming another kind of relationship with the reader. It attempts not the bond of commerce, but the bond of mutuality. The voice in the poems is, in fact, self-mutual, doubled and self-companioned to such a high degree in tone and stance that, indeed, we feel much relief in not being called out like the Mounties or inveigled to commiserate falsely. Ray is profitably his own interlocutor. The neighborliness and amplitude of the poems compel by a circuitry of strong emotional moments in which we join the events at a place beyond invitation. To our surprise we find we have come both to ourselves and our differences in another form.

Ray's appetite for inventorying domestic havoc is often relentless. We want to run from the room, from blear-eyed wisdom yoked to pain, to bitter fate: "She's caught / in the flywheel of a new love" ("Energy") or "far away— / another man is raising my children, / bedding my wife bedding my wife" ("Deschutes River"). The writer of these poems has outlived the world of no-remedy, and his artistic fortitude with the impossible encourages us toward our own forbearance.

The ravages of alcoholism and sexual betrayal give away to a new ease and largesse in the poems of *Where Water Comes Together with Other Water* (1985) and *Ultramarine* (1986), the work British readers first met in the collection *In a Marine Light* (1987), published the year before his death at age fifty from lung cancer. These poems expressed, among other things, a thankfulness even for his trials, and for having been delivered into a life he considered happy. This amplitude carried him into the final poems of *A New Path to the Waterfall* (1989), written in the last six months of his life. Art and life were his focus. Death, mosquito-like, hovered and supped at the periphery.

I recall in those last days being aware that I was, for Ray, the only reader of those poems he would have. I laughed and cried with him, reading them as they came. His humor, lashed as it was to pain, positively unraveled me. In "What the Doctor Said" we don't expect eagerness and the turnabout of thankful-

ness from a man receiving news of his oncoming death. But
that is what we get:

> he said I'm real sorry he said
> I wish I had some other kind of news to give you
> I said Amen and he said something else
> I didn't catch and not knowing what else to do
> and not wanting him to have to repeat it
> and me to have to fully digest it
> I just looked at him
> for a minute and he looked back it was then
> I jumped up and shook hands with this man who'd just given
>   me
> something no one else on earth had ever given me
> I may even have thanked him habit being so strong

It's steelhead season, early January 1996. I've been rereading
Ray's poems here at Sky House where he wrote so many of
them. Below in the valley, men are walking the banks of Morse
Creek, the river which became the central metaphor of *Where
Water Comes Together with Other Water.*

Just yesterday our neighbor, Art LaMore, recalled Ray's
amazing luck. One morning Ray had dropped a hook baited
with salmon roe off the footbridge and caught a ten-pound
steelhead. He'd carried it to Art's door, hooked over his fin-
gers by its gills, to show him. He had felt blessed beyond
reason. By the time I came home, he'd cleaned the fish on the
kitchen floor. There are still knife marks in the linoleum.
Men fish for years on Morse Creek and never catch a steel-
head. I don't think Ray knew this or cared. He simply ac-
cepted the gift.

We often walked along this river, sorting out the end of a
story, as with "Errand," or discussing our plans for trips. Al-
ways we found release and comfort in noticing—that pair of
herons, ducks breaking into flight upriver, the picked-over
carcass of a bird near the footpath, snow on the mountains—
the very kinds of attentiveness which bind his poems so effort-
lessly to our days.

When I think of the will that carried him through a lifetime
in poetry, I recall particularly one afternoon in the summer of

1988. We had finished assembling and revising his last book of poems, *A New Path to the Waterfall.* We were preparing for a fishing trip to Alaska which we knew would, in all likelihood, be our last. Ray wanted to go to Morse Creek once more, so I drove as close as I could get and we climbed out of the jeep onto the bank. We just stood together a while, looking into the water. Then, without saying anything, we began to walk toward the mouth where this freshwater river joins the Strait of Juan de Fuca, some seventy miles east of the Pacific. It was hard going for him and we had to stop often, to sit down and pull up, twenty feet at a time.

It was important, that walk, hyphenated by rests—his breath gathered inside him, again and again. We would talk quietly in those moments sitting on the ground, and I recall saying like a mantra, "It isn't far now." He was traveling on his remaining right lung, but carrying himself well in the effort, as if this were the way to do it, the way he had always done it. When we made it to the river mouth, there was an intake of joy for us both, to have crossed that ground. It was one of those actions that is so right it makes you able in another dimension, all the way back to the start of your life. We savored it, the river's freshwater outrush into salt water, that quiet standing up to life together, for as long as it was going to last.

"When it hurts we return to the banks of certain rivers," Czeslaw Milosz writes. For Ray, I think poems, like rivers, were places of recognition and healing:

> Once I lay on the bank with my eyes closed,
> listening to the sound the water made,
> and to the wind in the tops of the trees. The same wind
> that blows out on the Strait, but a different wind, too.
> For a while I even let myself imagine I had died—
> and that was all right, at least for a couple
> of minutes, until it really sank in: *Dead.*
> As I was lying there with my eyes closed,
> just after I'd imagined what it might be like
> if in fact I never got up again, I thought of you.
> I opened my eyes then and got right up
> and went back to being happy again.
> I'm grateful to you, you see. I wanted to tell you.
>
> ("For Tess")

Ray made the ecstatic seem ordinary, within reach of anyone. He also knew something essential which is too often sacrificed for lesser concerns—that poetry isn't simply reticence served up for what we meant to say. It's a place to be ample and grateful, to make room for those events and people closest to our hearts. "I wanted to tell you." And then he did.

Letter from Jane Campion

Australia
9th June 1998

Tess Gallagher
c/o Collins-Harvill
8 Grafton Street
London W1
U.K.

Dear Tess,

I'm sitting with *A New Path to the Waterfall* weeping my own salty waterfall so full of gratitude for yourself and Ray.

It is coming around to the time my baby boy Jasper was born and died eleven days later, a time which always catches me by the throat and for me it is greatly comforting to feel the company of others through sadness. I've never acknowledged to you that my husband and I used the poem "Late Fragment" as our wedding invitation when we got married for the first time at thirty-eight. We used it again on a plaque under a beautiful jacaranda tree planted in memory of baby Jasper in a seedy part of downtown Sydney, Kings Cross. It's the favourite hangout of many marginal people, lost children, prostitutes, and drug addicts and the little tree is still surviving. No one has pulled it over or broken its branches which in itself is a miracle.

I know it was wrong of me to use the poem without your permission, but I was criminally uncaring with grief and sad-

---

Jane Campion is the Australian filmmaker who directed *The Piano*.

ness at the time and felt such love from these words that I felt I had a right to them, that they had a right to be in Sydney next to that tree.

I have gone on to be very lucky and gave birth almost four years ago to a beautiful daughter, Alice Allegra, so there is much love and happiness in my life, but neither will I ever let go, nor do I want to, of the knowledge of grief, of my heart being held and gripped and squeezed.

Tess should you come to Sydney, please accept some hospitality from me. Please stay at my house, it's a beautiful, poetic house with nice trees and wonderful beaches nearby . . . or if all that from a stranger is too much, then a coffee.

I may be in New York next year working but what am I thinking?? This is not about meeting but about loving you and thanking you both for Ray's book of poems.

Yours completely unknown to you,
Jane Campion

Part 2

Short Cuts

Robert Altman and Tess on the set of Short Cuts, *Los Angeles, summer 1992. Photo by Joyce Rudolph, copyright © New Line Films.*

Letters to Robert Altman

The following letters, review, interview, and foreword attend the writing, making of, and response to, *Short Cuts*, a movie directed by Robert Altman and cowritten by Frank Barhydt, that made use of nine of Raymond Carver's short stories and one poem. Altman says in Mike Kaplan's documentary *Luck, Trust, and Ketchup: The Making of "Short Cuts"* that Gallagher was a "real contributor to the film." Indeed she saw and commented on several drafts and visited the sets and shooting location in Los Angeles for two weeks at a time during the filming. She also saw the final cut of the film in New York City, then attended the film's premiere at Lincoln Center in October 1993.

The film drew criticism from Robert Coles, famed Harvard child psychologist, in the *New York Times* as being unfaithful to the vision and characters of Raymond Carver. Gallagher's letters, both to Altman and to Coles, represent her own position regarding Altman's handling of Carver's work, but also a position she felt Carver would have shared.

—G.S.

To Robert Altman

Dear Bob,

Thanks for your kind note which arrived yesterday after you'd read *Moon Crossing Bridge*. Sometimes I get to feeling it's a pretty drear offering, that attempt to form the alchemy of personal suffering into something others can hopefully take back to their own sorrows and struggles. You hit it right when you said "the Blues"—finding the heart to tell it like it is. A Japanese poet, Shuntaro Tanikawa, has a line which goes something like: "Shall I say good morning while it's still night?"

I also love a thing I heard Cecil Taylor say on a radio program while I was driving around one day, something about how the best jazz works as much on the vertical as it does on the horizontal. I guess that's what I was aiming for in these poems too. Not just story or narrative which I tend to think of as horizontal, but more what Federico García Lorca called "deep song."

The editing on this book of poems is just now being addressed because my editor [Scott Walker of Graywolf Press] became a father two months ago. This is part of why I haven't been able to get back to really working with your script again. Also, a visiting poet and her two kids were here for a week. I essentially just had to surrender. Her husband (left behind elsewhere) was on the phone to her and they got into some long-distance malcontent that threatened to cast more than a little pall over the visit. Anyhow I think I've had psychic hangover (if there is such a thing!) from all that domestic wrangling.

As I told you, I watched *Nashville* but I've been wanting to watch it again without a two-year-old climbing over me. Seeing it confirmed my realization that you and Ray are a match. Why seeing that film should make that sink in, I don't know. Maybe it has to do with that haunting scene at the fund-raiser where the woman who can't sing does what's expected, what she thinks she has to do to succeed—she strips. The pathos, sadness, raw truth, and the harm of that is so close to what I get from Ray's work. It was a kind of self-rape for that woman, as merciless as that most American of dreams: making it. And, of course, the audience is also a participant in that self-wounding.

So I've just been carrying around *Nashville* in my head and letting it spark up against what I recall of the present script. Waiting until the scene clears a bit here. Life has been greatly complicated in the past two weeks by my having to edit this *Uncollected Carver* at breakneck speed before the contracts are even signed because the British publisher suddenly wants to bring it out in the fall! This means everything should have been done yesterday. A condition with which you will no doubt be familiar.

I think after I saw *Nashville* I also began to feel a little abashed at having volunteered anything toward your project, generous as you were to ask. I was frankly relieved and a little surprised that you thought I said anything of value in those notes and that letter. I got to feeling I'd been too intricate and that I need to plain-talk my way into it again.

Anyway, this is just to reaffirm that I think you're a class act, way out there ahead of what I can scantily bring to a reading of that script. Nonetheless I would have been useless to Ray if I hadn't been able to dust myself off from his genius and roll up my sleeves when he asked. So I will make time as soon as I can, then go at the script with mean-pen in hand for what little that may yield. This is just to let you know I'm trying to juggle a lot just now. (Taxes too!) I want to give clear, good time to this so I have to steady down the clamor on these other fronts before I can do anything worthwhile. So this isn't neglect, okay?! Thanks for your patience with me.

> All the best,
> Tess

September 25, 1992

Dear Bob,

This is just a little gift in the wake of my wonderful return to *Short Cuts*. I went directly from the plane, as it landed in Port Angeles, to Ray's gravesite which is not far and sat a while just to at least carry my feelings and thoughts to that place. It felt good just to sit there and be happy with the thought of him coming close a little through me to this fresh aliveness you've been bringing to his stories.

I'm sending along a copy of *Instructions to the Double*. I thought it might be a good talisman for the work you have ahead. Also, thinking of the cutting of the film, I recalled a poem from Chuang-Tzu, Chinese Taoist master, philosopher, and comedian—translated by Thomas Merton. It has all the instructions you will need for cutting the film.

> My whole being apprehends.
> My senses are idle. The spirit
> free to work without plan
> follows its own instinct
> guided by natural line,
> by the secret opening, the hidden space,
> my cleaver finds its own way.
> I cut through no joint, chop no bone.

Well the entire poem is marvelous, so I include it all. The title of the film includes Ray invisibly, since his name is Carver and his middle name is Clevie, which is so close to Cleaver, but also to cleave.

A funny thing happened as I was leaving Santa Monica for LAX in that my driver from El Salvador was asking me what I had been doing in L.A. I told him, working on a film and he wanted to know the title. "*Short Cuts*," I said. He acted very puzzled, and then I said, "You know, when you want to get someplace quick in your taxi, you take a short cut." He knew exactly. "Oh, yes! Yes!" he said. "I take them. Short cuts, many times."

If you want to include me later on, when you have shaped the film somewhat out there in New York, let me know. I believe I'm overnight there on November 10th and 11th to give a reading, and although the ticketing is set, I believe I have some time during the day or evening. Or I can make it! And if this is too early, perhaps I could come out later if it seems good to you. What I'm saying is just feel free to include me as you need and want. But of course I want to be of any use I can. I really was very moved by that scene from "A Small Good Thing" in the bakery. All three actors gave it their best. I hadn't seen Bruce Davison's face in the actual filming, and only at the dailies could I appreciate how well he portrayed the father.

> Well then, go to it!
> Tess

P.S. I'll be in Romania until October 6th. Good luck on directing the opera.

March 9, 1993*

Dear Bob,

I've been ruminating, in a writerly way, about the film and just wanted to share some of those thoughts with you on paper, which is my medium. I started out the morning with a letter to my Japanese translator and perhaps just reproducing a paragraph I wrote to her describing the film might be a good way to begin:

> The Altman film was really extremely affecting and I believe it's going to be a real treasure in American film history. Ray's work is well honored there, although it has been revivified by Altman's imagination—how it moves the scale into images and scenes in the flesh. I felt sad for the people's lives in the film, but there was a real vivacity and an exuberant kind of energy so evident in the artistry of the film that you had to respond on another level. I've found the characters' lives ricocheting around in my head ever since. That's the sign of a wonderful film, I think. So it was a

---

*Written after T.G. viewed the final cut of *Short Cuts* in New York City.

bright, good time and Altman treated me beautifully. We had meals together and got to talk in some important ways about the film, though I've left any changes completely up to him.

I saw Haruki Murakami and Yoko in New York and he came to see the Altman film. I think he liked it very much. Even so, he had that translator's fidelity of saying he would still like to see Ray's stories treated more exactly from the text.* Of course, that can be done, but perhaps it doesn't easily make good film. Would be perhaps even boring. I do think Altman's film is extraordinary for making a new use of the material and characters in the stories. He rather updates Ray to the nineties, I think. The film is meaner, more frank, and causes even more anguish than Ray's stories. There is something redemptive about the interior narratives in Ray, while in the film we are drawn in by the odd sense of ourselves as human beings akin to these human specimens who are in some chaotic swirl which is very mysterious and compulsive. As viewers, we are rather hypnotized by the spectacle of their behavior and we recognize ourselves in the deceits, betrayals, denials, the exposures and abandonments of these characters as Altman re-creates them.

In mentioning Haruki's reaction, Bob, I should add here that he told me he believed the film would be very, very popular in Japan. So that's an observation that might be passed along to the foreign marketing people. I can see that we will probably get some of this wishfulness toward the actual text of Ray's stories—completely inevitable when one uses a text of any sort. And I think it's natural for enthusiasts of the stories to miss the readerly intimacy of the style and the interior of the first-person narrative out of which the stories are spoken. As readers we are in a one-ness with this speaking and it makes us join the narrator's dilemma in perhaps a way which is more difficult to accomplish in film where we tend to become spectators and to witness and to observe, though we can be drawn in and emotionally affected in other ways.

What is present in both stories and the film is the sense of strangeness and compulsiveness inherent in human behavior.

---

*Murakami, after reconsidering the film in a second viewing, later expressed a more wholehearted appreciation for the genius of Altman's treatment of Carver's work and the film itself.

Both the stories and film are using the whole keyboard of human proclivities, it seems—But the film is huge with appetite and because it combines and interlocks stories, it has a ricochet power which the individual stories don't carry. I mean there are the reverberating themes of infidelity, denial, sexual exploitation, the alcoholic merry-go-round, the gripping reality of irrevocable loss in the death of the child, the more anonymous and grotesque death, then disposal of the woman's body in "So Much Water So Close to Home," and the disappearance of certain characters into fantasy. Throughout the film there is the surging of a current of frustrated sexual impulses that comes out as violence against things and people, the unreasonableness of the teenage suicide, and even the coexistence of the half-dead innocence of children with the often perverse range of adult life around them. The circuitry of the film connects these behaviors and themes to each other rather more prismatically than when one encounters them in the Carver text.

With the exception of the couple who lose the child (the Finnegans), the "So Much Water So Close to Home" couple, and Tess Trainer, all the other couples are actively involved in actual marital havoc and betrayal. (Tess' betrayal life with her dead husband is in the mausoleum of her memory.) The Kane couple experiences another kind of betrayal which hits at the root of their attitudes toward human valuing of life itself, and, I think, of women in their object-ness, their sexual plaything-ness. "So Much Water" is still particularly provocative for me as given in the film, because it seems to present both sides of the question of propriety concerning the dead woman rather evenhandedly, though women and men are going to come down on opposite sides of this, and viewers are going to be brought to recognize certain attitudinal differences between the sexes. (Ray's story is clearly tilted toward the female character.) The fact that we attach moral value to these actions or inactions toward the discarded body of a woman reveals a lot about us as creatures who are both pleasure-engines and desperate for some relief from human loneliness. With the stories brought together like this, we can see the stopgap measures toward loneliness as even *more* frantic than they appear in Carver. When these are played out in concert in the film, the driven quality of the lives seems amplified and perhaps even more hopeless, too, since a narrating consciousness in the written Carver stories gains some stature, some equanimity even when it seems to be baffled and grappling with the inexplicableness of what's happening to him or her. In the film the action is the meaning as we shadow it and divine it without intercession.

The questions which the film raises about women's complicity in their misuse in the American imagination as sexual playthings and as compliant with the American male need for anonymity of sexual access to them, are brought to bear on us freshly in the film. Even 1960s feminism tended to place the blame with the patriarchy for what happened to women in their sexual roles and lives. It largely avoided their own acquiescence to what was being done with their images. But the film definitely sees men and women in a dangerous partnership in these matters. This is going to provoke a lot of discussion among women as to whether the presentation of this complicitousness is a distortion, a magnification, or whether it really reveals women's own desire for themselves to be accepted at any cost. There is also a kind of matter-of-factness in, say, the character of Honey talking sex on the phone which just seems to acknowledge a view that gets women way over the line in thinking that this is what some men need and it isn't any big deal to give it. Especially when it's an easy way to earn money and you don't have to see what you do! The emasculation of the man in that instance is very compellingly played in the film and I felt surprised not to be able to simply stand in a place of judgment during one of the most violent moments of the scene when he kills the girl with the rock. That is, you see how he got there, how violence starts way out ahead of the actions themselves.

I'm not sure what you finally decided to do on the editing of that moment in the film. Whether you let it stand that the earthquake was seen as the possible perpetrator of the death or if the murder was left to stand on its own and the earthquake simply allowed to coexist with it. Of course I prefer the latter, since it's not so ironically overbearing as the way it was first cut. And letting the death hold its own there reaches back to Ray's story more truly, not of course that you have to be bound by that if your own artistry wants something else—it's just that this "something else" was too much a gouge at cause and effect to generate a credible perplexity. Anyhow, you will have felt this one out by now, I imagine.

I forgot to mention a little thing about the line the vacuum cleaner salesman says as he surveys the damage having been done by Peter Gallagher to the living room. That line was so truncated I didn't get it, didn't hear it in the film. Maybe that also has been worked with by now, or doesn't matter.

What I mentioned, about wanting to see the body of the girl in "So Much Water So Close to Home" before the men do, was probably connected to feeling the body "as a character" and as having *had* an aliveness. So far, as it's cut in, it just seems to stay a body and not to carry that dimension Claire finds for it—if we don't see it in its aloneness apart from the men. I don't know why the moment of discovery has to be when the fisherman is pissing on it. It's really more horrible to *know* that the body is there, then guess what is happening to it, that it is exactly where he will be pissing. But probably you've already thought this one out in your own way, too. It's just that all these things occur to me after thought.

I forgot to pass on that Marion Ettlinger* also agreed with me about there being perhaps too much emphasis on the clown faces by the end of the film. Maybe that was why I thought of cutting the song and dance of the two women in clown face.

I had been so impressed with Jack Lemmon's monologue in the dailies that, seeing it broken up with Bruce Davison's reaction shots, rather subdued that amazing performance. I spoke with Gerry about her cutting of it and, of course she's entirely right, that it *is* Bruce Davison's story in that he's carrying the main line of narration here as he hovers over his dying child, but the father is so out of proportion that the monologue is somehow rather truer to that, truer to his abstraction as a presence there—and that's why I think one could rethink how much to break that monologue up. I think Bruce Davison's reactions are quite wonderfully built in the present cutting,

---

*Photographer friend of Ray's, who attended *Short Cuts* screening with T.G. in New York City.

but the self-deception of the father is a real loose cannon here and I think we can feel that with fewer cuts to the son.

Mike Kaplan* and I had quite a good discussion about the hope factor of the film. The fact that the film leaves the viewer with a kind of pervasive sadness about the chaos of these lives. As we both know, art isn't obliged to provide the antidote for its revealed poisons. Ray also had to fight this notion from readers and critics—that the artist was supposed to do more than diagnose the condition of the characters—that he or she was also supposed to rise like the Statue of Liberty on the horizon and promise some sort of redemption. Well, it just ain't so! As with Ray's stories, the question of what we are going to do with the recognitions we encounter as viewers of this film, once we gaze into its mirrors, is really on our own ground, outside the stories and the film. That's the provocative nature of art itself. First of all, Art says what *is,* as honestly and truly as it can envision it. On this count both you and Ray are relentlessly true. What's going to be admired is the tenacity of your insistence on the unattractiveness of these truths. I think I said to Mike in one of our conversations that I thought your vision was indeed "meaner" than Ray's. And I didn't mean this pejoratively: I meant it as a definition of crucial difference in sensibility. Whereas Ray would put the knife in and bring it out more or less in the same spot, your way is to give the knife a small neat arc once it's in there. There's a great physicality to your handling of these scenes and characters. But it's the filmic scale of the effort, to both show the lived chaos and to organize it emotionally and intuitively as an artist must, which continues to astound me.

Well this does it for now. I'm sure I'll continue to refine and add to these thoughts. I got a copy of the final script from Jim [James McLindon, assistant to Robert Altman] and began re-reading it yesterday. As soon as you have a version of the script which is parallel to how the film has been cut, I'd love to have it.

Again, thanks for your generosity in continuing to include me in this process. It's genuinely one of the most important

---

*Associate producer for *Short Cuts.* Also producer and director of *Luck, Trust, and Ketchup: The Making of "Short Cuts."*

times in my life and I think I can safely say that Ray would have been very gratified by the way in which you've brought his scenes and characters to fresh life in the images and special language of your film.

With admiration and gratitude,
Tess

Reimagining Raymond Carver
on Film

A Talk with Robert Altman and Tess Gallagher
Robert Stewart

Raymond Carver, who died all too early—at fifty—of lung cancer in 1988, left a remarkable legacy of eleven volumes of short stories and poems, among them "Where I'm Calling From," "Cathedral," "What We Talk about When We Talk about Love," "Will You Please Be Quiet, Please?" and "Where Water Comes Together with Other Water." It is a body of work that brought him international acclaim while he was alive and that has now been translated into more than twenty languages.

It was his stories in particular, with their stark evocation of America's urban and small-town blue-collar world, that made the greatest and, perhaps, the most lasting impact. He'd come from there himself—a world of old factories and sawmills, of truck stops and diners, of bars, of run-down frame houses and the frayed nerves of the families inside; in short, a kind of life in the desperate zone, where the one thing one needs is a job, any job, but where all one does is stare at the tube and hang on, scramble, come up empty.

The appeal of Carver's stories lies in their raw, spare truthfulness, their grasp of what Freud, in his old age, liked to call "the foul realities," or what Carver himself might have thought of as just plain bad luck. Yet it would be an error to dismiss the strains of hope or the theme of surviving against the odds in his work, for these, too, are central to his far-reaching popularity.

To the millions of Carver readers here and abroad, one must now add the American film director Robert Altman. His list of films includes

The New York Times Book Review (September 12, 1993). Reprinted by permission of Robert Stewart. Robert Stewart was formerly the senior editorial vice president at Charles Scribner's Sons. He also edited *Carver Country*.

"M*A*S*H," "Nashville," "A Wedding," "The Player," and now the soon-to-be-released "Short Cuts," based on nine stories and a poem by Carver, which will open the New York Film Festival at Lincoln Center on October 1 (the stories and the poem are being collected in a paperback edition by Vintage Books this month).

In July I met with Robert Altman and Carver's widow, the poet Tess Gallagher, in Los Angeles to talk with them about their thoughts on the transformation of Raymond Carver's work into a film.

—Robert Stewart

Robert Stewart: How did the idea for *Short Cuts* first get started?

Robert Altman: In the early winter of 1990, I was in Rome planning to make a film there about Rossini. But the situation got very ugly and my life was actually threatened. I told my wife that we were going back to America right away, and I asked my secretary to give me something to read on the plane.

I always keep collections of short stories by various writers around, because they often make good film material. I had heard of Ray Carver, of course, but I had never read him, and now there were four or five of his books in the pile put together by my secretary.

Stewart: What were your first impressions?

Altman: I loved the stories. I read a couple of them during the flight. You have to understand that I was in a fragile state. I was coming from an aborted picture and a big defeat. I got off the plane, and I remember walking down the ramp and thinking, "There's a movie here." I think what I did is I made "Carver soup" out of these stories.

Stewart: Can you remember what happened next?

Altman: I went to Tess Gallagher, who owned the rights, and I made a deal* to option the stories. Frank Barhydt, a wonderful writer with whom I had worked before, started working with me. I went to Paramount, sold the idea to them. They gave me money to develop a screenplay. We bought some colored three-by-five index cards and put scenes from the

_____
*Actually no "deal" happened until much later when Paramount was contacted.

stories down on them and pinned them up on a big board. When we finished, Paramount hated the script,* turned it down, and sent it back to us. But I had sent the Carver script to Tess. I was scared to death about what her reaction would be. I had no idea of what she would think.

Stewart: What was your initial response, Tess, not only to the script but to the idea of Bob Altman wanting to do a film based on Ray's work?

Tess Gallagher: I had seen other scripts based on Ray's stories and they had been very flat-footed. Their approach to his work was to copy Ray's dialogue exactly, copy the character's movements exactly. You couldn't really tell what was going to generate the film's energy in those scripts. But I thought that Bob was really a perfect match for Ray, because he wasn't coming out of literature, in a sense.

Stewart: Do you mean by that that Ray came out of literature?

Gallagher: No, actually, Ray was very awkward in the halls of academe. He was a literary man by virtue of his writing and his reading. He was extremely well read. But the lives of the people he was writing about were the lives of pretty ordinary people and, in fact, that's what everybody was so excited about—that through Ray's stories these people started entering into the literature of the country.

Stewart: So of all the others, Bob seemed to be the right filmmaker?

Gallagher: I thought if anybody could do it, *he* could. I thought he was doing something very new. He was using the stories as a kind of sourdough starter, like yeast. It was generative. It was very interesting to me that he broke the frames of the stories in such a way that the characters began to interact with each other and to glance off each other.

Stewart: You're known to be careful about Ray's material. Were there reservations?

Gallagher: Well, there may have been one thing. I had seen *The Player,* and I knew that one of Bob's great gifts was his irony, that it was a great tool of his. I was very well aware that Ray eschewed irony, that he didn't distance himself from his characters or their dilemmas.

_____

*Paramount considered the film "too dark."

Altman: Yes, Tess made me very aware of that. I agree that real art is *without* irony. I think that irony is a product of something. It's not the reason for doing something. Irony is a cheap shot. But I can never get rid of all of it, because that's who I am.

Stewart: Can you give an example from *Short Cuts?*

Altman: After I had cut the picture, Tess made a negative comment about the ending. It's from the story "Tell the Women We're Going." A young girl is brutally assaulted by a sex-starved, violent character named Jerry Kaiser. He beats her to death with a rock. The scene is followed by an earthquake, and it is reported on television that the only known casualty of this earthquake was a teenage girl—the one he'd killed—caught in a rock slide, which, of course, has its measure of irony. And this was what Tess was responding to. So I immediately went back and recut the picture, the ending of it. I felt I was doing the right thing. Then I had another screening, and it went flat, and I said it's got to go back. When I took it out, it didn't give the audience an out, a way out of the picture somehow. If you just looked at that one moment, Tess was right. I should have taken it out. But if you looked at the picture as a whole, I needed it.

Stewart: You said earlier that you made "Carver soup" out of his stories. What exactly did you mean by that?

Altman: I meant that I thought of all of Carver's stories as *one* story. You know, I feel that all of Edgar Allan Poe's stories are really one story. I think of Shakespeare's plays as one big piece. That's the way I look at these things.

Gallagher: You saw Ray's *world.*

Altman: Yes, I saw his world. It was as if I was inside of an eggshell, *his* eggshell. I was inside of this kind of three-dimensional thing. Even the stories that we fabricated, the ones that didn't come from Carver's work, are *of* his work. Of course Carver is much, much purer. I love the work in the film and I'm not apologizing for any of it—but I don't think it has the power of the truthfulness of Ray's work. I think it has to do with the medium more than anything else.

Stewart: In what way do you think it has to do with the medium?

Altman: When you read these things yourself, you are

taking this information, this simple information that Carver is giving you, and you're taking it in and adding it to all the information that already exists in your brain; you are applying it to your own personal experiences, to things that you have seen, done, read, felt, thought before, and it's all judged and filed according to the information you already have.

Now a film audience does exactly the same thing. Except that we're hitting the film audience with visual material; we're hitting them with familiar or unfamiliar materials, which is the *actors*. When you look at Tim Robbins on the screen, whether you like it or not, your mind is judging everything you've ever seen him do before. So if you've seen *The Player*, that's rubbing off on you.

Stewart: So how would you describe what you do when you take one medium and put it into another?

Altman: I translate what I saw in Carver's work. I'm trying to use what was written and the effect it had on me. My authorship is shaky and doubtful in this. I'm trying to take an experience that *I* had in reading these stories and use elements and pieces of them to give a similar experience to a film audience.

Gallagher: It's a new experience. A fusion of the two consciousnesses, really, and visions—yours and Ray's—to create an entity which didn't exist before. What you do is move Ray's vision into the time in which we are living, the nineties. It's the difference between the vitamins the girl sells in Ray's story "Vitamins" and Jennifer Jason Leigh selling telephone sex in your film. Whereas Ray was considered a realist—and even called a "dirty realist"—you're showing us how much over the fence into fantasy we really live. There are any number of those instances in which fantasy is serving to prop up a reality which is spiritually bankrupt. Ray really had perfect pitch in the soul and spirit department. He knew what was coming down. And you're saying it *has* come down and this is what we're living now.

Altman: I think that he and I see life from a very similar window.

Gallagher: A lot of randomness and luck, but striving too. Many of Ray's characters tried to do better, really struggled against chaos and bad luck.

Altman: The whole thing about lady luck is that she has to pick a side. You can say it's the toss of a coin, but lady luck has to pick the side of the coin that lands face up. The poem "Lemonade" is the basis of the whole picture for me. I think the film, the whole film, has more to do with the idea of the chain of events—call it luck or fate—in "Lemonade" than it has to do with any of the individual stories.

Gallagher: It's a poem about a child's accidental death and about how sequences of actions cause other actions.

Altman: Yes, but it's not that those actions cause those actions, it's that, in looking back, we *blame* those actions. And the idea of calling it *Short Cuts.* From the very beginning people kept saying: "Now is that a very good title?" "Why do you call it *Short Cuts?* What's it mean?" I couldn't defend it very well at first, but now I can, because when I look at a map, something happens. A child dies and it's devastating to the people who are close to that event. So they say, "Why did that child die?" But instead of retracing the steps that led to the child's death, as in "Lemonade," you can just look at the map and you say, well, there's Sixteenth Street, Mulberry Street, the Pacific Coast Highway, Main Street. It's a kind of sign language that has nothing to do with the cause of the child's death, and yet it's the only thing you can trace.

Gallagher: Maps are like an aerial view of blame. It's a short-cut to understanding what happened.

Stewart: Ray said that he was a paid-up-in-full member of the working poor. And in the movie you moved the stories to suburbia, sort of raised them up in terms of class structure. Was that intentional?

Altman: In the way that I'm retelling Ray Carver this class thing is not necessarily an element that is making things happen.

Stewart: So you didn't try to consciously change from a poor working-class environment to a qualitatively different one?

Altman: No, but I probably consciously, and unconsciously, changed it to something that was more familiar to me. To do a whole thing about people who are out of work would give some sort of meaning to this picture that I didn't want to give to it.

Stewart: You didn't set out to reconfigure the class structure and bring it to Los Angeles, perhaps to appeal to a broader audience?

Altman: Oh, no, *au contraire.* My first reason for shooting the picture in Los Angeles was a practical one. I had a limited budget, and I knew I just couldn't go on location. Most of Ray's people were dislocated anyway.

Gallagher: Yes, from somewhere else, or going somewhere else.

Altman: I was also very conscious of trying to show that this isn't the Los Angeles of Bel Air or of Brentwood. Every house we used in every neighborhood was for sale. Across the street houses were for sale, cars were for sale. So there was an idea of transition, nothing was permanent.

Stewart: I have a question about a different issue. When I reread the fishing story, "So Much Water So Close to Home," I realized that the woman is telling the story, that Ray used the woman as the narrator. In the film, it's told from the point of view of the men. Did you do that on purpose?

Altman: Well, I thought a lot about that story because that story presented a moral dilemma to me. We sat there and I said, I don't want to take sides in this. I don't want to load this thing one way or the other. So Frank Barhydt and I and my son Steve, who was the production manager on the film, would just sit there and we'd talk. And we'd say, "O.K., we are just three guys, now let's really talk about this. Here's where we are. We've walked into these woods. It took us four hours to get there. It's close to nightfall. We find this body. What are we going to do about it? Are we going to fish, or are we going to report the body to the police right away?" Now Barhydt still contends that he would not have gone fishing, that he would have addressed the situation of the body. And I said I would do the same thing if both guys agreed to that. But if they both said, "Oh, we're gonna fish," I wouldn't argue with them. I'd go along with them, which is what happens in the story. I could easily have done what those men did and not feel guilty about it. Now when he gets back and tells his wife about it, there's not a question in *her* mind about the moral irresponsibility of what he did.

Gallagher: Yes, and if you had had four women going fishing, it would have been different. It couldn't possibly work out the way it works out here.

Altman: You're probably right. And if it's true, Tess, then something of great value has been said in this story.

Gallagher: You have told us something we didn't know about the difference in the sexes.

Stewart: Does that mean that you shifted the narrator from the woman because you didn't want to get into sex differences or feminist issues?

Altman: Yes. I didn't want to make any judgment whatsoever. I even had the guy take a leak on the body—and my wife, Kathryn, said, "Why did you have to do that, that's disgusting"—and I said, I know it's disgusting, but the point of it is that all he did was take a leak in the water. There happened to be a body there, and when you see that you think, "Oh, there's something revolting in that, that's a violation, that's a terrible thing." But I kept that in on purpose, because I didn't want to make it easy on anybody.

Stewart: Do you worry that some critics may find your handling of the story sexist?

Altman: I don't care about that. When I made *M*A*S*H* there were a lot of accusations. A woman stood up in a five-thousand-seat auditorium in Ann Arbor, Michigan, and said, "Why do you treat women the way you treated Hot Lips?" She hated me. She called me a misogynist. "Why do you treat women that way?" I said, "I don't treat women that way. I don't think women should be treated that way. This is the way I *see* women being treated. You make the moral judgment, I'm not going to make any moral judgment. That's propaganda."

Gallagher: I think Ray's story avoids propaganda, but he still manages to show that woman's revulsion at what her husband has done.

Altman: I think we did that in the film. And that's why I had Claire and Stuart make love that night when he comes back from the fishing trip. I thought that was a good balance—nice, loving, happy—they made each other happy. She says after they separate in bed, "Oh, you make me so happy." And then he says, "Claire, we found a dead body up there." And two minutes later she's in there and she's saying, "You're making me sick." And she's washing the slime out of her. The next day she gets in her car and she drives seventy-five miles to be at the funeral service for the dead girl.

Gallagher: In the story, Ray made more of a point of the man not telling his wife about the death of the woman until the next morning, until he had his "sexual welcome" so to speak.

Altman: I think we did that, too.

Gallagher: I guess I mean that you *feel* the delay more in the story. Time somehow collapses in films.

Stewart: In the story "A Small, Good Thing," in which the child gets hit by the car, Ann asks her husband to pray for the boy. I was just wondering, Tess, if Ray ever thought in religious or spiritual terms, if he believed there was some kind of higher power in the world?

Gallagher: Well, Ray was a recovering alcoholic, and I think he did adopt the attitude of a higher power as a help to us. But he never articulated this. And he never preached to anybody, and I don't even know if he believed in a hereafter, really. He pretty much thought you had to do it all here. But he believed in right action.

Stewart: I'm curious about the element of classical music and jazz that you've added. And you've created this character, Tess Trainer, a faded jazz singer, whose husband has died and whom you've named after Tess.

Altman: I did that simply because I wanted to have a reason for the music. I didn't want the music to come from a sound studio outside and amplify the emotions. And yet I know that music does that. I knew I couldn't do this picture without music. That's tough for an audience. But I didn't just want to *apply* music.

Stewart: Whatever the reason, you succeed rather well in creating a story that doesn't disturb the rest of the film.

Altman: Actually, it's the least Carveresque of the stories. Most of the people who have criticized the film have said, "Oh, you can do without that story."

Stewart: What do you think of your namesake, Tess Trainer, Tess?

Gallagher: Well, widows don't get much applause in America, and there's a lot of applause built into this film for Tess Trainer. She's a real gift to me. I love her stamina, her wry courage, even her loneliness. "She's seen some things," as Ray would say. I certainly recognize some of the widowhood things from my own life, and the painful quality that seeps into things because of how they used to be. I think you even poke fun at her—in the way that you make her so nostalgic. I mean I can even laugh at myself through her in the film, the way she's always looking over her shoulder at the past. Am I wrong?

Altman: Well, no, how can you be wrong if you're telling me what you received? But about the nostalgia. I think that's what music *is.* I think it comes from singing those same songs every day in bars and clubs. My feeling is that the music made her what she was, and the music made her daughter commit suicide. I think it was the sadness of the music.

Stewart: If you were asked to review this film, Tess, how would you deal with the question of the adaptation of Ray's work?

Gallagher: I would be very careful about the comparative, in the way that I'm careful about metaphors. What I mean is that to say that something is like or unlike something else is already a kind of invasion. I would try to protect the integrity of Altman's and Ray's vision. At the same time, I would say that I missed a certain *interiority* of the characters in the film. The suffering in Ray's stories is more palpable; the empathetic qualities in Ray's characters are more present. I also think Altman's film is more societal than Ray was in his work. Ray got inside the individual and any societal ideas that Ray may have had were very much a by-product. But Bob actually makes that more his terrain.

Stewart: Do you think one of the things that might come out of this film is that more people will start reading Ray Carver?

Gallagher: I hope they are going to discover the great richness in Ray's work. And the interiors are going to stand out a lot more in the stories because so much of the film is action. Now they're going to go inside in a new way. They're going to take a story like "So Much Water So Close to Home" and wonder about those choices.

Stewart: But despite the differences, Tess, the sense I have of it is that Ray and Bob would have gotten along extremely well.

Gallagher: Oh, absolutely.

Altman: I kind of think so. I think we would have argued a lot, but a kind of "discussing" arguing, the way I do.

Gallagher: I'm sure you would have laughed together, too—and told a lot of stories like the one in a poem of his in which a man goes walking by the river and an eagle drops a huge salmon right at his feet.

Compassion from Carver, Male Swagger from Altman

Robert Coles

With the arrival of Robert Altman's highly praised *Short Cuts*—inspired, he has declared, by a chance reading of Raymond Carver's stories—some of us who have loved those stories and used them in our teaching, have had to watch our step lest we be dubbed "Carver purists." It is a phrase that has already been used by some reviewers to defend the film against potential criticism.

Raymond Carver's sensibility was that of a late twentieth-century secularist, many of whose stories nevertheless hinted, through pity and compassion and attentiveness to life's detail, at the redemptive side of human suffering.

Mr. Altman's Carver is quite another matter: The director gives us a movie full of male swagger, with women always at the edge of things; a movie that lacks Carver's gentle humor and prompts laughter *at* people; a movie stripped bare of human ambiguity; a movie relentless in its cynical, sardonic assault on anyone and everyone, as if America itself is beyond the pale morally and psychologically; a movie in which gruff, smug detachment keeps clubbing empathy over the head. Alas, that last attitude (to be cool, cool, cool) has been noted by some reviewers with no great alarm.

Mr. Altman's own values and beliefs come across loud and

The New York Times (October 17, 1993). Reprinted by permission of International Creative Management, Inc. Copyright © Robert Coles, 1993. Robert Coles is a child psychiatrist who has regularly taught a seminar on Raymond Carver's fiction and poetry at Harvard University.

clear in the movie. As I watched *Short Cuts* and took note of its harsh, derisive tone, its mean and bitter attitude toward women, its almost frenzied pace, I had no trouble distinguishing between Carver's world and Mr. Altman's. The former is not to be found in the latter.

Short Cuts is a collage—episodes in Carver's stories are jumbled together by a director who knows how to use music and who is not afraid to visit ruin on everyone in sight. The viewer is given acts, a tumble of them, rather than character portrayal. People do things, but God forbid that we (or they) ask why. The camera goes everywhere except inward—to the hearts and minds and souls of people who speak of a world going nowhere fast.

To this world, Mr. Altman adds two characters all his own, a jazz singer (played by Annie Ross) and her cellist daughter (Lori Singer). The mother is an egoist, indifferent to all except her own whims, moods, and fancies. She sings poorly, boozes it up, and is blind to her talented, distraught child, who eventually kills herself. Two women in the film's parade of doomed women—and what, one asks, are we meant to make of all this?

We are informed by Mr. Altman that his movie is based on nine Carver stories; and in a new introduction to those stories, brought out this month by Vintage Books, the director tells of "collaborating with Carver." Whenever a film is connected with a piece of fiction, we are likely to hear disavowals on all sides that one medium is not another, that an attempt to be literal is doomed. (In his introduction, Mr. Altman worries that "Carver fans may be upset" with what he and his cowriter, Frank Barhydt, have done.)

Mr. Altman has tried very much to associate himself with Carver, who died in 1988. The characters in *Short Cuts,* he announces, do a lot of storytelling in the film and speak frequently of events in their lives. He goes on to clarify his relationship to the storytelling writer: The scripted situations, he says, "are Carver stories or paraphrases of Carver stories or inspired by Carver stories, so we always tried to stay as close as possible to his world, given film's collaborative imperative."

In fact, as has been noted by some critics, Carver's "world" is nowhere near the hyped-up, fast-moving, multicolored, upside-down one around Los Angeles that Mr. Altman's folks inhabit, a world in which each person it seems, is more disturbed (and disturbing) than the next. Carver's world of small towns in Oregon and Washington where men and women barely scrape by, a world of ordinary working people whose way of saying things the author had down cold ("She was having a dream, is all," "Ain't that something?" "Scoot over"), goes out the window, to be replaced by a uniform narration fit for a mostly upscale Los Angeles suburb.

Mr. Altman has explained why he is not particularly interested in echoing Carver's vernacular: The characters, he says, "could be talking about anything. Which is not to say the language isn't important, but its subject doesn't have to be X, Y or Z. It could be Q or P or H."

With that, the director gives himself enormous leeway. Again and again in *Short Cuts* he changes the subject, or refuses to pursue the very subject Carver had in mind. In the story "They're Not Your Husband," Earl Ober tries to lord it over his wife, Doreen, who works as a waitress in a diner. He stops by for coffee, notices men evaluating his wife's body with no great enthusiasm, and decides to make her lose weight so she'll appear more attractive. She reluctantly agrees, and the outcome is wonderfully funny, a thorough reversal: Earl's pitiable weirdness becomes obvious to everyone; Doreen's amused patience reveals her to be the stronger of the two. She shrugs and goes about her business after replying to another waitress (who asks, "Who is this joker, anyway?"), "He's a salesman. He's my husband."

Ironically, Doreen's lonely, dependent attachment to Earl is the only sustained connection of any poignancy in the entire film. Mr. Altman has Doreen (Lily Tomlin) clinging desperately to the callous Earl Piggot (Tom Waits), who often treats her poorly—a far cry from Carver's interest in turning the tables on the husband.

To be sure, Carver's husbands and wives misunderstand and mistrust and misrepresent one another (a staple of short stories since Chekhov), but for Mr. Altman things go no further than that. Or things get worse, and the woman suffers or is at fault, or is reduced to apparently pointless or crazy provocations. The director has combed Carver country for hurt, troubled women, made them even more hurt and troubled or made up his own version of them.

One character in the movie (played by Jennifer Jason Leigh) provides phone sex, her children nearby. (In Carver's short story, the woman sells vitamins door to door.) Her husband ends up viciously attacking a young woman with a rock. Another woman (played by Frances McDormand) sleeps with man after man, indifferent to the implications for her young son.

A woman (Anne Archer) learns that her husband and his buddies encountered a dead woman in a river while on a fishing trip, only to continue fishing and drinking without apparent unease. (One of the men notices the dead woman while urinating on the water that flows over her.) Yet another woman (Julianne Moore) is relentlessly questioned by her jealous husband about a possible affair years earlier and ends up giving him (us) a frank sexual display. (That scene has already become somewhat notorious, which will no doubt increase the amount of money the film will earn.*)

It is not that Carver necessarily turned away from such episodes in his fiction. He was not shy about sex or violence. He knew how seductive or mean people can be—sometimes seductive out of meanness, sometimes out of rock-bottom despair. But in his stories the narrator indirectly searches for explanations (or the characters search quite directly)—and in so doing, individuals move toward one another, even if their prospects together seem dim.

The woman whose husband found the body in the river in "So Much Water So Close to Home" is moved not only to wash herself after hearing about the fishing trip, which Mr. Altman shows, but to reflect on human nature, especially that of her husband and his friends. In the story she emerges as a much more thoughtful person, with her own reproving voice—one earned gradually in the course of some trenchant exchanges with her husband, a man who tries to make up by using sex, only to realize that his wife has other things on her mind.

---

*Short Cuts, although judged a critical success, never earned enough money at the box office to break even, despite its slim (by Hollywood standards) budget of twelve million dollars.

In the story "Will You Please Be Quiet, Please?" a husband and wife return to a moment of marital jeopardy. But his possessive prurience and her guilt and shame do not become an excuse for self-loathing, as happens in the film to the characters played by Matthew Modine and Ms. Moore.

Carver was hardly a sentimentalist. His men and women are barely able to stay afloat financially, and they are often in deep trouble personally. He was not afraid to expose their limitations of judgment, vision, feeling. But his stories are also given over to an unmentioned yet palpable hope that life will turn out better through a friendship, a love, or an enduring family life. Even in one of his most enigmatic stories, "Tell the Women We're Going" (which Mr. Altman draws upon to create the scene in which the married man, played by Chris Penn, hits a young woman with a rock), a reminder to the reader that people who suddenly go berserk sometimes give warnings.

In this story, as in so much of his work, Carver was trying to fathom the inexplicable, as well as render it: "Bill was getting to be deep, the way he stared all the time and hardly did any talking at all." By the time Mr. Altman's character strikes the woman, our three hours with the film are about to end, and we have become used to seeing women degraded, insulted, demeaned, scorned. As a result, this episode seems understandable only on those terms—a mere final pounding.

It is interesting to think of all the entrancing, stirring, and tender (or wryly comic) stories *not* summoned for *Short Cuts*, stories that, by the power of the craft that shaped them, have lifted their maker from yet another observer of domestic manners to one mourned, upon his untimely death at fifty, as "an American Chekhov." I think of "Cathedral" and "Errand" and "Elephant" and "Bicycles, Muscles, Cigarettes" and "The Student's Wife,"* each haunting and unnerving in its honesty and wisdom, each able to offer a generosity toward people, no matter their limitations.

I think of "A Small Good Thing," not the version given us in "Short Cuts" but rather the great tale in which a baker helps

---

*Several of these stories were under contract to another filmmaker at the time Altman optioned available stories for *Short Cuts*. Essentially he was working with stories that were available.

to heal parents broken by their son's death. In today's hip laid-back Hollywood, however, it seems impossible to have that kind of communion, with the suggestion of bread and wine, of forgiveness, that Carver wants so much to convey.

Letters to Robert Altman and
Robert Coles

October 21, 1993

To Robert Altman

Dear Bob,

I just wanted to share a bit of the glow from my having just introduced *Short Cuts* in the heart of Carver Country at a showing at the Harvard Exit in Seattle. This theater is wonderful—one where I attended movies as an undergraduate at the University of Washington. The hall was packed. I don't know exactly how many people—maybe six hundred or so. But it has been the most intelligent audience I've been a part of, this having been my sixth viewing. The audience laughed and were silent, and participated in the film. There was a live and prickly current like the static electricity that sparks off clothing and hair sometimes. People couldn't seem to contain themselves and rushed up to me to shake my hand, congratulating me—which I quickly deflected, accepting for you and Ray. Which they meant of course! I had spoken for just a few minutes before the showing and that seemed to put the film in a good place with people. What I loved was feeling their respect for your work and for Ray's, since many of these people were personal friends of ours, people who knew the stories and who heeded the difference and were smart enough in their response to enjoy seeing the stories take on a new impetus.

I had a card today from my childhood friend, Jack Estes, who was with me when Ray died. He was a member of the audience and wrote that he absolutely loved the film. I enclose a Xerox of his postcard.

Mainly, I just want you to know the film got a open-arms reception here. The day of the showing the *Seattle Weekly* came out with a quite good review. The woman writing it had evidently been at one of our roundtable interview sessions in New York and lashed me a couple of times about the head and shoulders for answering a question not posed to me. Female insubordination again! Intolerable for her, another female, of course. Anyhow, the rest of the *Weekly* was taken up with a long retrospective on Ray's literary and public status.

The Robert Coles piece was finally forwarded on to me by Mike Kaplan today. Frank [Barhydt] said you weren't much concerned about it. I'm still on the road with the film, heading to Charlottesville and a gruesomely titled panel on the "challenge of taking literary material to film."

Of course it's some difficulty to me personally to find myself so far afield from Coles, a man whose values I highly respect. It's just one of these instances where reasonable people can and do hold greatly disparate views.

Well I hope things are going well for the new work. Meanwhile I'll be at three different film events here, running through November 6th.

> All my warm best, and greetings
> to Kathryn—
>
> Tess

November 5, 1993

To Robert Coles

Dear Bob,

I'm just back from the Charlottesville, Virginia Film Noir Festival and have a bad cold out of it. Those independent filmmakers like to stay up late and tried to make a teenager out of me. Got back November 2nd to the clip finally of your piece in the *New York Times* "Arts & Leisure." I felt the lavish wash of your love for Ray's work, first of all. Though it can't modify your own true reaction, there are also many letters and reports coming in here which, while being deeply attached to Ray's stories, do admit to respect and reception of Altman's view as it intersects and even extends elements of Ray's.

About swagger, I also know a thing or two. I live in the heart of swagger here in the Northwest. All these out of work loggers have almost nothing left but swagger now that the timber cutting is all but gone. My father was the king of swagger—had his nose broken at least five times in brawls, and all because of a certain kind of prideful carriage that belongs to his sex and yes, to having to put your body on the line when it's about all you have. "Swagger" is a working-class word and notion.

I value your passion in the piece and understand that wish to protect and present the tenderness of Ray. But this is a new making—this film. I always protect that sense of art as a means to discovery. As Louise Glück puts it so well in her introduction to *The Best American Poetry 1993:* "Art is not a service." Ray had to fight that misconception his entire life. People wanting him to cheer them up, truffle hunting in his stories for hope and calling the stories "bleak." So ironic that Robert Altman is now in an even darker boat. I wish you'd read Glück's intro, because she says things so intelligently. Her wish for art to dislodge assumption, I find very important. And her requirement that "it bring one to feel that a whole new territory in the mind had been suddenly opened," that "it *be* unsettling." As she puts it so well: "The need to avoid 'the homage' that simulates what it cannot generate."

My attraction for the Altman reconstitution of Ray's stories is vested in exactly the fact that it refuses to take its marching orders, is full of volatility and not constrained even by the wishfulness of our weary hearts for compassion. Of course we need it, always and ever. And Ray gave it to us even when he seemingly withheld it. But as a mandate, it seems to belong more to that world of personal conviction that lines up its truths so firmly it can't then discover.

What I connect with in this whole enterprise is the sincere effort of Altman to postulate from Ray's territory into his own. Stanley Kauffmann is right—it *is* "Altman the Devourer." And if it were Ray using Altman's work, it would be "Carver the Devourer." The true artist is closer to cougar than house cat.

Ray had no compunctions whatsoever in taking for use any material which came to him, no matter how tender and personal. No matter if the "Fires" essay he wrote would hurt his son. He *had* to write it. Did write it. Did injure and wound the son on the way to his truth.

Those who want to make use of art as if it were only a tool kit to representing the working-class plight, or marital misconduct, or collapses of trust in its many varieties—all those agendas—those sorts, should better go to sociology, to my way of thinking. Service and usefulness are added entities. The maker and the seer have to step away from the perceived requirement, even for consolation, even for simple "dignity" and "goodness." For "in our error (rests) the defining energies of cure" (that's from A. R. Ammons in his poem in *The Best American Poetry 1993*).

Even film, which seems to live so fully in the presentation of bodily forms and motion, should not invest its energies in reiteration. True, as you say, this may be the only film-embodying of Ray's stories. And of course I can sympathize with your wishfulness that someone could snap these stories up into images which live the pages exactly as we read them. But I have seen enough such attempts to know it wouldn't work, except in a piecemeal and deadweight fashion. A slack parody has been the ultimate result. Frankly, Robert Altman is the only one who had the vigor and yes, audacity, to take on this material. But nowhere in my dealings with him was he ever anything but amazed, curious, and intrigued by the stories of Ray.

In your article you chastise him for using just *those* stories, and why not others—well, at the time, fourteen of the stories, and some of the best ones were indeed under option and ultimately sold to another filmmaker [Jill Godmilow] who had no ability to make the film, to get backing. She tied up the work for ten years and ultimately the stories came back to me due to a reversion clause. So the bulk of Ray's stories were not even available to Robert Altman.

I've understood Ray's artistic generosity as if I lived out of his own heart. Ray did not see art as an enterprise simply of individuals. Artists contribute to the general font of art. He perceived art as a joining venture in which individuals did the best they could to render up their immersions in life not only as they saw it, but as they could reenvision it.

Hope, as an entity for Ray's characters, was always a hook no fish was ever going to bite. But how strong we see even the *voicing* of hope became! How much even the gesture of hope sustained his characters! It's a world roughly ten years down the road that Altman takes us to. And it is *down* and dirty, full of deceit and wrong turns, self-delusion, velocity of lives driven beyond their wills. As with Chekhov's view of peasants, Ray was under no delusion about the innate goodness of what he called the "working poor." He knew their cunning, their carelessness, their misuse of one another, their venial gropings for sex and self-esteem. I think two or three of his later stories, because of their epiphanies, tended to throw back over his entire work a kind of roseate glow. But I do know that glow coexisted with the primal dark of the life he had before he met me, a life he nearly didn't survive. Ray and Altman both survived alcoholism. Altman and I had a talk, in fact, in the backseat of a taxi in NYC in which he allowed for his belief in a higher power or some entity out there which is present, even if it doesn't direct, but is there at least in witnessing. Altman's differences don't make him immune to his own immersions, even if these stun and harm us into awakeness with our reception in this quite amazing film.

In approaching all of this I have as example and direction those times Ray and I did look together at various scripts which came to us based on his work. He was largely uninterested in these. Did not want to participate, but also gave a free hand to those who wanted to try to make filmic entities out of his stories. The best one we saw together was one called *Feathers* by an Australian director. It was pretty close to the story. But Ray didn't have much investment in these things and wanted really just to write the next story. (If you'd like to see a video of it, I can send one on loan.) After our own encounters with Hollywood, in which nothing ever got onto celluloid and we spent quite a good deal of time on lapsed projects, he felt rightly the real investment should be with his stories. He often used to quote Ezra Pound who said, "It doesn't matter who writes or makes good literature or art, only that it gets made." In this way he was divesting the whole enterprise of personal greediness in the sense of showing up the pride in one's gifts and accomplishments.

If I read your piece in a certain deadly way, Bob, I would have to feel I had betrayed both Ray's work and his person, not to mention his devoted readers. And I have hovered there on that, deeply considering it. Assigning myself that corner to see if it fits. And if it did, I must tell you I would be so torn to the core there would be nothing left for me but to go out to Ocean View [Site of Ray's grave] and pull the granite over me. For I feel deeply charged with my responsibility to Ray's work. My permission and my participation in the film effort, proceeded out of the hope for dialogue between these two forms, recognizing that Ray's view of art was not of its containment, but of its ability to reemerge, to relocate itself, to reinvigorate others—even with the possible eclipsing of some of his own predilections.

Well I must go now, as they are flying me to Toronto to appear on a program about Ray's books for all of Canada. I long for poem-time again. The mail is crushing at the moment, but I wanted to take time to speak to you, because your understanding and your recognition of these concerns out of which I've been operating are important to me. Even if we disagree in the end about the use of Ray's stories in this film, it is important not to be out of range of hearing and considering and understanding with that deeper heart.

My best,

Tess

November 19, 1993

To Robert Altman

Dear Bob,

I heard from Frank [Barhydt], who called from Paris this morning. Sounds like he's having a good time there and also getting some work done. Yesterday Olivier Cohen called me from Paris, also—so that's two mornings in a row Paris has woken me up! It seems like plans are still on for me to be there the first week in January, although no tickets have yet been purchased.* I'll be hearing the details before too long and will let you know. I guess everything will revolve around a television program introducing Ray's book *No Heroics, Please* and perhaps my own book of poems as it comes into French. I've had a couple of faxes from my French translator [Christine Rimoldy], trying my best to unravel some of my compacted English phrasings for her. But fun trying to do it, even though it feels like failure. An invigorating failure at that.

Hope all is going well on *Pret-a-Porter*. I'm getting set to introduce *Short Cuts* about an hour from here at the weekend.† Advance tickets sold out in one hour. I'll read something from one of Ray's stories and then speak a few minutes about the film and be there for questions afterwards. We're also bringing books into the occasion. Ray's *Short Cuts* volume with your intro has sold over forty thousand copies and is on the "Top 10" list of the *Village Voice Supplement*. Great, huh?!

I introduced the film at the Olympia Film Festival (about two and a half hours from here) a couple weeks back. It was the first time anyone had lined up in that town for anything for years, my host told me. The place was packed and when I came out onto the stage there was a great roar of welcome. The film had a wonderful reception there.

The next morning I flew to Toronto to appear on a live televised broadcast called *Imprint,* with four men, discussing Ray's work. They showed the clip of the scene in the bakery, but didn't discuss the film on the program. I think it was prominently mentioned in the introduction to the discussion.

Well I'll look forward to hopefully seeing you in January. If anything exciting comes up, I'll be in touch.

Here's greetings to Kathryn and any of the *Short Cuts* crew who are about—

Fond best,

Tess

---

*Ultimately the trip never materialized, since *Short Cuts* did not receive an Academy Award.

†Showing of *Short Cuts* at the Rose Theatre in Port Townsend, Washington.

Ricochet Power

Someone has cut the power to the motorized, body-thick duct of cool air that had been shushing into the space through a second-story window. At dawn the crew had cloaked the house in black tarp to shoot these night scenes. *The camera is rolling.* It is the quiet of unfinished arguments, of Mafia hats at dawn—the air impending and alert. But what a population looks on! Members of the crew hover unobtrusively in doorways and crannies, crouched and leaning in the stairwell, stilled like children in a game of statues on a postage stamp–sized lawn.

Robert Altman sits next to me on the bed with Anne Archer in her cotton nightie squeezed against him, his hand balancing at her waist. She readies herself as "Claire" to cross to the bathroom where she will speak back toward Fred Ward (Stuart) from the *Short Cuts* script.

By then I've read the script in at least two different versions. Before that I'd seen revisions and published versions of the story, "So Much Water So Close to Home" by Raymond Carver, on which this scene had been based. In its final form it had appeared in Ray's last collection, *Where I'm Calling From.*

The reverberation of this current connecting Ray's writing with the script by Altman and Barhydt, passing into these flesh-and-blood characters being fixed on celluloid has begun, in the cramped space of that room, to cause my molecules to chatter and collide. The half-threat call of "Rolling!" has gone out and Walt Lloyd, the cinematographer, is bent to the camera. *Film is rolling.*

"Ricochet Power" appeared as the foreword to *Short Cuts: The Screenplay,* by Robert Altman and Frank Barhydt, Capra Press, 1993. Copyright © Tess Gallagher.

There is a vibrant calm at the center of fire. This is the calm I enter in the unbearable heat of the tiny bedroom of Claire and Stuart on location for *Short Cuts* as it was being shot in L.A. in August of 1992.

Claire looks back at her husband, Stuart, who's just told her that for three days and nights he'd left a woman's body tied in a river while he fished with his friends. *The camera is rolling.* Claire's expression of bafflement shifts into slow but steady disbelief in the icy flicker of the monitor which shows what the camera is picking up. Her face seems enormous like anything newborn because, I suppose, of that special amplification time takes on when you know its images are being preserved.

The moments I was living had been a long while arriving. All the way back to a newspaper article which had sparked Ray's story, forward to Frank Barhydt's sister giving him a book by Carver in 1988, the year Ray died, and then to Altman on a plane coming home from Italy, reading Carver stories as aftermath to his own changed direction.

The curious thing too was that, even with all the import of filming I've just described, there was also a casualness about what movement did take place around the shooting. Casualness and ease. Someone, something, or several someones were in control. Everything was going to happen the best it could and if things went wrong, there would be a way to handle it, even to use slippage to advantage. This agility of spirit Altman brings to his work seemed to free everyone to do their best. I was to appreciate the consistency of that spirit during the numerous visits I would make to the filming locations in August and October.

There is a feeling of brine and high seas about Robert Altman. He's scow and schooner, scrappy and tested. In stature his six feet, two inches, his love-to-eat heft, uncannily reminded me of Ray. Directing, he's like a genial, no-nonsense captain with a tender, flexible grip on things, even though he seems to be relying on everyone else present to do exactly what needs to be done, largely without him. When he does speak, it's calmly, as if he's teasing things out, yet with an exactitude rooted deep in the heart of the action as it's evolving from the script. But he's most live to what's coming through the actors in that crucial moment of shooting.

This exploding yet controlled time of the camera-rolling which I've tried to describe would have been sheer chaos without the firm scaffolding of this fine script, initially drafted by Frank Barhydt, a lean, down-to-earth man who laughs easily and whose laconic manner is quietly disarming. Having met him first on the page in his work on the script, I knew myself to be in the company of an impressive writer on his own ground. He also understood the way Ray's characters thought because he had down how they talked. I liked it that in person he didn't seem to need to prove anything to anyone. His relationship to Altman goes back through his own father who'd been Altman's boss in some past era. Barhydt has also worked on three previous projects with Altman.

After discussions with Altman, Frank had roughed out the *Short Cuts* script. Then they had put Carver's books aside for the next phase. Over the following months, Altman and Barhydt began to eat, sleep, and live Carver's world in its essences, imagining how it could find new life in film and in the things they each had to offer. Frank's Missouri-twanged voice picks up color and velocity remembering how they worked, the way their ideas began to feed into each other out of Carver, so that in the end, it's hard to remember who gave what.

The two would perform variations like jazz musicians on the Carver stories, inventing their own characters to add to his, getting scenes onto colored note cards that let them visualize the wide mosaic on the wall behind them at the initial production office in Malibu. Once, on the phone, Bob and I had talked about how scenes could go more than one way. The scripting of the stories began to reflect this variability of direction. I mentioned to Bob in a follow-up letter that such exploration was deep in the spirit of poetry, all the way back to Aristotle who says poetry deals with "a kind of thing which *might* happen, i.e., what is possible."

But behind, under, and inside this script remain the nine short stories and one poem, "Lemonade," of Raymond Carver. His clarity and precision, the intimate elisions of his characters' speech, the ways they glance off each other in conversation— bruise, circle, plead, lie, or seek to persuade—are unmistakably carried forward. As Frank is quick to acknowledge, much of Carver's dialogue was just too good not to use. But it couldn't simply carry at other times. Film, as Frank puts it, is "wordier." Sometimes an action demands two lines in film where one serves on the page. Sometimes a written thought or attitude will take a series of actions to translate onto film.

Besides the collateral of Carver's wonderful ear for the spoken word as it carries the unspoken, the script also had the charged fabric of Carver's quicksand world in which those life verities one depends on might, at any instant, give way. Altman and Carver probably join at this strange hinge "luck," both of them chancers and creators willing to stake their lives, artistic and otherwise, on the precarious rim of possibility. They've known the dive and swoop of fortune which takes us a step beyond mere courage to that helpless place we all hit at some point where we realize anything could and does happen, and to us.

What I keep admiring in this film script is the way the stories more than coexist. The failure of so many scripts of Carver stories by others I'd seen prior to the Altman-Barhydt project had been to stay so close to the originals that a robotic pandering to the text resulted. They were like someone ice skating with an osprey's egg on which the bird is still nesting. Nothing new came to the stories and they were damp with overpoignant silences.

Altman and Barhydt broke the frames on the stories and allowed the characters to affect each other's worlds or not, as if to suggest that we are both more "in this together" *and* alone than we ever suspected. There is a high element of surprise and delight simply in remeeting the characters *Nashville*-style in unexpected conformations. These interactions moved Carver into new territory. Often it seems Altman and Barhydt are using Carver to cue what *might* have been said or done, but was under the surface in the stories.

The trick in this scripting is, of course, to give enough of the unsaid while somehow communicating Carver's gaps and darkness. The shuttle motion of picking up and dropping stories at intervals is one mechanism the film uses to suspend us in its current, then allow us to reapproach what's going on downriver.

In early March of 1991 I'd sent Bob five pages of notes, what I called a "champagne read" of the first script I'd seen. I would later send "hard read" notes. But early on I was simply cheerleading. The caliber of that initial script verified my early joy at Altman's having undertaken to use Ray's stories in a film. I could see that he and Barhydt honored the spirit of Ray's work, knew how to give its Kafkaesque "gay and empty ride," its shadows as well as that Chekhovian side Ray came to in the last seven years. I'd read the scenes with what I called "dead-alive eyes," meaning I'd tried to let Ray, as I'd experienced him in our many collaborations, look through. I'd felt how amazed Ray would have been to meet his stories interwoven on one huge canvas.

Early on I'd realized that literary widows can get sickeningly nostalgic with "he would haves." So I ration that assumptive verb tense. Nonetheless, it serves honestly when I think how much Raymond Carver truly *would have* hated missing the glow and sweep of what has gone forward in the evolution of this scripting. It has passed from his stories to Bob and Frank, to the contributions of the crew, the inspiration of the actors, then into the cutting room, and now into theaters around the world, embraced and chastened, galvanized and amplified, reinterpreted by the many-headed hydra of collaborative intensity which is filmmaking—admittedly a galaxy away from the solitude in which Ray's writing was accomplished. But Ray was a realist who knew the difference between the action of the hive and of the cleaver. This scripting is amazing for how it orchestrates for both.

Risking trespass, I will say I believe Ray's attitude toward Altman's use of his work would have been one of permission to an artist of equal stature. Ray's capacity for delight is legendary. He surrendered to those things he loved. He was a straight-on admirer of Robert Altman, whose *Nashville* we'd watched more than once on video together and considered one of the most inspired, patently American films yet made.

Ray would have shown a generous curiosity about the new shape his stories would inevitably take. I imagine him exuberant at the dailies, swilling lemonade, laughing with his whole body at his smaller violences of snipped telephone cords becoming larger, more surgically destructive in Stormy Weather's chain saw massacre of his wife's living room furniture. He would appreciate the shifting of emphasis in Altman's version of "So Much Water So Close to Home"—how he uncovers something about the differences between the sexes by being more evenhanded with blame in a story which belonged firmly in Carver to the dilemmas of its women, dead and alive.

Altman and Barhydt both have a great sense of the dryly comic and they've brought to the surface Carver's own willingness to laugh with, not at, his characters. The most cautionary advice I gave Bob was the sense that Ray never raised himself above the plights of his characters. He was nose-to-nose with them, feeling the ruptures in intimacy and coherence which split their lives apart. This was to hint at restraining one of Bob's most potent and incisive artistic tools—irony. I typed up and gave him lines from Rainer Maria Rilke's *Letters to a Young Poet* which, while admitting that irony "cleanly used is also clean" advises that one "shouldn't be governed by it. . . . Seek the depth of things: thither irony never descends."

While such advice smacks perhaps of the confinements of the literary, it is also true that irony, in the more public mediums of television and film, often becomes the contemporary escape hatch to avoid genuine feeling. Ray's story "A Small, Good Thing" would have set Bob's compass in this regard if I'd said nothing. Because it centers around the death of a child, it required and got Bob's consummate skill in keeping the depth, yet not tipping into sentimentality or drawing away from the emotions. It is the story left most intact by the scripting, and, along with the Jack Lemmon portrayal of the adulterous father, it is one of the places the film lets the suffering of the characters open out most—hands and heart on.

Altman's difference from Carver is that he often shifts the cries of the characters into the wider arena of the audience by withholding them on screen. For instance in a Carver story like "Jerry and Molly and Sam" the adulterous husband silently asks himself, "Is there a chance for me?" But in Altman we see Gene retrieve the family dog he's abandoned, then return home as if he's never betrayed anyone—though he has, and the fact that the audience knows it serves as the inner ache he is too compulsive even to acknowledge.

Carver's characters grapple with their fates in the matter-of-fact voices of his narrators, but in film this all has to happen as action, not introspection. The effect of this necessary translation is at times to toughen and speed up what is tender and circuitous in Carver. Altman and Barhydt's intuitive feel for the need to restore tenderness can be felt in moments of vulnerability with characters like Doreen Piggott, the waitress played by Lily Tomlin, when she runs after the child she's hit with her car, pleading with him to let her take him home— realizing aloud to her husband (Tom Waits) later, then to her daughter (Lili Taylor) that her whole life could have changed if the child had been killed. The audience must bridge this near-escape to bear the truth—that the child *does* in fact die. Doreen's ignorance of this engages the audience's pain register each time she repeats how close she came to killing the child.

With Altman we can't escape the steepness of the ravine rushing up at us. If Carver fans miss the redemptive interior voices of his baffled middle-American characters in the film, it's because in the stories these brief glimpses of their hopes being blunted by realities do serve to cushion our fall.

I'm reminded of a remark by Pablo Neruda's friend Roberto Matta: "One has to be in despair about everything, in order to defeat despair." This hard assignment—to feel the pervasiveness of the American malaise—seems crucial to Altman and Barhydt's revisioning of Carver. The film audience, to a large extent, becomes it own interior narrator, a dazed character eventually forced outside the theater who keeps ruminating the half-articulated, glancing-off, unresolvable pain they've just witnessed.

Both stories and film use the whole keyboard of human proclivities, but the film is huge with appetite, and because it combines and interlocks stories, it has a ricochet power which the individual stories alone don't carry. There are the reverberating themes of infidelity, denial, sexual exploitation, the alcoholic merry-go-round, irrevocable loss in the death of a child, anonymous and grotesque death in the neglect of the woman's body in "So Much Water So Close to Home," and the disappearance of certain characters into fantasy.

Throughout the film there is a current of frustrated sexuality that erupts as violence against things and other people, and against the self. Even children coexist in half-deaf innocence within the perverse adult life around them. The circuitry of the film connects these behaviors and themes to each other rather more prismatically than one encounters them in Carver's individual stories.

Good films and good stories raise important questions. This film questions, among other things, women's complicity in their misuse as sexual playthings in the American imagination. They are seen by Altman as compliant with the American male need for an anonymity of sexual access to them. The victim-oriented feminism of the 1960s tended to place blame with the patriarchy for what happened to women in their sexual roles and lives. It largely avoided their own acquiescence to what was being done with their images. It knows better now. In this respect and others, Altman rather updates Carver to the nineties. I think the film definitely sees men and women in a dangerous partnership in these matters, and this is going to provoke a lot of discussion as to whether the presentation is a distortion, a magnification, or whether it reveals that women, in their wish to be loved at any cost, do in fact often contribute to sexual usury.

There is also a kind of checked-out matter-of-factness regarding sex, say, in the character of Lois Kaiser (Jennifer Jason Leigh) talking sex on the phone while she diapers her kids. Her character seems to indicate that this lack of intimacy is what some men need and that it isn't any big deal to supply it, especially when it's an easy way to earn a buck and you don't have to see what you do! After all, it's just imagined—right? The sell-out oblivion of this character is an Altman figure a step beyond Carver.

In Altman's vision throughout, the connective tissue in American life between what is imagined and what is real is being severed. The emasculation of Lois Kaiser's husband (Christopher Penn) is very compellingly delivered. The moment in the written script when Jerry Kaiser kills the woman with a stone had made me wonder if this action could really credibly be brought off. It had taken many drafts from Ray even to get it to work in the story. As it turned out, I was shocked in viewing the film that, unlike in the Carver story "Tell the Women We're Going," I could not simply stand in a place of judgment during one of the most violent moments of the film. Altman makes us scarily complicitous because we *feel* how Jerry Kaiser got to this action.

Altman and Barhydt's scripting keeps the calamitous momentum of action up all the way to the end by scooping up the characters in their separate but joined quiverings in an earthquake. This is a step past the mock, symphonic finale of *Nashville*. The blues singing of Annie Ross as the widow Tess, played off the cello-undertow of Lori Singer, is also an Altman-Barhydt addition to Carver which joins the stories' purgatorial world seamlessly from the inside. Altman's is probably a franker, even more lost world than Carver's—and therefore more anguished for its unattended wounds. Tess sings "To Hell with Love" to answer Carver's "What We Talk about When We Talk about Love"—for her, the talking is so over it's raw utterance and rasping good riddance. Such dialogue between Carver and Altman-Barhydt is provocatively alive throughout the script. We have to ask ourselves: what is it we've left behind if, with Tess, we say "to hell with love" which—for the record—is not what Ray said.

When, at last, in January of 1993 the film was assembled in its bladder-breaking three-hour-and-ten-minute version in the cutting room in NYC, Altman held a special showing for me. There were celebrities attending, but I wasn't able to spot most of them without cuing from my photographer friend, Marion Ettlinger. (I did recognize and meet Lauren Bacall in the elevator!) All the better to focus on Altman and the film with the lively ghost of Ray beaming in on me.

The fan of images was projected in that small crowded viewing room. Time again slipped out of itself. The jigsaw tapestry of the lives on the screen began to intersect with my own, to make a kind of earthquake in my solar plexus. I was absorbed by the spectacle. It was as if the film compelled its audience to recognize its own deceits, betrayals, exposures, and abandonments as Altman re-creates them from Carver and adds his own. By the end, the beautiful flawed confusion of human lives had worked its spell on me. Yet it was beyond spell, out into that territory which John Updike says demands "great natural health" in which we are asked to sustain life without illusions.

There was a pervasive sadness and loneliness in the room when the film ended. But also a palpable exhilaration that comes from having been through something large and inexplicable, more achingly comfortless than anyone had guessed they'd have the stamina and will to experience. But we had. We'd come through. When the lights went up we belonged to that world. The fusion of Altman-Carver, made visceral on film—naked, obsessive, palms up, rawly innocent, chaotic. It was a poetry of the impure, as if we could suddenly see ourselves worn away by the acid of not knowing what's happening to us as we do what we do—the poetry of food stains and shocks, doubts and stupidities, of loneliness and pirated rooms, injured sex, clingings over hospital beds, splinters of glassy hearts in the freshly vacuumed carpet.

It was natural in aftermath at the restaurant to want to talk about hope, that elusive Carver-manna heaven is always intending to drop. Had Altman inscribed our brows with William the Silent's "One need not hope to undertake"? Were we cut off as a people from our pain and suffering because we don't know how or what to hope for anymore?

Art as distinct from the purely entertaining isn't obliged to provide the antidote for its revealed poisons. Ray also had to fight this notion from readers and critics—that the artist was supposed to do more than diagnose the condition of its characters—that he or she was also supposed to provide, like the Statue of Liberty on the horizon, some sort of redemptive light.

But in Altman's film, as with Ray's stories, the questions *are* the redemption. What we do with our recognitions, once we gaze into their harsh and tender mirrors, is really on our own ground, outside both the stories and the film. That's the provocative nature of art itself. It says what *is,* as honestly and truly as it can envision it. On this count both Altman and Carver are relentlessly true. They both reach these truths lyrically. Altman's lyricism works by dislocating the narrative, by jump-starting it, by allowing it to love its lost causes even as it leapfrogs them onto the wet cement of the next enormous instant.

On one of my last nights in L.A. at a meal at the Granita restaurant, Altman and I had been talking about our mutual fascination with doubles, the wild probability of gaining that extra likeness which might extend your life into the secret fruitfulness of the path not taken. "Ray was a Gemini*," I told Bob, in my by now habitual reflex of keeping Ray present in our conversations. We also spoke about poetry—Ray's love of it. I said I felt Ray's stories had the hum and leap of poetry inside them. Later, as we left the restaurant, Bob came back from the car to where I was standing with Frank at the curbside to plant a kiss on my mouth so firmly it was brotherly. "Goodnight, Poet," he said, and, without a beat I answered: "Goodnight, Other Poet." Thinking double.

---

*The third sign of the zodiac; the Twins.

Part 3

Conversations

Interview with Bette Tomlinson

In her essay "The Poem as a Reservoir for Grief," Tess Gallagher says: "It is important that our inner nature be strengthened by the wisdom of our grieving. . . . Until individuals maintain a responsible relationship to their own losses and changes, there will be no such thing as a hopeful future." This essay was written several years before the death of her husband, Raymond Carver, a widely respected writer of fiction and poetry. Moon Crossing Bridge *is the record of her responsible relationship to the grief she experienced. She succeeds in strengthening, with wisdom, the inner being of her audience as she strengthened her own.*

The six sections of Moon Crossing Bridge *follow the complex movements of a heart's response to, and the attendant gestures of, the death of a beloved. The signal poem, "Red Poppy," introduces the images of a Bedouin god, a desert canopy of sleep, shaggy ponies, and a gallant hussar. The obsessions of childhood as metaphors of love give these poems the authority of innocent, devoted love.*

In Gallagher's essay "The Poem as Time Machine," she speaks of her childhood: "I was six or seven years old and already leading a double life as an imagined horse disguised as a young girl. . . . There were several ridges behind my house which our horse-selves delighted in. Some of my freest moments still exist in those images of myself standing silhouetted on the highest knoll, pawing with one foot, tossing my thick pony mane and neighing for my friend with such authority that a real horse pastured down the block began to answer me." These images of horses repeat themselves throughout Moon Crossing Bridge, *changing as the stages of dying change, and as the freedom of moments on the ridge take on complex and mortal wounds.*

The moon is the phenomenon of spirit in grief, and all other images are its epiphenomena in this cohesive and mysterious collection. The moon is the repository for souls, and in the beginning poems, it is the

From *Kinesis* 4 (1992). Reprinted by permission of Bette Tomlinson. Copyright © Tess Gallagher and Bette Tomlinson. Bette Tomlinson is a poet and critic living in Missoula, Montana.

light of the mourned one. Gallagher uses this image with subtlety and suggestion. In "Trace, in Unison," she brings the moonlight into her body, as her body has reached for him: "Buds of jasmine threaded through / her hair so they opened after dark, / brightening the room. That morning / rain as it would fall, still / falling, and where we had lain, / an arctic light steady / in the mind's releasing."

Later, in the title poem, the moonlight joins Gallagher and her love outwardly: "Only what we once called worship / has feet light enough to carry / the living on that span of brightness. / And who's to say I didn't cross / just because I used the bridge in its witnessing, / to let the water stay the water / and the incongruities of the moon to chart / that joining I was certain of." She says, later still, in "Two Locked Shadows": "Their joining is the way a buried self / exerts its chill in order to ravish / the greater light around it."

That greater light points the way to a return: the possibility of loving again. In "Sea inside the Sea," Gallagher affirms her own flesh and its insistent relation to what moves in rhythm with the moon: "Silk banner embossed / with the myriad invigorations of the blood / pulling the tide toward us / until our bodies don't hoard eternity / but are spun through with a darting vehemence, / until the abundant thing made of us spikes free / of even its ripening, that moan of white fingers at a depth / that strips the gears of the soul."

The telos of loss, to reconnection to the world, is driven by moonlight and understood by the romantic compulsions of childhood. In her essay "Sing It Rough," Gallagher says that "[the reader] wants order and magic at once. But the magic of poetry so often works against the taxidermy of logic and the reasoned apprehension of experience, that the poet turns outlaw when the reader wants to bulldog a poem into one-two-three-four meaning." The compulsions, expressed through the desert imagery of a nomadic people and a horse's apprehension of the natural world and its relationship to its rider, gift these poems with the innocence of the child-as-animal which is reclaimed and renewed through loss. Gallagher delves into annihilation to emerge victorious in a desert of loss, rain, a canopy of stars, and with bells woven into her mane.

Moon Crossing Bridge is rich with a power to carry the reader to profound understandings of loss and recovery while celebrating the initial awareness of the distant past of childhood. Tess Gallagher uses the unexpected and the traditional to capture the tidal movements of loss.

At what point in your grief were you able to begin bringing it to language?

I didn't start writing poems until about six months after Ray's death. At first I was just stunned, and language didn't come to me. I found that I was quite silent. There are certain states that are very hard to bring to language. As a poet one attempts, and poems are a record of those attempts and failures and small successes.

Would you say that in those states of experience there is fundamental meaning that can be revealed?

I think so. I went back into that place that I couldn't bring toward language. For instance, the last moments of being with my loved one. To go back into that time and live it with full consciousness, and full strength. I didn't self-censor. I wanted to see exactly what the gestures had been, and to recall just how they happened. Especially "Red Poppy" and the poem called "Wake." Some things which happen around death are never spoken of, and even though they are very difficult and strange occurrences, I reported those things. The last kiss after my husband died and actually lying beside him—those are things that I know have happened before, but they haven't been given a life in our poetry. They certainly are very private moments. They remind me of a poem of Rilke's, "Washing the Corpse," where we feel the power of both the living and the dead.

Rilke believed that Being speaks to the poet, as opposed to Valéry, whose tradition is one the language poets express—that the artist creates meaning.

I think that it's really a combination. I was just reading a book about the life of Akhmatova. She says: "We do not remember what happened, only what we remembered one day." I feel as though that's what happens in these poems. One day I remembered these things, and I added to that memory. I refreshed that memory with the present moment in which I was writing.

The coalescence of a moment of memory and a presence of spirit?

I think that this book has a very strong presence of the spirit of the one who really revisits, through memory and through actual feeling. Someone who has had these feelings might relegate this to superstition, or . . . I don't put a heavy religious significance, either. I just feel that these things happened and that I could make them palpable in the poem.

What role do you find that language plays in the revelation of spirit through memory?

The language itself does help you to reenter, as well as to create. Language is the new adaptation that you bring to the experience.

In your introduction you mention that a visit to Japan allowed for a certain spiritual development. Would you say that in writing Moon Crossing Bridge *you were influenced by the Oriental use of the tradition of imagery? I'm thinking, for example, of the use of the moon as a repository for souls in the Western tradition.*

The moon has been that mythic place where souls went between reincarnations, and the unborn were there, also. And, of course, all of the tidal connections with the moon. I'm always noticing when it's high tide and when it's low tide. There is a poem called "Kisses from the Inside," where I say that the tide is everything and the speaker says, "I have never seen the sea." That again is evidence of presences and powers which we only vaguely understand. There is that sense in which we never *see* the sea. It is too huge and mysterious.

Your book uses philosophical and religious allusions to tie your experience to a whole tradition of a people and an art form and to give it weight and depth. Certainly the Japanese have that tradition. Would you say that they influenced you that way in recapturing this experience?

I walked across the bridge whose Chinese name means "Moon Crossing Bridge" and I thought, "That's my title." My way of making a bridge across the loss. A spiritual bridge. The crossing-over goes both ways. My crossing over *into* those boundaries. I think for a long time I was crossing over the death boundary and bringing back what I could, and trying to be with Ray in that new state. Then I have that line in the poem which is a kind of injunction not to build your house on the bridge. I think that the book begins to realize this—that it's self-instruction, that I have to get across the bridge. The last section seems to me to be rather schizophrenic and tentative. It's the beginning back toward some sense of being able to love again, but it's terribly guarded. When it seems to break, it breaks rather suddenly, and begins to self-encourage. Rather than encouragement to the speaker, it's encouragement to the other; the participant, the hoped-for one.

Change does have the feeling of being abrupt, but we know that healing has taken place gradually.

In the poem "Glow," I commiserate with the Japanese women and then ask, or choose, that waiting not be my state. In rereading that poem, I actually get permission from my lost love: "The light from the moon belongs more to me." And then the book does go on and takes it that step further. That's when it seems schizophrenic, where it seems to be invitational, but it also is holding back. The strangeness of trying to enter into intimately knowing someone again after the intensity of a very extraordinary relationship.

You have stated that our society's inability to grieve might be more central to our problems than we have yet been able to recognize. Does the expression of grief play a major role in the creation of a culture? In grieving do you get to the depth of a kernel of experience, and of language, in the passion of the grief—that the highest moments of a culture can be expressed in grieving?

Akhmatova's poetry, the strength of that poetry, comes from its ability to acknowledge that a loss has indeed occurred. If you can't lose anything—if you are a person or a culture that doesn't acknowledge that things pass from us, or that people pass from us, that we make grievous errors and then we have to reinstate ourselves spiritually and actually—you're in a very bad place if you're unable to do that. You're going to be a very destructive person, or a country whose behavior is terribly rash and erratic and unconscionable. I think a lot about the Vietnam War. A poem in *Portable Kisses* deals with what happened to a lot of women during that time. The psycho-erotic effects. My poem is called "Sugarcane."

You're addressing what happens when we don't grieve, but what about when we do grieve? Aren't amazing truths manifest in ritual and music and poetry? That is to say, a whole culture created out of grief?

I've come to a lot of understanding through the map I made in language of my own grieving, and I've rejoined my new understanding back to my life. I think it helps to see someone do that. I don't believe in disposable death. I believe in an ecology of death.

What was the stance that you took with the experience that encouraged language to come to you?

I wanted the poetry to reflect the depths and also the moments when I had recognition and even joy from realizing how important that love was to me. If I've written well, you should feel the greatness of that love.

Rilke says that we lose ways of experiencing the world when we lose the language that describes them.

Yes, we lose the capacity to grieve if we don't keep redoing, frisking the language.

It seems to come back to courage—the courage to go back into those experiences and risk emotionally and psychologically.

I'm generally against the notion of courage in this matter. Everyone has their own timing in this process. I think that there will honestly be people who won't be ready for this book. Still, I can't not write it or publish it because of that. While feeling generous toward individuals and their grieving, I do feel a general lack of stamina in America for some of the most demanding experiences in our lives and in our consciousness as a society, a country.

Yet some people could read this book and realize that they want that stamina. Language as an agent of the spirit.

I hope that it hits them in the spine so they feel things that they didn't feel before.

Interview with Megan Sexton

Your poems travel through moments of tenderness, moments that are almost unbearable to be so conscious of, but you sing us through it and we are closer to being whole when we get to that other side. I'm thinking about "Stepping Outside," when you say, "Your words would have made a feast of what ate you." How do you come to describe these events that utterly change your life? Do you let them incubate and call you when it is time, or do you force yourself to describe them until you can let them go?

Essentially you're asking whether I wait for the poems or if they just compel me. It's really different with each poem, but I would say in many I work close to the event. That's not true for a poem entitled "Sugarcane" which is in *Portable Kisses.* That poem took twenty-three years to write. There are elements in my history that come together with the present moment I'm writing about so that it's never all one thing. If you read my essay "A Concert of Tenses" where I talk about past moments and present moments coming together and if you look at each poem, you see a poem is never all one time frame. So in that sense, even though I may be working close to a present event, it's nourished by other times.

I'm afraid of letting certain things slip away by waiting too long to write about them.

You lose certain attitudes, certain inflections to the emotions. Louise Bogan said that poetry was essentially an emotional medium. It's not used that way in a lot of poetry that I

From *Georgia State University Review* (Spring 1992). Reprinted by permission of Megan Sexton. Copyright © Tess Gallagher and Megan Sexton. Megan Sexton is a poet who teaches at Georgia State University. She is the managing editor of *Five Points: A Journal of Literature and Art.*

read, but that's how I first came to poetry—it affected me physically; I felt it in my body and nothing had really affected me in that way. And that's why poets in the beginning were feared, because they could affect people's feelings. They could sway them, and that's a danger for the poet too, to keep free, yet be responsible for how you sway people.

I guess we don't have that sense of danger so much in this country as say a country like Russia has had with someone like Akhmatova, for instance—we don't imprison our poets for writing. Is that the kind of danger you were referring to?

I was thinking of it as the poet's responsibility to the readers not to be carried away by their own music in some wrong direction. But yes, of course, if you put out news that nobody is ready to hear, and in fact the government doesn't want to hear, you ended up in prison in Russia, or in Romania, and a lot of other places. In Belfast, where I have many strong friendships, you have to be very careful because of the political climate. Mindful of repercussions. What you say could put your life in danger, or the lives of others.

I think poets need to guard themselves from hubris, the feeling that they know too much. I had a conversation a long time ago in Ireland with Seamus Heaney about a poem I wrote which he thought I wrote too soon, and I think there is such a thing as writing too soon, before you understand something. However, I also think that even your ignorance can be useful, at least making you pose questions, because if you know everything you're not going to ask those questions quite the same way. I should say that in "Sugarcane" I talk about the psycho-erotic effects of the Vietnam War on women, and I don't think this has really been addressed in any serious way. It's taken time for this to be absorbed and brought to language. We heard a lot about the POWs; we heard a lot about the trauma that veterans suffered after the war; we've heard a lot about how we didn't celebrate their sacrifice, and all of these are things which the national attention has eventually been turned toward to one degree or another. But the women who were attached to these men, thousands and thousands of women—there has been virtually nothing offered toward those lives and thirty years have passed. Maybe one movie I recall entitled *Coming Home*.

In "Linoleum" and "If Poetry Were Not a Morality" you seem to long for a simplicity that is not endorsed by our materialistic culture. What are "the right things" for the poets to give up, so that they may attain the clarity and simplicity needed to be open for poems?

You know this is so very different for every poet. I didn't start out thinking, well, I'm going to give up being married, I'm going to give up children, but I did, and now I've even given up my job teaching, at least temporarily. I didn't know that I was going to give up having a home for all those years I was living like a gypsy throughout the seventies. I didn't really know what it required to be a poet. I just knew from the very beginning that there was really no other choice for me. That I loved poetry and had a vocation there and that whatever the cost, I had to pay it. I'm surprised at all I have been willing to do for this life in poetry and writing.

I don't feel in any state of anguish about these things I've surrendered to the process and, in fact, feel lucky. Imagine getting here thinking, "Oh, I should have had five children like my mother, then my life would have been full and right." But I did make these choices and I think they came out of the necessity of what I thought it took to be a woman writing poems during that time. Ursula LeGuin was able to have children and has a wonderful essay about her own mother who had children and then, when they'd left home, started her writing. Ursula LeGuin, it seems to me, has a husband who was very helpful in raising children. I never attracted men who would have supported me in that way, unfortunately or fortunately, as it turned out for my writing. My first husband would have, I feel, but the war did us in, in so many psychic ways, that we weren't able to continue those dreams, and that's the topic of that poem "Sugarcane." In a sense, I lost my children not because of my poetry so much, but because of that war, because I refused to raise children in a country that was going to surrender its young men to those kinds of wars, and of course if I had had a child, that child might have been sent to fight in Iraq, and as you hear now [March 20, 1992] our president is threatening again to bomb Iraq.

But we were talking about the things a poet gives up. I think you find those things as you move through the territory. I recently gave up full-time teaching, and I loved my teaching.

It was also a gift. I've been very lucky to have two gifts, teaching and writing. It was extremely hard for me to make that decision because I had to give up my tenure, and I had worked very hard for this. I was the only woman, and still am to date the only tenured woman writer that Syracuse University has ever had. I am the first and only, so it was very hard to leave because I thought it was an important precedent. I would have liked to have been able to sustain that, but I needed to take leave and it was a longer leave than was usual and, when it was disallowed, I had to resign in order to get the time that I needed to write these poems. I could not have written these poems and continued to teach. They demanded I go into my solitude. The poems couldn't have been made in the usual stream of academic public movement. I really had to withdraw in order to get into the territory where these came from. No one can tell you to honor those things, and no one is going to protect the possibility of your poems. The university will never protect the writer; they will never come to the writer and say: Look, we think you need to take a couple of years off and attend to this particular material. First of all, they don't know your material, and they don't assume those needs of solitude. They want the writer in the stall, available to the student. And there is one particularly odious word one often hears as the reason for this from administrators: *continuity, continuity.* When most of life and even much of learning comes from certain discontinuities, certain fortunate abutments and even "wrong turns."

Do you have any encouragement for novice poets living in a culture that seems to nurture very few of us?

I feel that poets have to be extremely resourceful about finding their nourishment. You can't go about expecting to be taken care of—that strange expectation being an unfortunate by-product of writing programs. They can give the poet a false sense of what's really going to be out there. In fact I think there are more supports in this country than there are in Ireland, although some have developed in Ireland since I began going there in 1968. There are now some stipends, but there are no writing workshops in Northern Ireland. In the Republic there are festivals such as the Yeats Summer School and poets will go there. I think in England there are a few workshops springing up in a two-week seminar kind of thing or in a summer session. So writers meet instead in cafés and in their homes and they're not always talking about poetry, which I think is pretty healthy. They're talking about music; they're singing to each other, entertaining each other; they're telling stories; they're going for long walks along the Giant's Causeway, singing to the sea.

I think it would be very healthy for American poetry to get a little less ingrown. I'm sorry when I find my former students still teaching English composition for very little money, and doing this for two and three years, waiting for the break to get their poetry book published. Then I meet a young writer who was a student of mine and she's doing something quite else. She has decided that yes, she is not going to get that book published right away and that teaching composition is not satisfying, so she's gone back to school and she's gotten a degree in social work, and she's enjoying that. She has understood that the time we're going through demands something else, and I really think that it is a time for young poets to be out in the community. My battles will be different because I'm living where I was born, this town, this land which is at the heart of the struggle for saving this forest environment, these rivers I love.

You do have to make time for the poems because no one else will make that time. I find I write in periods. Times I go every day to the poems and then other things will start to happen in my life and I will be carrying, accumulating that kind of energy a writer needs as a contemporary creature.

Do you find a similarity in the landscape of the Pacific Northwest and that of Ireland?

Well, Ireland doesn't have these forests. When I was in Tucson I saw David Ignatow. You know the poets in New York talk about *a* tree, *the* tree. I talk about forests. As I talk to you, I'm looking at the Olympic National Forest which wouldn't be here except that it's a protected entity. There is a sense of that forest around me here and the sense of being close to wildlife, though we can't even really call our parks wildernesses anymore. Wilderness is gone, so that we have parks with wild animals *in* them. Ireland seems very tame in that respect, very domesticated. But there is a kind of time there which is close to the kind of time I feel here, a slowed-down kind of time that you can get into, partly because of the proximity of forest here. In Ireland the slowing down of time is more agrarian, especially in the Republic where you have all these small farms. That was my environment during the writing of *Under Stars*. I lived near several of these small farms.

I have saved a quote without a citation from Gail Godwin. It says, "A quality that serves well: self doubt so deep it is indistinguishable from vanity." Do you agree with this?

Gail Godwin is a fiction writer and the things a fiction writer needs are a little different from what a poet needs. I think that as a poet you need a certain amount of confidence in order to write, to assume anyone will listen. I think if you hear the early stories about Yeats going around in his velvet tie and cape in Dublin you understand there is a certain posing that young poets do early on to get some kind of inward stature and public credibility. I do feel I understand what Gail's saying, in that every time you write a poem you're playing chess with yourself in a certain way, because you're looking to see what is the accepted idea for the subject you are trying to write about, and then you're trying to surprise that accepted idea, and then you're trying to go further—you're trying to abandon it, to unseat it, put some spin on it. Whatever the accepted political view is, you are challenging it. So that's the kind of doubt that interests me more than self-doubt. I think we've had a period of women really just finding confidence, and that's why we've had so many women writers evolving during the past twenty years, since Sylvia Plath's time, and this has demanded more confidence than doubt.

So you think you find that kind of confidence within yourself and try to focus in on that?

I suppose you borrow your confidence. I think the women's movement has helped women feel that they can legitimately put their energy into their art. If you think of Louise Bogan, she didn't have as much encouragement from the community at large as I feel I've had, even though when I started out my immediate family thought I was crazy to be doing this. I come from a working-class background and no one ever thought a poet would come out of this nest. I have written an essay about my own development entitled "My Father's Love Letters."

When I was first writing I never met women teaching writing. Jean Garrigue was there teaching in a literature course. But I never had a single woman writing teacher in the writing program at University of Washington or at University of Iowa. That hasn't been true of the young women I've been teaching, and that's one of the reasons I've stayed in teaching so long. I felt that this was a special entrustment, to be there for those women. I have a community of women who nourish me now, but I didn't have that very much in the beginning—although I'm still in touch with a woman, Joan Swift, who was in Theodore Roethke's class with me. She's in Seattle, and there is a community of poets in Seattle and I see them when I do readings. Madeline DeFrees has been a close friend for a very long time. Lucia Perillo, a former student, is a friend of mine, and she lives not far from me, in Olympia. Alice Derry and Karen Whalley are poets who live in my town. But mainly I think I've found strength from reading poets in books. Reading Akhmatova has been very central to my work all along, for instance.

In the essay "The Laugh of the Medusa," Hélène Cixous states, "Woman must put herself into the text—as into the world and into history—by her own movement." Would you discuss what this statement shares with "The Story of a Citizen" and the following lines:

I
whose only patriotic act had been the continued
love of myself in the body of a woman.

And would you also like to discuss the image of the dog and what it represents for you in this poem?

I did go back and reread that poem. It's a very complex poem. I was trying to define some of the things I felt not just as a woman but also as a citizen. This poem was written at the time when we were all feeling the threat of nuclear war strongly, the buildup of armaments, and I was realizing that women and men—I mean we're all in the same boat—we're all soldiers, we're not civilians anymore. We can all be destroyed by a nuclear bomb, this hardly imaginable destructive event. "The Story of a Citizen" is very ironic in tone, and when you ask about the lines "I / whose only patriotic act had been the continued / love of myself in the body of a woman," well it *has* been a struggle to live in this woman's body and to meet all the challenges of being a woman, especially through the time in which I've lived.

Those battles we thought we had won now have to be fought over again. This is what's so ironic to me, that as a young woman, seventeen years old in Seattle, first time away from home, birth control was just beginning to be available. The fear in those years of possibly getting pregnant was incredible. It was a terror. To think that women are having to go through that again. Having to regain the right to deal with pregnancy as an individual right to have control over their own bodies. Many women didn't make it out of my town. They got pregnant and bore their children and they stayed here. You're not very portable once you have children. I forget what the statistics are now, but so many women now are also raising their children alone. To be a woman in this time isn't really at all easier.

I think that was the early thing the woman's movement tried to say, that at least we should be able to determine what happens to and in our own bodies. The book *Our Bodies Our Selves,* a handbook of information for women about their bodies, is still an important book—and for control of our bodies to still be a priority after twenty years tells us something, doesn't it?

My poem, "The Story of a Citizen," was really off a poem of Robert Hass'. In his poem they're discussing the Vietnam War; it's a conversation, and there's a lot of anger. There's one character in my poem who talks right out of his gut, "It makes me want to puke." That's real working class. I think we're still living in a time of what I call "blatant political pornography." I was surprised in rereading the poem at how much still remains true. It's interesting that you're the first person since I wrote the book who's asked my anything about this poem.

You ask about the dog image and that's a very complicated image in mythology. The dog bays at the moon because it's communicating with souls, according to mythology. I think I was reading in the *Woman's Encyclopedia of Myths and Secrets,* a wonderful sourcebook that I imagine women poets across the country must all be reading. I'm sure I had read the whole section on "the dog" before I worked on that poem. There were certain goddesses who were accompanied by the dog, the bitch goddess Tharma, she was accompanied by what they call death dogs. The divine huntress Diana also. The fate goddess, her symbol was a dog. I think I mention "the eye of the dog," that's the brightest star in Sirius. And Spakeo was another name for bitch goddess. The dog is a mixed symbol in American life. Some people care more about their relationships with dogs than they do about human affairs, and at times they sadly even seem to be right, human affairs being as muddled as they are!

Do you know the saying "Man's best friend is a dog, doesn't say much about the dog?"

No, exactly. Well, I think that women have been man's best friend and so in that sense sometimes they haven't always been their own best friends. I think we've come to a period at least where women have been alerted to this and have made more effort toward becoming their own best friends.

I mean the dog in that poem to be an ironic figure, so you can't explain it in only one way. It shifts in the poem so you have the "I" kicking the dog, insulting the idea of ownership of even this dog, and being able to kick it, just as we are able to act as if we're the policemen of the world, and bomb Iraq repeatedly when we get ready to assert certain kinds of ownership or economic needs. I think this is an American preoccupation, ownership. But, I mean, our kind of ownership is so frivolous. We buy these things and then they're soon in the trash. So in a sense our form of ownership is very peculiar—ownership without responsibility, and that, I think, has to change.

Do you think that women poets today are successfully writing the female experience without internally censoring themselves? Has backlash affected women's poetry in your opinion?

I think it's very dangerous to write only out of the politically accepted view. I think there are women poets who are suffering from the politically accepted feminist point of view. You have to be aware of what those views are. You can't work in ignorance. With a poet like Linda Gregg, I think it's possible, at least as I hear her work being talked about, that it somewhat suffers unfairly in the way it's been critically misapprehended. The feminist view that one isn't now allowed, as a woman, to authentically suffer for love, that injures us all. To suffer for love, according to certain feminist currents, is not a viable option, and yet it happens, and the poet has to reflect what happens. Women are still suffering in the kinds of love they find. So I would defend Gregg's right to reflect her suffering for and from love. Of course her poems are so rich and complex, I think these critics ultimately fail to rob Gregg of her stature as one of our finest lyrical poets.

When I visited Tokyo and then went on to Kyoto, I visited a particular temple especially for women who suffer from bad situations in love. They were copying out the sutras and trying to heal in that temple. And I think that if Linda Gregg had simply followed the feminist mandate to live only for your own ends—remember that the early feminist mandate was to be an independent woman and to find those ways in which you could get the kinds of work you wanted and earn respect as a woman doing what you wanted to do—if she had obeyed only that, Linda couldn't have written those incredible poems. Her independence is vested in her spiritual and psychic journeying and venturing.

Now there were a lot of sacrifices made along that independent route, and our relationships with men were challenged greatly in that we suddenly became unwilling to sacrifice our own careers simply for our love relationships. I think that this book of love poems I've written for Ray is outside the usual parameters of what a feminist critic would *like* to see me doing—to have spent this time honoring this love and understanding the kind of loss involved, and the hope of new love, that possibility at the end of the book. These are erotic explorations toward the end of the book, the experience of being without the mate and admitting that this is a very strange state of being, to which I then try to give form. If I had just sat down and thought "What do women need?" I might not have been writing these poems. I think you have to write out of your own personal urgencies.

It's a culture that avoids death. I go to the graveyard and there's no one there but me. Time after time I think: well, nobody dies in America. Or that our deaths are so portable that they don't need even the simple ritual of visiting the burial site. But I have allowed myself a free reign. What is excessive for one person won't be for another. You have to find what's right for what you feel, and do those things. I have gained a lot from the fact that there is such a thing as a feminist view. At the same time there is a problematic side to it.

I think I've also gained quite a lot by coming to my poetry in the era in which I did. I look at my mother's life and feel very glad that I didn't begin to write my poetry when she was a young girl and have to write out of those strictures. I had a lot of ground under me when I began to write. I miss her poems nonetheless; I would have been glad to have any poems she might have written. In fact her life, and the sacrifices of her life are the very ones that have enabled me and charged me not to be silent. I write a lot out of my mother's silence.

Here's my mother, who worked as hard as any man out there in the logging operation with my father, a woman who was injured and who had to leave the woods, who had great physical strength and who worked side by side with him. As a result, I never really believed a lot of the propaganda of the fifties about women's ability being any less than a man's. I always believed women were extraordinary. They *are* extraordinary.

I am really lucky to have this mother. She's still my most amazing friend. I see her every day, and people who meet her are also struck by a particular quality. Many of the stories I wrote in *The Lover of Horses,* which has just been reissued, I owe to her in some degree. She's a wonderful storyteller.

One thing that young writers should be aware of is that as a poet your work doesn't travel the way it will if you're able to write fiction or to write essays. I've also written journalism, film scripts, and essays about artists. Do try different kinds of writing. Look at a writer like D. H. Lawrence—he was writing novels, short stories, and poetry. Not everybody will be ambidextrous, but I'm so happy my stories have been translated into several languages. They just appeared in Swedish, and they're been translated into Japanese. I wouldn't have Japanese readers except for my short stories.

I admire the many perspectives you achieve in your poems. For instance, "You hear me, but you don't / hear me, the motor says / to

the fish" from "Boat Ride" reminds me of the way Joyce has the cake of
soap commenting in the Nighttown scene in "Ulysses." I think you
bring mystery to the ordinary this way, is this your intent?

You're always trying to find a way to indicate how mysterious events and objects and states of being truly are, to find a way to give these things form. We have the sense of mystery in all its forms most acutely when we're children, and then things seem to get more and more ordinary as we get older, so we have to restore the mystery. Akhmatova, when she wanted to bless a poem, would say, "There's mystery in this poem." I came to poetry because of mystery. If I write a poem which is only flat-footed and matter-of-fact, then I've left far behind those burning elements which first brought me to poetry.

I see poetry as preserving, in a sense, the mystery in our lives and preserving key elements that affect us. This is perhaps an "old" view of poetry, and when I teach with Galway Kinnell and Sharon Olds, I'm the odd one out. They feel very creditably that you approach the mystery by going head on with it, looking at things as clearly as possible. This was also Raymond Carver's view. I'm still with Yeats and Lorca and Akhmatova.

I think Raymond Carver did have a way of finding mystery.

Yes, he did. I think his work is very mysterious, and yet he has a good exactness, preciseness also in his work. My way is different, and what's different from his way I can't even make explicit. I haven't applied critical tools to my own work. I've really left that for other people, even though there really are no strong critical voices working now on contemporary poetry, or if there are some critics scrabbling about out there in poetry, they go to the far ends of the spectrum talking about language poetry which is something so obviously different from a poetry which is still involved with memory and coherences even as we contrive them.

I think it would be interesting to write an essay on mystery and contemporary poetry. I would like to do that at some time. But even if I knew how I came to my own mystery, I probably would not tell. I really don't think I *can* tell you how I find or create the mystery, just that it is something that I'm conscious of hoping for in my poems. I get a lot of my mystery from allowing states of being to be spoken of which wouldn't normally be voiced. My challenge is really to cross boundaries, speak of things that are taboo. In *Moon Crossing Bridge* there's a poem titled "Wake" where I climb onto the bed next to my dead love. That kind of poem is a challenge to write, to give that so that it can truly happen, so it causes us to take a step in a direction in which we wouldn't have gone.

Yes, and I find that you do that in your work, as I was saying in the first question. You bring us to a point where we can accept that these things happen to us.

I don't set out to write those things but I allow myself full freedom, not to censor, but to go ahead and write those poems that no one else is writing or speaking about. I did that in the poem "Each Bird Walking" in *Amplitude.* Nobody was talking about the relationship between the mother and the son and their forbidden, but natural bodily intimacies. That poem had never been written. Ordinarily I suppose one would have expected a man to write that poem but no one had, so I wrote it. Any number of men have thanked me for having written that poem. If we don't have examples of men in their tenderness how can they be moved out of the fixities their more aggressive stances encourage, the "warrior stance" we see being asked for.

Yes, and I wonder if the men's movement is going to help that or hurt that, that men will come closer to writing about tenderness or further away from it.

I just found the Sharon Doubiago piece in the current *Ms.* very interesting on challenging Robert Bly's call for the warrior in men, and the unfortunate fact that this coincided with the Iraq War. It must have been an ironic thing for someone like Robert Bly. Someone so active in speaking out against the Vietnam War. I don't think he intended for that message to coincide with that war, but it did do so.

I read recently an article in the "New York Times Book Review" about how the men's movement is denying a place for women once again.

Doubiago's also talking about that. I think everyone should read it to get the dialogue started. I immediately called one of my woman poet friends who is also a fine critic and asked her to read Doubiago's piece so we could talk later. I have male friends who have been to sessions with Robert Bly who have felt that the men's movement has been extremely important to them. I believe them.

Some of the things I guess I can agree upon but other things I can't, like this warrior aspect. A friend of mine thinks that it's women who have put men in the warrior position and men have had to deal with the burden of that.

I find it very hard to believe that women have put men in Iraq, except through their political ambivalence. I feel very sad about the sorry state of women's political engagement. I feel that they should be taking a much stronger hand in their state and local government. I spend a lot of time writing my congressmen and my senators—I know their names, I'm calling them. I would urge young women to get involved.

I do think that sometimes there is so much to respond to that we get into this white-out of "dear God, what shall I give my time to," and it's hard to make those decisions. There are so many causes at the moment, and you don't want to be eclipsed by everybody else's mandates. You have to figure out those things you genuinely want to affect, a couple of things, and give some time to them.

Think of poets in countries which have undergone revolutions. Those poets' energies are entirely turned toward political acts. We have great leisure in this country to write about our loves and our inner lives. That's not a possibility so easily in a country that's being torn apart and reorganized. So I feel my poems for Ray couldn't have been written very easily if I'd been living in Croatia, say Dubrovnik, or if I had been living in Bucharest, where my friend, the poet Liliana Ursu, lived under Ceauşescu, with bullets flying into her apartment from the secret police.

The title of your new book "Moon Crossing Bridge" alludes to the Japanese and the poems within are filled with images of Asian culture. The poem "Glow" describes a place we do not seem to have, but desperately need in this country. Why do you suppose our culture cannot give us the images we need to express our grief in love and death? and how did you come to discover the language that you use in these poems?

A very mysterious process, how I came to the way I'm speaking in these poems. I can tell you that the poems came more or less whole. That I didn't do the kinds of revisions I may have done if they had been less formed when I wrote them. I think your question about why our culture doesn't provide these images, why I had to go to Japan, is that our culture is still young in its interior investigations. Its physicality is very powerful. It's *doing* energy. It has a lot of reach to it, a lot of daring, but the inner reach of this culture isn't old. It hasn't found those kinds of interior images readily available. So I found myself borrowing from Japanese culture.

That poem "Picking Bones" is perhaps an example of how developed Japanese rituals are around death. I describe how they actually take chopsticks and pick the bones of their loved ones from the ashes. To an American sensibility, this may be terribly gruesome and it's nothing I'm suggesting we adopt; it's just there as a neighboring reality so we understand how our own compasses are set, and that they can be reset. It's not necessary to do what I did, I'm sure—for everyone to go to the gravesite every day as I did for two and a half years. (I go once a week now.) But it was necessary for me personally to do that.

As I've been going around giving these readings I've had an opportunity to talk to widows who've come up to me afterwards. Their relief has been very palpable in hearing what I've acknowledged in my own process. One thing they say to me again and again is that everyone else wants their grieving to be over quickly and for them to return to some idea of "normal," and a couple of times women have burst into tears telling me this because they're right—it's not humane treatment of their situation.

I think the culture has to learn more patience with everyone's timing, their process of incorporating loss. I also have some energies coming to the poems from my friendships with my Mexican friend Alfredo Arreguin, a painter in Seattle, his wife, Susan Lytle, also a painter, and other Latin friends, and from my readings from Pablo Neruda and Federico García Lorca. As the book comes to a close it moves toward more Spanish impulses and it may be that from the Spanish culture we have a kind of love-energy of bodily, earthy sexuality. The book and my own experiences seem to have discovered that as a way of reentering the life process. I think that a poem like "Corpse Cradle," for instance, is very sensual, erotic at the same time it is spiritual, and I think this poem may be an important instance of these elements coming together strongly in American poetry. If you read Rilke you realize you're very much in the realm of spirit. He finally does not turn out to be a very bodily poet, a bodily focused poet. So this may be one of the important things I'm offering in these poems, that spirituality has a physicality to it, and that the words are sensually alive in their approach to this subject of loss.

Taking the Kiss:

Interview with Merle Bachman

This interview was conducted after Tess Gallagher's Berkeley readings at Cody's and Black Oak Books in March 1992. Despite a plethora of other poetry events on the same evenings, Gallagher drew crowds eager to hear her read from her newest books, Moon Crossing Bridge *and* Portable Kisses. *Although the books are very different, they both have their source in love—the eleven-year relationship between Gallagher and noted fiction writer Raymond Carver.* Moon Crossing Bridge *chronicles a passage through her grief in the wake of Carver's untimely death on August 2, 1988.* Portable Kisses *collects poems published in a limited edition in 1978, though most of the book was written from May to September of 1991. Mostly in a lighter vein,* Portable Kisses *represents the poet's return to the world of sensual love.*

The poems in Moon Crossing Bridge *are among the most complex, rich, and challenging that Gallagher—or perhaps any contemporary poet—has written about the universal process of loss. Given the poems' preoccupations, they are not without controversy. Some critics have found the poems' absorption with the grieving process to be excessive.* Poetry Flash's *own Richard Silberg, in his brief review (March 1992), finds that* Moon Crossing Bridge *is almost too much. "Gallagher is almost too self-aware, mourning, unable to let go. Yet she understands herself, gets it down on the page as she stretches to the borders of sanity, between people, life and dust." In this interview, Tess Gallagher speaks as much about "crossing the bridge" of grief as about*

From *Poetry Flash* 231 (June 1992). Reprinted by permission of Merle Bachman. Copyright Tess Gallagher and Merle Bachman. Merle Bachman, a poet with publications in many small press journals, is a student and teacher of Yiddish language and culture. Her chapbook, "The Opposite of Vanishing," was published by Etherdome Press in 2000.

*her work itself—and, being someone who is obviously filled with life,
she laughs quite a bit as well.*

—Merle Bachman

*I was struck by what you said last night about being the fish, not the
ichthyologist, when it comes to your newest work. Does that mean you
are still discovering what these poems mean? Is there something about
going on tour and reading before different audiences that exposes
different facets of the poems to you?*

Yes, I certainly am learning. Even reading what the gentle-
man from *Poetry Flash* had to say—it gave me pause, and I had
to recognize that as a possible reaction to the poems, even
though it's one person's reaction. It may be a precept of these
poems that they exceed what would be "normal" for what
people *think* should happen during grieving. And when I ac-
knowledged (at the second reading) that that could be pos-
sible, some people came up to me afterwards—women who
had experienced what I am writing about—and said they
didn't think it was excessive at all, but that it was accurate.
That these poems, even in their severity, *especially* in their
severity, and in their demands, were not exceeding what was
necessary but were accurate.

*You also noted last night that you were just learning how these
poems "fit into the scheme of American life," considering that "this is
not a culture where people spend time in graveyards."*

I went every day for two and a half years to that graveyard
[where Raymond Carver is buried], and I could be sure of
solitude there. Really, the only people there were often walk-
ing their dogs, because the beach was down the hill. And on
certain holidays people would come; Memorial Day there
would be flags and a lot of attention out there, Easter . . . So, it
brings up questions. How is the culture handling its deaths?
Maybe those deaths are being absorbed in quite another way,
and so my noticing this is unfair in this regard. I don't know,
but I suspect the absence does reveal something.

In light of that, to bring out Moon Crossing Bridge *seems to me
to be an act of courage!*

It's a very un-American book (laughs).

*Do you feel it would be more of an Irish book or a Japanese book,
from your experience of those countries?*

When I went to Japan I did read many of these poems, and I really loved my audience's response. They were very ready for these poems. Not that the audience here isn't, but I did feel, as you saw in both readings, that it was necessary to prepare the audience. When I read in Tucson, I had a very hard venue there, because it was in the middle of the afternoon and people couldn't really settle down, and I had to read after a friend who had a very rollicking repertoire. Quite rightly, that's his style. But then to try and follow that was quite difficult. So I have to find a tone in which to make an arena for these poems to live.

Do you think it's felicitous that Portable Kisses *came out earlier than you'd expected, at the same time as* Moon Crossing Bridge, *so that you have a way to balance the readings?*

It's been very helpful. I would feel quite comfortable in Japan to do nothing but read [from *Moon Crossing Bridge*], but here I feel like I have to let some gaiety in before I come to the end of the reading. Also between poems—both for myself and, with these audiences, for their listening—there has to be a certain amount of human space between the poems, in order for the listeners to enter the next poem, because of the density and the demanding nature of the experiences. I can't do as some people do, just read poem—silence—poem—silence . . . Even though it may seen concessionary, to add some lightness, I think it helps the listener to take in—if you let up a little bit—then it helps to move the experience to a deeper level.

Like taking a breath before going back in.

And this is what I'm discovering in the readings . . . how the poems affect an audience, how they are heard. And I'm happy that they are getting received; I like the listening. And it improves as the reading goes on. . . . [But in this culture], we seem to be able to be more together with each other in our happy natures than in our more complicated, grieving selves.

In Japan is there a more communal aspect to peoples' grieving?

I think so. It's kind of ritualized, because they do go to their ancestral grave plots every year on August 12, and they don't go alone, they go together, so that every year they make touch with their ancestors. Also, there's more silence in that society, good and bad silence (laughs). They have a special word, I wish I could remember it, for gestures which speak; and because they have many of those kinds of gestures, language sometimes isn't necessary. It's not necessary to verbalize everything; you do certain things with gesture. Silence, I think, is a very helpful medium for poetry. An audience that has a very developed silence, a receiving silence—an active receiving silence—that's what I experienced in Japan. Sometimes the silences in American audiences are terribly nervous—and jittery. Because our attentions are so fractured here.

I wanted to ask you more about Japan, how it was that you went there, and how you feel the experience had an impact on your writing. Obviously some images found their way in, and how some of that silence may have found its way in as well.

Well, I went because I had a book of short stories, *The Lover of Horses,* published by Chuokoron-sha—it's a publisher which also publishes Raymond Carver. He's better known in Japan than he is in America, and they love his work there. Haruki Murakami, a distinguished novelist, is Ray's translator, and he's vowed to translate all of Raymond Carver's work, and he's well on the way to doing so.

Emiko Kuroda, my translator, and my editor, Mr. Norio Irie, put together a schedule for me and really stayed with me through the whole experience. I gave a reading at the American Center in Tokyo, and I gave many interviews to Japanese reviewers, and they treated me very respectfully. They really had read the book thoroughly, and it seemed to be quite a good translation. Emiko Kuroda, who did the translation, visited with me for two weeks at my home. She had also initially translated Raymond Carver's poems. So we worked together on her translation of my work. It was a lot of fun, and I learned a good deal from her during that period. Then she and I traveled together during a bit of the trip.

One of the most affecting parts of my time in Japan was a visit to Jyakucho Setouchi San. She is a nun who had earlier been in a relationship called a *furin,* something that's almost an institution in Japan—a rather sad one, in that women accept certain partialities in their lives. What happens is a [married] Japanese man will take a lover in the city or the suburb, or elsewhere and go between the two women. And that was Setouchi San's life—she was the other woman, the forbidden love. She laughed when she talked about it, saying that men

Tess and Jyakucho Setouchi, Buddhist nun and novelist, at the temple where she resides near Kyoto, Japan, 1990.

managed to have both. She had read my stories and had read Raymond Carver's work.

Setouchi San and I had a two-hour conversation about matters of the heart, love and loss. She had not been able to be with her lover when he died, because he had died at home with his wife, and she said it was terribly painful to have been absent then. She said to me that the hardest loss on earth was that loss of one's life companion—going on from that, finding a way to go on. I know she's right, from my own experience.

She didn't enter her life as a Zen nun until some years after her lover's death; she didn't do it in a reactive way; she wouldn't ever agree to that. Eventually she was given this temple, and after she began to speak there, women started to come every day to copy the sutras. These were women who had suffered in matters of love, and she tried to comfort them and to give them a way to address their grief. There are so many people who come to see her now that they have to have appointments to get into this little temple.

It was a very moving experience. I came away with a tape of her voice and the translator's voice moving between our voices; Setouchi San doesn't know English. She invited me to come back again. She's probably sixty; she writes novels, and she was just a great inspiration to me as a person; she has the most beautiful smile. My editor was there, and he said, "You don't get a smile like that easily." It reflected that she had managed to somehow transform her grieving, not into tranquility, even; it was something beyond that.

One minute she and I were perfectly calm; then we were laughing; then I was crying; then we were laughing; the visit just went through all these different inflections, as if we had an immediate way to talk to each other. It was only supposed to go for an hour, but she wouldn't let me leave; she kept me there another hour and showed me the temple. Afterwards, my editor and I, along with a women's magazine editor, went across the Togetsu Bridge. I hadn't a title for my book at the time, and when they told me that the bridge name meant Moon Crossing Bridge, I said, "Well, this is my title," because that's what these poems are doing; they are on this "soul terrain." I always think of the moon in that old way of being the repository of souls.

When you started writing these poems, did you have the sense the book was going to be a bridge for you?

No, I knew that it was carrying me, but the word *bridge* did not come until midway in the book. Once it came, I also didn't obligate myself to it very fully, I must say (laughs).

There's a lot of back and forth on that bridge!

Yes. And I wanted it to be, as the title poem suggests, something less tangible than we usually think of as a bridge. The word *bridge* is so very sure, it has that *d* and that *g* together. It seems to really ground you. But if you look at the poem by that title, "Moon Crossing Bridge," you understand it's a kind of walking on water, that the image of the light across the water is the bridge I'm talking about—the light I'm able to put into the experience.

There were some aspects of the poems that brought to mind a Zen experience for me. When you mention the "negative" of a thing, as in the "no street in no universe" ("Spacious Encounter"), and in "Blue Grapes," "no world, no meeting."

Good. Zen has been a part of the fabric of my thinking since the early 1960s.

More on how the book came to be: you touched on it briefly last night, how for six months you couldn't write, and how then the poems came in moments of necessity. What was that process like? How conscious were you of what was going on?

I was conscious in a poem like "Wake" and like "Red Poppy" that I was writing about subjects which were essentially taboo. That it would be beyond the range of what most people would be ready to hear, that you climbed into bed with your dead mate, or that you kissed your dead mate and received—received *for* him—you *took* that kiss. That's the important verb there. You had a certain right in the matter, that went beyond life; so it's an assertion, and with the dead we have all of these decorums that are meant to cut us off from them, from certain kinds of contact with them. And I think the poem was testing those boundaries. Just as in an earlier poem, "Each Bird Walking," I test the boundaries of what's allowed between son and mother, when I describe the young man in that reversal of roles, washing the place of his birth, the vagina.

The "birthlight" place.

Yes, the place of his birthlight. I hoped that this would allow a return of touch, that good and kindly touch between sons and their mothers. I grew up in a family of three boys, and I can see how much that needs to be restored in its good fashion in this culture, because I witnessed its refusal.

In terms of the consciousness of pushing the boundaries, of taking risks—

I didn't think, "I'm going to take these risks." I knew that those things happened, but that to write about them was a crossing of boundaries which hadn't perhaps been done before. So I just said, whatever the consequences are, these were important moments for me, and there were discoveries here . . .

The poem called "Ring" was based on something that actually happened, but then the poem takes these matters further. I explore what it meant to try to give away that precious emblem of love, the love ring, to send it out, and then to be aware that it was in a drawer, and to still have these connections with it. And

167

then to retrieve it, to try to figure out what to do with these love emblems.

And certain things you feel are solid—like earth—aren't solid anymore. You feel through the x-ray vision of a poem that you can look straight down and through the earth. In one of the poems, "Fathomless," it's as if the speaker's hairpins drop all the way down through the ground. The imagination makes everything permeable, and that is a good part of this grieving state—you live in a much more permeable environment. The boundary between life and death is quite different, dissolved almost.

What you were saying the other night at Cody's about objects taking on that power: "You go into a pagan state; it's as if the world's reanimated with a strange power . . ." And how "objects create silences." And you took out Raymond Carver's tie and hung it on the edge of the lectern. What are the barriers to poetry's ability to represent things that are just present in their silence? To me this book is your faith in language being able to represent and transform that experience, but I was wondering whether—

It's also a failure. The poems fail. That's what taking Ray's tie out was to signify. That the book was an attempt. As an artist in words you only partly succeed. There's so much that got away from me, so much that has to stay silent. But the intricacy of how I do move in the language, that complexity and perverseness even was a necessary representation of the unsayable. In the poems too, I keep trying to give that sign of partiality, of the unsayable.

One of the things I noted was the existence of a lot of hyphenated phrases—the "not-coming-backness" ("Cold Crescent"), the "more-than-real" ("Red Poppy"), "me-of-the-last-of-his-lastness" ("Crazy Menu"), "At the-Place-of-Sadness"—that signified a way to translate into words something that an individual word couldn't carry. Did you feel you were searching for a new language—if such a thing is possible?

Sure. Or that I was going to have to use the language I had in a new way. That's why I made these "word trains." It seems an honest way to indicate that the language is in a situation of formation. And I think it's another sign of trying to get into the language this sense of permeability I was talking about.

That language is a lot more cellular and hungry—the words themselves are voracious sometimes.

Did you write the poems over a very short period of time?

No, I was working on the poems right up till September, last September [1991].

Was there a lot of revision that went into it?

Some poems didn't see very much revision, but I did enlist two friends, very closely. One is a Swiss friend, Harold Schweizer, a literary critic who teaches and runs a Mellon Fund grant for facilitating dialogue between critics and poets at Bucknell University, in Lewisburg, Pennsylvania. He saw the poems in early versions and commented and encouraged me. And also a friend from my college days at University of Washington, Greg Simon, a poet and one of the best translators of Lorca, who lives in Portland; he saw copies of the poems. It was very hard for me to work without Ray, because he had always seen drafts; and it really took these *two* men to . . . (laughs).

In terms of what you just said about missing Ray in this context— in terms of this working relationship—in addition to everything else!—that you built up over the years—how do you see your work, your process changing, in the absence of that?

I think a very healthy thing has happened, in that both with Greg Simon and Harold Schweizer I have two readers who are able to accept and nourish my most complex self. I have a self which is not only lyrical and narrative, but intellectual and sensual. With Ray, a more matter-of-fact, clarified self had to be present, for his understanding and encouragement. So these poems likely couldn't have been written with him at my elbow. And that's a very ironic statement.

I think that Harold Schweizer kept this more mysterious side of my poetry alive during my relationship with Ray. I owe him a great deal for that.

From reading Moon Crossing Bridge *quickly, I did feel a conversation between two types of images. One is simpler, more elemental: birds, sleep, snow, shadows that recur, and flowers, the nature imagery that's so beautiful, and the "place-ness" of the Northwest. At the same time, these other images that are so extreme in their richness and exotica—the Mongol tribesman in "Black Pudding," Balinese tapers in "Crazy Menu," the "ancient sacrificial bodies dragged to death by chariots" in "Legend with Sea Breeze," and the recurrence of words like "sacred," "talisman," "sacramental," "ritual." I was wondering, do you invite these images in consciously?*

It comes from my reading. I have a notebook, and when I encounter those images, I write them down. When I read the notebooks again, sometimes those images will rush in to join the simpler elements, to give another dimension. Much like painters who are pattern-painters, such as my friend Alfredo Arreguin, will collect certain patterns which they then inlay behind the main subject matter and use to enrich, or to bring forward, or to background.

I just love the image and the language and the complexity—the added dimension of considering a "Mongol tribesman," and finding the metaphor to carry the particular kind of spiritual severity in the poem "Black Pudding." Making poems is always a matter of finding a vehicle to carry what it is you feel impalpably, that which you somehow have to make palpable. In *Portable Kisses* there's a poem called "Palette" and I describe the artistic process that belongs to Arreguin, how he works *into* his oils. He says, "My painting is my palette." And I feel that's true also for my poetry. I don't set out with an agenda. I will have absorbed this material about the Mongol tribesman, and I will then find the ways in which that image can carry these psychic and spiritual and emotional elements in this poem.

Considering the intensity of the subject matter, it's not surprising that so many of those images find their way into the book. There's a pagan quality that's almost archetypal.

Yes, I'm trying to get back to that, because that's such a part of this experience, that you are not able to behave in a quite civilized fashion, and to operate on purely reasonable dictates. You're not in the simply reasonable world anymore. You're out beyond, and you think that you know things that you shouldn't know, that you can't know. But you believe you *do* know them. And you have no process for certifying that knowledge. So these poems are ratifications, in a sense, of areas of feeling and emotion, and a kind of mapping of that territory, for others as well as myself.

Death is no stranger to your poems.

This book is well prepared for, in the sense that just six

years before Ray's death, I had my father's death to deal with, from the very same situation, lung cancer. There's a real sense in which I couldn't have written this book if I hadn't passed through that territory with Ray as deeply as I did; also, if I hadn't helped my mother nurse my father, I couldn't have been with Ray so well.

It is heartbreaking to read some of the poems. That one line [from "Infinite Room"], to "know with the wild exactness of a shattered window."

Yes . . . knowing what's irretrievable. That this person, this golden time is never going to come back; you will never see them again; you will never have that life again. You somehow have to reinvent a way to go on, and so the poems are helping me do that. Even if all they do is carry me to the end of this book, they help me. John McDermott is right; he has that essay—"Why Live?" I think is the title of it. We're trying to figure that out, every day. It's not a given that we should keep on living, just because we have these lungs and can breathe. We decide, some of us, *I'm living today. I'm going to go on living.* And why am I living, I'm asking. In the poem, "Two of Anything," that question occurs between the speaker and the "you" of the poem. That conversation actually did take place between Ray and me, where I really just felt like I didn't know how I was going to go on—and I even proposed that I not have to go on. Luckily, that condition didn't prevail.

Do you feel with this book that a chapter has been closed? When you look ahead to whatever next book is forming "out there," do you feel that it will also be for or about your husband? I'm sure not in the same way . . .

I really am not looking very far ahead at the moment. I think one of the things which happened because of being so close to him in his death is that it forced me into . . . the moment. The future is a quandary; I really don't know and I'm not very worried about what I will write. I think it will be there; whatever I will write about will be there.

I'm thinking more toward prose now; I'm thinking of the emotional urgencies under which this book was written, and even some of the poems in *Portable Kisses,* although that's an ostensibly lighter book, it really isn't . . . I think the books overlap quite a lot. Actually, the last section of *Moon Crossing Bridge* was kind of floating between the two books. I finally decided that it was okay to cross the bridge and to put those last poems in *Moon Crossing Bridge*. But then the writing just continued, and *Portable Kisses* was on its way. So, I think that *Portable Kisses*—I don't know how to characterize it—it's more sexually adventuresome, I think. One of the things I suppose I discover is that life force is very much connected to the sexual for me, at least at this time in my life. That coming back fully into the body meant those explorations again, those acknowledgments, those receptions . . . *Portable Kisses* and the last section of *Moon Crossing Bridge* are the evidence of that return.

The sense of not being too preoccupied with the future and living more in the present . . . I know one of the poems mentions the "lost future tense," and that struck me because in your essay, "The Poem as Time Machine" and in other places you've talked about the intersection of tenses, of poems being a magnet for these "times." I was wondering how will this affect your poems, if there's a certain "future tense" that's absent?

I'll probably keep trying to, in the sounds of the poems, acknowledge the grief of that . . . I think that since American life is so future-bound, everybody's living for the future. They're out there running their five miles a day—I'm not!— so they can live their five years longer when they're eighty. More power to them! But I would like to live very fully in the hours of this day, whether I make it to eighty or not (laughs). My sense of fate is a lot more fickle.

And that there is such a thing as "fate" is not an American concept.

Yes. I feel closer to that through my reading in Russian and Spanish poets and Irish myths, than perhaps many of my colleagues.

Speaking of Irish myths . . . the Irish presence is not as great in these poems as in some past, and I was wondering about that.

Well, in order for it to be present, you have to have been there, and most of my Irish friends seem to have been coming to me lately. Medbh McGuckian came and stayed with me last spring for four days; she's a very close friend, a wonderful Belfast poet, and I read and love her work. So I think some things from Medbh are in these poems, but you wouldn't recognize them unless you know the poetry of Medbh McGuckian. Especially poems in *Ballycastle Beach;* there are some wonderful things syntactically that Medbh does; I don't know whether she got them from me and I then took them back or what; we have a good reciprocal acknowledgment of the other writer's presence and consciousness that happens in our work. So it may be that there are more Irish references or influences inside the writing than you're aware. And there is the poem I wrote while I was on holiday at Medbh's house.

It has an Irish place-name in the title?

Yes. It's called "A Dusky Glow at Glenstaughey." Glenstaughey is where they have their summer cottage, Medbh and her husband. And I helped bring in turf while I was there; it was quite an experience. But it seemed to fit into this book because of the sense of this twilight which happens at the end of the poem: "Strange we are / in the blue air that stores its night. / Strange, like figures crowded off the edge / of memory." And that seemed very much to belong to what was happening in this book. So I put it in.

This book is more visibly influenced by Japanese awareness, Zen awareness, enlivened or challenged by Spanish and Russian. I love the severity of Akhmatova. That she would really reveal her stringencies and require that revelation of herself. Sandra Gilbert and I were talking about the unrelenting feeling we share that we had to be honest and accurate about these loss experiences we've had. And the severity is a part of that. And its healthfulness and its bleakness, the void of it. Not rescuing one's self too quickly. American consciousness wants to rescue itself before the pain-echo has even begun to fade. So my book's full of revealed, transformed, but unrescued pain.

I have just a few more questions, if that's okay. What are some of the projects relating to Ray's writing that you're going to be involved in during the coming months or years?

I just finished the PBS film,* and that's been released. I finished writing the introduction to *No Heroics, Please,* to be published by Vintage this summer; it's already come out in

---

To Write and Keep Kind, PBS documentary on Raymond Carver, 1993, produced by Jean Walkinshaw.

hardback in Great Britain. There is a volume of versions of Ray's stories, variants of stories, that will be edited*—we've already begun the process—William Stull has done the work of collecting those. And I'll do nothing but write an introduction. It's time to see what we can learn from those versions; I think it will be very valuable to people teaching and studying Ray's writing process, and regarding writing in the way which Ray did, not simply writing but as rewriting. He discovered his stories in the rewriting. And so you'll be a part of that discovery as you read this book.

We are feeling some need to pace these projects so that there isn't too much coming out all at once. We'll need to make a collected poems at some point. There are some stories in the drawer in various states of preparedness, and I could conceivably take a look there and see what could be published—not a lot of work, but some.† And then there are Ray's notebooks. He began to really keep notebooks during our time together, our eleven years, and he was keeping them before his brain tumor was known—that would have been March 1988—during the early part of his struggle with lung cancer. And then, when the brain tumor hit, things dropped off a bit. But those journals have these little snippets, and sayings, and self-revelations; they might be interesting to publish at some point—that's way down the road I think. Hope I can still read his handwriting by then (laughs). There are letters that could be published; I'm very shy of doing any more biographical work, because there's been such a bad trend in regard to writers of making the life too firm a text and pretext for the work. And this is especially dangerous for Ray, whose work *seems* to move in such a realistic way. It would be easy to think him less an artist than he was. And also, the human elements of the biography would take me back into difficult emotional territory. So, I think that can be delayed endlessly. I would prefer to be dead when all that takes place (laughs), because it's going to be fictional, anyway. So it may as well be

---

*This book has not yet been published.

†Since published in Great Britain by Harvill Press as *Call If You Need Me* (2000). Includes five previously unpublished stories as well as other prose.

good and fictional. I think people should go back to Ray's work, read his work, instead of biography.

It seems very American to want to know about the person.

Yes, people would rather read biography than read the work.

I'm interested in form, in the lyric poem itself as a form. And since [in "Poem as Time Machine"] you talk about how poems "dissolve the boundaries" of past, present, and future, since they coexist in the poem, I was wondering if you had ever been tempted to dissolve the boundaries of the lyric poem. Or whether you feel that you have.

Well, I wrote an essay which introduces the term, *lyric narrative,* and that as a kind of new animal. "New" as of about fifteen years ago, since I wrote those essays in *A Concert of Tenses* twelve or fourteen years ago. And in a poem like "Incomprehensibly" that's what I'm doing. B. B. King is a blues singer I admire a lot, and he used to say, "I don't *have* to play all those notes—I'm interested in the *sound.*" And there is the sense in which my poems do play a lot of notes, some of them, like "Incomprehensibly"—but still manage to have a *sound.* There is a *sound* to them. And it's not unrelated to blues. Because of the grieving—the resilient capacity of grief. Now that's a contradiction in terms (laughs), but I think it's true. If you're able to hear the grief, it's already a sign of having absorbed it, and being able to carry it. That gives strength, confidence of a sort.

There is that sense of carrying Ray with you, of that being the task now.

Yes, privilege more than task, and in poem like "Black Violets" [from *Portable Kisses*] then, of binding that presence, and feeling that that presence accepts the ways in which my life has to move on.

To Go Naked on Horseback:
Interview with Gabrielle Idlet

A couple of years ago when I was just out of college I read Moon Crossing Bridge, *Tess Gallagher's volume of poems addressing the death of her husband, writer Raymond Carver. I was struggling through a suicidal depression, and her book worked for me like a compass, offering orientation in darkness. Refusing to draw facile conclusions or skip over the nuances of pain, Tess honored the mystery inherent in her experience. She was willing to explore the unknown territory there without leaping to safety. And her bravery helped me to navigate the baffling terrain of my own suffering.*

Working at my own fiction and poetry, I became increasingly interested in Tess' thoughts about her process and material. I asked her for an interview, partly to learn more about her work, but also to let go my awe of her in favor of a deeper, more complex understanding of her as a writer and as a person.

What follows is the text of that interview, which took place in March of 1995 at her home on Washington's Olympic Peninsula. The material was augmented and revised through the mail over the following several months.

—Gabrielle Idlet

From the standpoint of your writing, what was lost and what was gained in the aftermath of Raymond Carver's death?

After Ray died, there was a lot of silence inside me. As if somehow, by obedience to this silence, I had to admit that there was a huge quotient of the unapproachable and the unavailable, for a while.

From *Indiana Review* 19:1 (March 1996). Reprinted by permission of Gabrielle Idlet. Copyright © Tess Gallagher and Gabrielle Idlet. Gabrielle Idlet, an essayist and fiction writer, was most recently Writer in Residence at the Sundance Institute.

So I was just very patient, and accepted that. I waited. I'd watch late-night movies until two A.M. and fall asleep on the couch. I didn't really decide to, but it happened that I let myself be extremely empty. I didn't write for six months.

Gradually I began to have a sense of an approachable body of material, of images and a general fruitfulness that was going to come. I knew that in order to be able to receive it I had to prepare a time in which I didn't have a lot of public engagement. So that's when I gave up my teaching at Syracuse—I knew that I couldn't be giving in that deep way you do when you're a teacher. Maybe the necessity of solitude was an extension of the earlier silence. I knew I must try to find a language for feelings I'd really never had before.

So it turns out that my silence was very fertile because those poems, when they came, seemed full of a kind of vibratory resonance. Harold Schweizer, a poet and critic at Bucknell (who reads my poems and who saw them in draft as they were being written) said to me after the book was out for some time, "Tess, I don't even think you know how amazing the poems are in there." At first I just thought, "What is he talking about?" But when I go back to them now, I do sense that they're beyond my ability even to write them somehow, strange as that may sound.

And I understood for the first time what Rilke's feeling must have been when he "received" the *Duino Elegies*. For me the arrival of my poems represents a similarly miraculous emergence of presence. I look at the book now, and I find those poems so completely strange, so completely unexpected. Because I feel very humbled by the sense that I was at all able to write that book, to exceed my personal ground as a writer, going beyond what I thought I could do.

There was a crossing back and forth across the threshold— an interpenetration of spaces, an enlargement of space— because of the death of a loved one, which caused a communicated reach. You're wishing you had solitude, both nicely aggravated by the presence and fervently engaged by the absurd fertility. That's what I felt, a great fertility of space. It would be almost more than you could bear, really, some days. A potency that so exceeded yourself.

Soon after the death?

Yes. You would have moments that could just come like a javelin, right toward you, when you least expected it.

But what was lost, you ask, after Ray died. Well, so many things in the sharing aspect of my art and life. That delight of running to another room with a draft and saying, "Listen to this!"—which is so immediately rewarding—that was lost. And he had such delight. You could just surf on it for days. He would appreciate and laugh and take enjoyment in something you'd done, and likewise me with him. So that wasn't there anymore. It was an extremely quiet house with only my movements and my needs, my thoughts. But as I say, consciousness of him would intersect very importantly with me as I went through those days. So that's what those poems try to record, the time when the moth flew against me in my bath, and it became an extension of the world's caress, but also made me shudder as an omen does.

When you say he would intersect—

His spiritual dimension. Or my investment of his spiritual dimension into the moth.

You're not sure which?

No, I don't really need to assign. I don't know whether I invest or whether it's there. But it amounts to the same thing, really, because you're moved and you're engaged, extended into the world by it. The mystery is fluttering all around you. It's tender and horrible all at once, the way it caresses you with wings that could be lips.

Tell me about the interplay between your process of writing poems and your recovery from the grief.

Your word "recovery" is interesting to me. Because I didn't so much recover as just travel along *inside* the grief as if it were a sort of cocoon. I really was not very interested in getting out of it, I must say. I was interested in the exploration, in going where it went. Like I say at the end of the poem "My Black Horse": "I just want to ride my black horse, / to see where he goes."

Horses run all through your work.

Yes, yes. I love discovering a spirit-emblem. And just letting it come into the poem or not, and again, not trying to delineate it, to overassign it. Because if you do that, it won't visit.

Your horses won't visit you. They only have essence and meaning in your poems if they have permission but no duties.

Would you say that you're still riding that "black horse"?

Well, I don't know if they will continue to occur in my work—horses. But "my black horse"—well we have a lot of associations with black horses historically and culturally, and so it has an aura around it. It's initially funereal. But I also see Joan of Arc who had such credence, was so able to urgently embody a set of symbols that she appears at Vaucouleurs in a red dress and rides away in armor. Then there was that beautiful black horse she was given by Charles I, the duke of Lorraine. I actually had a black horse, as a child, named Angel Foot.

But in my poems it's a metaphorical horse, and that's what carries—the metaphor. That's always the question—What is carrying you? The poems are *my* black horse. They are carrying me, and I don't know where. I do have to "see where they go."

In that period, writing the poems after Ray's death, it was important to trust the horse to take you. To be able for passing the pigsty where the horse is going to be terribly frightened and veering, eyes wide and glaring. Maybe to ford a river. I remember riding horseback in Missouri on my grandfather's farm as very exhilarating. This was during my adolescence and also young womanhood. There's a beautiful kind of exuberance and power on loan to you when you ride a horse with which you have a relationship. You know that horse. You have certain things you agree about, also certain habits the horse has that you accommodate. It's amazing how rich going out into the countryside will be. You're inside the horse's mind and it changes the way you breathe. Even the ground itself takes on its rightful dimension of hazard and delight.

Are you still riding that "funereal" black horse—in the sense of writing out your emotional experience of Ray's death?

Well, not as pointedly these days. No, I had my arena, and then I moved on. There are joyously unrestrained love poems, you know, toward the end of *Moon Crossing*. When anybody reviews the book, they seem almost embarrassed about the fact that it goes off the top of the desire scale. They don't know what to do with these love poems in the last section so they just don't mention or acknowledge them.

They wonder, "What's a widow doing writing like this?"

Exactly. I imagine it seems a sacrilege. If you're a widow, you're not supposed to be erotically ecstatic too soon. You're certainly not supposed to bring great conjugal loss and the joyously erotic into proximity, or to cause them to overlap as I have.

You're supposed to wear black.

That's the easy part. But it's taboo as a widow to reveal oneself as sensual or full of desire. Again, Harold gives me these words—he says, "You're transgressional." This is what the critic does for you! (laughs). I do know that I couldn't have gone as emotionally high in those final poems or gained their spiritual and psychic dimensions except for the great delving down of the earlier poems.

You said earlier that after Ray died you waited to find a language for the experience. I'd like to hear about the language in "Moon Crossing Bridge." The work that you were doing up through "Amplitude," just before Ray's death, seemed to be increasing in accessibility. But Moon Crossing Bridge *is remarkably complex. What happened?*

I think with Ray I got more and more narrative and linear, while trying to marry that to lyrical bursts inside the narrative. From writing short stories, I used quite a lot more character and scene in the poems. After Ray died, I went back to being the intricate, semioblique poet I'd been maybe all the way back into my years with Michael Burkard, my second husband, who is a wonderfully complex and rich poet.

The poems I wrote in *Moon Crossing Bridge,* I wonder—I think Ray would love them. But he would find them difficult. I don't—and I've said this—I don't think I would have been able to write them very easily with him as my first reader. I would already have felt his mind accompanying me and not knowing what I meant and feeling left out. But it was terribly important for me to be able to write and *not* know what I meant, to be perplexing even to myself in certain ways.

In preparing for this interview, I came across Mark Jarman's review of Moon Crossing Bridge *in the "Hudson Review." He criticizes your complexity: "The obscure and ornamental predominate in the book. There is so much of them that . . . I ask myself why she does not stop more often." How would you respond to his argument?*

I'll just ask Mr. Jarman, why "obscure" and "ornamental" are buddies in his formulation, linked up by this "and." Why *that* pair of elements? That my poems should be accused of being "obscure and ornamental"? If something is called ornamental, is the criticism lodged in some idea that it's inessential? For me, ornament is sometimes extremely telling and primary. It has a certain tilt, the ornament. In Irish writing, the ornament will often be vested in the adjective. In my own work, the verb can mystify or throw you, or whole rifts of phrasing can elude linear comprehension. That's my impression. I would have to look at my book like a critic again, to articulate this. But any sentence element can become ornamental and quirky in my poems. An ornament in musical notation is that little flurry of activity which happens around a clear melody note. And you will just veer off it onto the next note. It will sometimes be a chromatic movement. You may double over and past the melody note, then prolong it again. But this key note, your melody note, will have been changed, shadowed or haloed by your having visited this bouquet of other, neighboring notes.

So the ornament is not *just* the ornament. The ornament is active *in relation to what it veers off of and what it returns to.* It ghosts importantly.

Given that your sensations after Ray's death went beyond anything you'd known, it might have been impossible to express them simply through melody, without those "flurries" of ornamental activity that took you into mystery.

Well, it would be, was impossible. And it wouldn't be of any interest to me. It would just be flat journalistic narrative. It would not have tension. What the ornament does is to give the narrative its leap—or I should say, its escape from narrative—many of those poems are escape from narrative—and that's also what lyric elements allow, a leaping past simple linear narrative.

I think the poems invite the reader to be situated in some moments, but swept away in others. Tony Hoagland, in a review of ecstatic poetry, talks about my swept-away moments, where I just let the poem completely take over and suddenly we're quite offshore, and we might have to swim for it to get back. But if I only had density and offered you nothing—no place to stand or to rest, then I could see this lack of consideration for readership as a valid sort of huge complaint. Thank you, Mr. Jarman. But I have to write this way, anyway. Because it wouldn't interest me otherwise, at this point. Besides, the things I've been writing out of wouldn't allow strict narrative.

The experience dictated the shift.

And a return to my most complex self, which had been unnecessary during my time with Ray. In living with Ray, things that had been very unclear and difficult—things you would have brooded about and worried into some misery for yourself—just didn't accumulate that kind of energy at all. And living in that more clarified space also had to affect the work. I think this also affected the tonalities of his work as well.

So during your time with Ray, your work came out of a simpler emotional framework?

Yes, because in our life together I was on that clear current with him all the time. When he was gone I moved back into this more complex psyche in the arena of my poetry, while I've tried to keep the clarity in my daily life.

Let's see now. We didn't deal with "obscure." We dealt with "ornamental." What does it mean to be obscure? We should look up that word. (Opens dictionary.) "Lacking or inadequately supplied with light" is one of the definitions of obscure. And also "sheltering, covering." Ah—that's what I'm doing when I obscure something: I'm sheltering and darkening the entrance, in order to give it another kind of significance.

Earlier we were looking at Hopper's artwork, and I was remarking on the viaducts in his paintings. We were admiring the one with the three equestrians who were going to ride under the viaduct into this darkness. There's a kind of ominousness, but also a wonderful power. The sense of the riders way up on those horses, and that their heads might scrape the top of this viaduct—there's danger in that. And yet the painted viaduct is a mental enclosure.

So for me, to obscure is to enclose. Yes, I turn off the lights. Even here at Sky House I actually switch off the lights so that I can see the way the night is shining, the lights of the ships passing through the Strait. In *Moon Crossing* I wanted to see how the night is shining, as much as how the moon is shining.

Reminds me of "Yes":

> Now we are like that flat cone of sand
> in the garden of the Silver Pavilion in Kyoto
> Designed to appear only in moonlight.
>
> Do you want me to mourn?
> Do you want me to wear black?
>
> Or like moonlight on whitest sand
> to use your dark to gleam, to shimmer.
> I gleam. I mourn.

Yes, in order to use your dark. You do both. You use your light and your dark. So that's what I'm doing when I'm obscuring. I'm using the "dark" of the reader. And if he or she won't volunteer their dark, well, I'm sorry! (laughter).

Speaking of subjects with obscure meanings, I want to ask you now about how you speak of the soul in your poetry. You've said that you belong to no religion but the "church of the poem." So where does the notion of the soul come from in your work? What exactly are you describing? And is there an outside religion or a reference point to which we can connect your concept of soul?

Poetry is a great reviser and evader of definitions. I've kind of amalgamated what it is I address when I say the word *soul*. It moves around a lot on us in contemporary life, what we can mean, you see. So that's why I say in every poem I'm revisiting the word, trying to see, like the moon—what's it going to shine on? What luminosity can I squeeze out of the idea of soul? Is it still able to ignite or to activate thought? Creditably?

In Moon Crossing Bridge, *you use as an epigraph a terrifically evocative quote from Jeff Keller: "If we believe in the soul, then perhaps we have more in common with the dead than the living."*

Yes, right. Because the dead have gone entirely into their presence as souls—if we accept that sense of the dead as disappearing into soul. Jeff Keller studied with me when I was at Kirkland College in 1975. He's living in upstate New York now. He's extremely wise in what he offered as a casual remark to me in that letter.

You've been talking about resisting the pressure to define. But in

Moon Crossing Bridge *it appears that you are struggling to define indefinable qualities and essences. Would you elaborate a bit on this question of definition?*

Well, I think definition can be a kind of anathema to poetry. Because if you just had in mind to fix things, to equate this with that, then you easily become reductive. And you're immediately dissatisfied with the outcome. What you want, in talking about the soul or any other amorphous concept like that, is to throw doors open, not to shut them. And simple definition tends to limit, to constrict. You want rather to make a constellation of relational elements, so that the idea gets rich and finds fresh expression. Poetry is not a butterfly-pinning party. I admire the painter Morris Graves, the way he stops right on the edge of abstraction and exactitude. I take instruction from his restraint. One doesn't always approach tenderness by joining the other, for instance. The space between is often the tenderness.

Just so, in language—you don't always get the payload of the energy language releases simply by being frontal and "clear" or informational or narrative. In fact, poetry exists in order to remind us and to prove to us that language, as the fabric of our communing with each other, is enormously vibrant. That light shouts from what is showing of the language's iceberg. "Fleeting plenitude"—that's what Graves says his art is all about. Mine too!

I love your poetry for exactly that reason. You refuse to reduce to solidity what is intangible in life, and death. You embrace the mystery, with all its risks.

Well some people like to stay down on the flatlands. I'm alpine.

You are! I read a travel piece you wrote for Vogue *about hiking on the glaciers in Canada.*

I was up in Banff, hiking in the Bugaboo Mountains. That's a great thing, you know, if you live in the Northwest, when *Vogue* calls you they want to give you assignments to be on the top of glaciers.

Flown in by helicopter.

Yes, and we had a wonderful lodge there in the Bugaboos. And you'd hear these gruesome stories, of course, about rock climbers who'd just fallen the day before off sheer granite walls you were looking at as scenery. The people you meet on mountains, you don't forget. There's a very close association. And there are moments which occur there that remain poignant even—especially—when you come down from the mountain. And I think poetry is like that.

I can remember a young Austrian hiker who was with us, who found, in the middle of summer, a patch of snow. He ran pell-mell out into the middle of it, and leaped onto his hands, and did a handstand in the middle of this patch of frigid snow in July. I will never forget this. He just stood there upside down. Then he began to walk in the snow on his hands! Suddenly we were all just laughing and rippling, just magnificently somewhere else, being-wise, because of this audacity of his. His beautiful delight and silliness.

So my lunges at obscurity are also a kind of audacity maybe, a kind of walking on my hands in a recalcitrant patch of alpine snow. We're not supposed to walk on our hands. We're supposed to walk on our feet. But how boring, you know. Once in a while, can't we do a handstand? And can't we discover some snow that's going to chill us all the way from our fingertips down to our rectum.

Or up, as the case may be.

It would be up, yes! in a handstand.

You said something once, talking about starting to write fiction again after Ray died. If I remember correctly, you said, "I decided to do it because I realized that I had stopped writing stories after his death." What struck me in that statement was not so much just the fact of your returning to fiction, but rather the unusual tenacity and resilience reflected in how you framed your writing process. That because you recognized that you had given it up, therefore you must resume it.

Yes, I'm like a horse that's out there setting up the jumps for itself, you know (laughs).

Spliced species, there.

Yes. There's the hurdle, and I'm going to get my haunches over it. Take that, Degas!

In your introduction to Carver Country *you wrote of telling Ray to straighten up his business affairs and quit acting like a loser—how did you phrase it?*

"You better change your luck," I said.

That was it. And you've also talked about Altman and Ray having that in common, the question of luck, and the gamble.

Yes. You're on the edge of fortune, and you don't know which way it's going to fall—bad or good.

Does this outlook have class roots?

Very much so. I mean, when you're working class, a lot more depends on luck—at least in my mind.

You have a poem about that at the end of "Amplitude," where you're driving around town in the Mercedes thinking—

Yes, "How did we manage this? It's astonishing." I was thinking that when I was down in Hollywood, too. "How did I manage this?" It's just beyond you. So many writers in America and actors and directors and actresses would have given the small digits on both their hands to be there. Somehow, luck and fate and song had played out in my favor. I had been able—this is what was amazing to me. I had been welcome. A contributor to the effort.

Do you apply the notion of luck to loss at all, as in bad luck?

Certainly I've had my share of misfortunes. But you know, misfortunes join you back to everybody. So they're not ultimately bad luck because they don't allow you to stay isolated in the exclusivity of that individual experience. Rather, your misfortune overlaps with everybody else's losses.

Yes. I believe in your essay "The Poem as a Reservoir for Grief" you were talking about the leap of faith the poet has to take in writing about loss because each loss is "singular and an only." One interesting thing about Moon Crossing Bridge *is that you were addressing a loss that many people felt—of Raymond Carver.*

But it was also very singular because nobody held our particular closeness. I was joining everybody to something of my singular experience of Ray, yet also beyond us, too. And they were experiencing me again, in quite a different self, a state of self discovery.

Regarding your resilience, you used the image earlier of the horse setting up its own hurdles. I was thinking about something you reported in an essay—that as a child you used to neigh at horses and they would neigh back to you. Tony Hoagland said that your work requires an "intuitive response" from readers. It occurs to me that like a horse, you're doing a neighing which forces the reader to neigh back—to respond to the work in a nonlinear, nonintellectual way.

Yes! It would be good preparation for anybody wanting to read me to go outside and find a nice field and just try to neigh. And see—especially if you're out in the farm yards, in the farm area—whether you might be answered. But just to hear the voice going out in quite another resonance. That's what I want to do in the poems. To send the voice out through the feelings and sounds as they're released into wide space.

If you, as a human being, try to neigh it can come out very ugly and strange because you don't know how to do it, you know.

But children do.

I think so. I was answered by horses. I bet I could do it today and find some willing, reciprocal horse. But it's a very raw sound in your body, when you make it, a neigh. It takes me all the way back to childhood when I do it. It was one of my childhood languages—neighing.

Why don't we talk about the mythic figure you portray in the Annie Liebovitz photograph up at Ridge House. [In the photo, Gallagher holds a mask over her face while sitting atop a horse in a shimmering ankle-length gown.] Before the interview you told me that the Kiss as a character may have begun to "appear" in that photograph in 1980. You were portraying the goddess . . .

Epona. The Celtic goddess who used to go about on the back of a horse through the villages. She's a relative of Lady Godiva.

Through the mythic lineage?

Through the fact that they both went about on horseback. Of course Godiva was supposed to be humiliated, by being forced to ride through the town naked with just her hair to cover her. But in fact she was so valiant that she was raised above the assignment of her assumed humiliation and became mythic. Her actions involved courage and the breaking of a public taboo—that is, one does not appear naked in public. And to go naked on horseback was extremely sexual and powerful.

Which is a good metaphor for what you've been doing lately, toward the end of Moon Crossing Bridge, *and in* Portable Kisses. *Jeanne Heuving gives a feminist critique of the taboos you're breaking, your "transgressions" as she calls them, in both of those books* (Northwest Review *32 (1) 1994). She acknowledges what's required for you to address the loss of a man who happens to have a tremendous literary legacy, and then again what's required as you assert a sexuality despite your widowhood.*

Yes, an important transgression, because you know they try to steal the vitality from you in widowhood—the community. They don't mean it harshly, but it's just so embedded in widowhood—to still have your sexual and sensual vitality intact is very threatening to the community because you're unmated. So you can impact upon those in couple situations. And I think that's where the sense of taboo comes from, that sense of transgressional sexuality attached to the widow. There are lots of jokes, after all, about sexy widows in every culture.

And what sets widows apart from virginal women?

They're experienced.

They've had a taste.

They know what they're about. Something *will* be satisfied. And a powerful interlude is likely to take place for any lover a widow has.

Who are the "they" that view widows as a threat?

Well, I suppose "they" would be whatever community in which you find yourself. I was rather a gypsy poet before I came home, and in that circumstance you have mobility, which also makes you a threat. And of course widowhood is a complex state of invitation and denial. The "they" may be imagined. It may, as I'm using it, refer to the exclusion that widows inevitably begin to meet in whatever social or communal arrangement they attempt to enter. It can be anguishing.

I remember after Ray died, being in Syracuse, and—there was no malice involved really, it just happens with all the naturalness of whales rising, then sinking into the oceans—suddenly you notice you don't find yourself in company with the couples you had been with, as a couple yourself, with your mate. My company became instead all these marooned individuals living singly. We were a loose-change bunch, but vigorous and actually more exciting in a lot of ways in our unsettledness and our curiosities than some of the couples I knew before Ray's death. I met the Kashmiri poet Aga Shahid Ali at that time and he's one of the most exuberant people in my life. But we've also companioned each other through the death of his mother. I recall feeling so happy for his flair and kindness during that time and since.

How does widowhood contrast with divorce, which you experienced too?

Well, the wounds were very different. I mean I felt like everything with Ray was at such a state of completion that it wasn't as if flesh had been torn from flesh. Because there had been a letting go on one level. But the reaching after his death was actively going on, and I was trying to find an approach which was still possible, given life and death.

In a divorce, at a certain point you're not reaching in the same way at all. In widowhood you're trying to amalgamate that life you had together, make meaning of it, absorb the pain, and get some alchemy going that will allow you a fruitful "next."

Did people respond differently to you though, as a divorcée?

Gee, I never really made those comparisons, so it's kind of new ground. What I remember about being divorced, I mean it could be quite similar. In the social end of things.

However, the suffering has a different appraisal. The currency of widowhood is different. You get a little credit in the bank (laughs). Whereas what's accorded to the divorcée—at least in 1976 when I last experienced it!—was pretty much in the debit lane. But some men will love you for your debts. The fact that you have been humiliated by life to that degree. Again it joins you back.

We've all gone through various humiliations.

Yes. I mean, one great reach toward others for Ray was, as he said, that he'd been below the floorboards and he couldn't go any lower.

Which is why droves of people felt so much for his stories.

Including the fact that they were extraordinary. Yes. Because he could acknowledge his having been really lost. That it could happen to anyone.

Why don't you talk some about the fiction you're working on now.

It began as a kind of challenge to myself—realizing Ray had given me confidence, and a lot of his time, his faith in my fiction writing, and how very much I had come to love the short-story form. Loved it in his hands. And I had missed it, just as I missed him. I missed having stories being written in the house, and hearing them, looking at them with him.

Sitting on the couch in the library, going over them with him. I really longed for that. Even if I couldn't have that part of it with him, I thought, Why am I denying myself stories? I should write some stories again. So I began to write them.

I conceived the idea of the book—which actually helped me get going—before I had even written the first story. I sometimes read books on subject-oriented matters. And there was this book on anger. It quoted a proverb which really struck me. It said, "If you contemplate revenge, dig two graves." I really thought that was a powerful statement. I also thought, I wonder if people take revenge and think they get away with it. They dig the grave but they don't get into it, you know. They walk off from it. Is there a delicious, even fruitful revenge which really happens? The proverb would tend to put you in the corral and say: no, no, if you take revenge, you're going to be punished too. So you wonder, are there escapes, and if so, what are they? You wonder what the terms of revenge are, if in fact they're reciprocal. And you begin to look for instances.

What I found was that the book began to generate itself. I would just quote the proverb in company, and all of a sudden people would be telling me stories. It was amazing. And of course, those tellings would become the initial kernels generating the story. I would take those stories and think about them, and at some point they would become fertile. Then I would begin to write. I would use some elements and throw away others.

Is it a political book?

It's not moralistic. It's not judgmental. Except in the sense that you do see in some instances the person is brought to ruin, something we'd all like to avoid! And other times people do these things to each other, and they gain a certain resilience even from their bad acts (laughs). So I don't know if it will be political. I'm not sure what the reaction will be. You can't really think about that—what the reactions will be. You have to be faithful to each story as you write it. I'm still drafting. The whole book could change emphasis.

I was telling you earlier about a young woman who wanted me to write role-model birth mothers in my stories because she didn't like the fact that when I read a story, "The Mother

Thief," about a birth mother, here in my hometown, there was laughter at some of the behavior of the birth mother. I didn't write the story to deride or ridicule the birth mother. The actions were in themselves just hilarious. They were over the top. And I think laughter is wonderfully intelligent, in those instances. This woman's profession was to help adopted children and birth mothers connect and she was terribly single-minded in this—believing she had a right to subdue my story to her needs. My story contradicted her notions so she wanted me to rewrite the story to suit her sense of propriety toward birth mothers. I think that when you're so invested in—what would you call it?—your advocacy, that it becomes a disservice to one's intelligence and one's humors—then we're vested in the rabid, ruinous thinking that now has this country by the throat and is shaking the life, the graciousness out of it.

Your unwillingness to circumscribe the story goes back to your resistance toward limiting the potential in a poem by striving for simple definitions.

Indeed. There is a portion of the American population for which a kind of madness of rectitude blots out the humanity of others. It's deadly and invested in an advocacy that condones actual violence to others. It is also a violence to my imaginative life to assign me to write propaganda. I don't want to live in China during the Cultural Revolution. It's a terrible comment on the ramifications of free speech in America that we have doctors being shot here. These people behind the bullets are so entirely without the balance of their humors and their tolerance for other ways of living, that they believe they can assign everyone else's fate and values. This is what will kill the spirit and kill freedom in America. And I don't mean to use freedom in any casual sense. I mean responsible freedom, of which even people with differences are capable.

So, this kind of mad dog slavering frightens me greatly, where the reader or the listener writes to you and says, "We don't want to hear anything unfavorable or funny about those birth mothers." In a short story, anyway, it's not a documentary, it's not a tract, it's not a road map for how you live your life. It's an instance. As a writer you may not be drawing that character as fully as you might in another story, but you try to make it true to the circumstances of *that* instance.

Does the book of stories you're writing represent a movement from introspection to looking outward?

Yes, very much. This is what I love about short fiction, you have to have other people. You cannot just say, "myself, myself, myself," as you do in the lyric. Or as my teacher Theodore Roethke used to say in his letters, "*sweet* myself" (laughter). So I really find it quite more communal to write stories.

I think as a widow you need to make those forays very ardently back toward the community. Frankly, in American life, for widows, there is not much reaching in *your* direction, so you'd better be actively investigating how to get with everybody. I love that about my friends who are widows in this town. (I don't meet very many my own age.) Lu Mealey, a widow, lives down the hill. I have a cup of coffee with her and we have a good chat from time to time.

But I so admire them, and I learn so much from them, about how to be fruitfully engaged while alone. I don't think I give off the aura of loneliness, when anybody's around me, even though I spend a huge amount of time alone in my days when I can possibly manage it.

Are you lonely?

Not in the aggrieved sense. I've come through that. You'll find yourself there, now and again, of course. I think I've told you about New Year's Eve, where I usually would be with a specific group of friends. This year, I just didn't go. I stayed home. And they were all very put out with me. But I said, "You know, ever since Ray died, I've never spent a New Year's alone because I was just terrified to be completely alone on New Year's. I have to do it now." That was our favorite holiday together because it was also the day that we had joined our lives. January 1, 1979, that's our anniversary. That's when I moved to El Paso, in 1979. So it's probably—it's the most difficult holiday for me.

Now I really enjoy Valentine's Day. And people may think this is funny, you know. Even without having Ray, I still feel a great abundance of amorous and sensual and friendly and communal love. So, I like to celebrate this day, and this year I had my friends around. I put up crepe paper streamers and tinfoil hearts, just like a little kid, you know. I went to the supermarket and got those little candy hearts that say "Be Mine" and "Yours Forever" on them.

Reading your fiction collection The Lover of Horses *recently, I saw that in the title story the children hold all the energy.*

Don't they! They're just wild, and ricocheting around out there in the night, and oh, I loved writing about that because it really brought back my own childhood. I was right there again with those children. You know, there's a way in which you run, when you're a child, full speed, and in the dark, it's so great! And you so seldom do that again when you grow up.

You don't have kids.

No.

But the child figures often in your poems and your stories.

I have myself as a child. And I have my brothers as remembered playmates. My sister came later. I remember them very well as children. And I have my friends' children now. And of course, I have nieces and nephews that I've been an important figure for as they've grown up. So I think I gauged things pretty well—that I've made a better aunt than I might have made a mother. Although I have lots of mothering experiences, too. Because I'm a mentor, and that's what you are when you're a teacher. So you'll always be doing some mother-duty. I treasure that part of being a teacher very much.

Did the decision not to have kids have to do with the question of being able to come into yourself as a poet fully?

Well, I think if I had read this essay of Ursula LeGuin's, where she talks about—kind of laments all the women who give up motherhood for art, maybe I wouldn't have gone on the journey I did. But very early on, if you read the handwriting on the wall, as a young woman, you begin to understand that it is extremely hard to carry both, art and children. Unless you get a husband who will carry the child-rearing *more* than equally, as I understand Ursula LeGuin's husband did.

I had grown up in a family where there were five children, and I had my children then, you see, because I was the eldest of five. There were various problems in the family that caused me to carry a lot of the child care. Also, because my mother fell ill, I was a de facto mother at age thirteen when my little sister was born. So I experienced motherhood very importantly at that age. And in some ways really wasn't able to cope with it all, although I did, in fact, do just that. Cope.

You know, I love my sister very much, while realizing I had that experience of mothering too young. She was an important way toward my freedom. It being okay just to give myself to art. But now she's also the one in the family who gives me shelter as I tried to give it to her in that crazy, tormented household.

Taking care of a child at such a young age was instructive.

Yes. So my attitude toward motherhood became: "Well, I don't need to do that. Done that." Although I did very seriously think of having children—you know, I really am quite surprised to find myself without them in the end, because I really wanted to have children before the Vietnam War. But the war was a defining moment. I found it repugnant, all of the women around me rushing to have babies before their husbands went off to fight the war. Remember, I was married to a jet pilot in the marines. I mean I understand their impulse perfectly, of course. At the same time, I turned back.

Well you know, I've been discussing with a close friend whether or not she will have children. Some of my friends are about ten years younger than me and they still are not at the cutoff point. So they bring these questions to me because they see that I've survived quite well without children. I have plenty to do, and I am fruitful in other ways. I'm not *too* abject (laughs). So I listen. And one says, well, the man she's involved with, he has had his children at this point, and how many more forty-five-year-olds is she going to be able to find, you know, who will travel along with her? Maybe she just ought to give up the idea of having a child, she says to me. And if she has a child, maybe he'll abandon her. He says it's finished, their relationship is finished, if she has a child.

And I think back to my talks about this with Ray. There was never any sense where he limited my need or possibility toward having a child. In fact, it was, "If you want to have a baby, I'm with you, Babe. We'll do 'er." So, he was not going to at all impose the fact that he had already had children, you know. He would never have shut down my needs in this way. I didn't tell my friend that, because it would too heavily impinge upon the situation she's in. But I thought this was a wonderful gift from Ray—to give me the full possibility of *my* decision. If he had shut me down, I might have at some point resented it, especially as I was so young when he died. But no, it was, "We'll do 'er, Babe."

The two of you had a lot of children after all—your joining as writers yielded books.

Oh, yes. We're still having them. I'm at work on his *Complete Poems.*

I think of A New Path to the Waterfall *as a real companion to* Moon Crossing Bridge. *Do you?*

Absolutely. You know I often dream that some day they'll appear together under a joint cover or something.

They should. They companion themselves in time, you know, the before and the after. And there's also a kind of gendering to each of them. When I read them together, they played back and forth.

Yes, great.

So what's next for you, Tess?

I am going to London now—the publicist at Bloodaxe Books is arranging a tour of England. Then I'll go to Sligo, in the west of Ireland, where I spent time writing *Under Stars,* near Abbey Ballindoon. I've been going there since 1968.

I'm stitching all of this past back into the present. It's wonderful to feel those continuities. The rest of American life tells you it's all falling apart, you know (laughs). But I have a lot of connective tissue in my life.

Part 4

Unending

Introduction to *Carver Country*

As Bob Adelman and I set to work on this book I was aware that I felt somewhat baffled as to how to regard the coining of the term "Carver Country" as it relates to Ray's work and life. It seemed at once integral and antagonistic to our project. That is, I mistrusted the catchiness of its ready-made, haiku-like smugness, and its seeming assumption that we might be able to locate the qualities of Raymond Carver's world by simply pointing to physical landscapes out of his past or to the kinds of people who had appeared in his stories. Nonetheless, the term became a helpful clue to certain tangible aspects we wanted to define in Ray's work and, with its limitations in sight, it seemed possible to use it in an exploratory, even an inspirational, way.

The book gradually began to evolve so that it became more than a collection of photographs positioned against passages of Ray's work. It became a story, both of Ray's life as a writer and a man, and also of our lives together as writers, lovers, and helpmates. We decided to add selections from Ray's letters, as well as photographs of his drafts and notebooks, those totemic items he kept on his desk, and photographs of people important to Ray's life.

Finally, as we worked on the book it began to occur to me that Carver Country was, in fact, an amalgam of feelings and psychic realities which had existed in America, of course, even before Ray began to write about them. But because of his writing we began to give these feelings and patterns more

---

Carver Country: The World of Raymond Carver, photographs by Robert Adelman, introduction by Tess Gallagher (Scribners, 1990; Arcade Publishing, 1994). Copyright © Tess Gallagher and Robert Altman.

credibility. This elusive interior had to be carried in the tonalities of the photographs, in the informal, possibly even furtive, moments of Bob Adelman's artistry. A current of benign menace seemed to pervade Ray's fictionalized world at its inception, and would have to be a strong element in defining the invented territory we are calling Carver Country.

Ray's stories carry their own particular brand of tension—what William Stull, one of the most knowledgeable writers on Ray's work, termed a "purgatorial intensity." Critics have described this ominous quality variously. Marc Chenetier's phrase is a "motherlode of threat." Michael Koepf writes that although there is a Chekhovian clarity to Ray's stories, there is a "Kafkaesque sense that something is terribly wrong behind the scenes." It is this Kafkaesque quality, combined with the quotidian reality, which I feel Bob Adelman's photographs capture most palpably.

The later expansive, more inclusive and generous aspects of Ray's development have been represented perhaps best in the story aspect of our book—its movement from early life, through his recovery from alcoholism to our marriage and his final days. Bob has approached Ray's writing and life with an emphasis on Ray's early life which was formative of his artistic vision. This emphasis was also occasioned by a letter Ray wrote to Bob early on in their discussion about the project.

Ray's letter was an encouragement to Bob's work, and its flavor and enthusiasms are so particularly Ray's that it seemed natural that it accompany and explicate many of the photographs which form the nucleus of the book. The text of this letter centers around Ray's childhood and early adult life in Yakima in eastern Washington, and moves on to other locales such as the Grand Coulee Dam on the Columbia River where his father had worked, then onward to the rolling hills known as "Horse Heaven" near Prosser, Washington, commemorated in a poem of his called simply "Prosser."

The years in which Ray and I made our life together in a cross-country commute between Port Angeles in northwestern Washington State and Syracuse, New York, have been represented in portraits of some of the people close to us from these places. They include my brother Morris, Ray's hunting and fishing partner; my friend Jerry Carriveau, who is blind and

on whom "Cathedral" was modeled; our painter friend Al-
fredo Arreguin; those named in the poem "My Boat," our
colleagues and friends in Syracuse, California, and New York
City; and also in the portraits of Ray near Hurricane Ridge or
at the mouth of Morse Creek as it feeds into the Strait of Juan
de Fuca.

The physical proximity to water, in fact, became a source of
inspiration for Ray's later poems and for his last book, *A New
Path to the Waterfall*. The sense of removal and wildness on the
forested Olympic Peninsula with the snow-covered Olympic
Mountains, bordered by the moody waters of the Strait be-
tween Canada and America, allowed Ray the actual solitude in
which to write the stories and poems that would, in the last
years of his life, enlarge his work, spiritually and artistically.
It is amazing to realize that in the eleven years we were to-
gether in Port Angeles and in Syracuse, he wrote eleven
books, having written his initial two books of fiction and two of
poetry during a period of twenty years, ten years of which
he'd been suffering from alcoholism.

Landscape did ultimately become crucial to the way Adel-
man was able to suggest a forsaken quality in the lives of Ray's
characters. There is nothing, for instance, to give cover in the
photograph of Wenas Ridge and, in this, it is like the floodlight
intensity of Ray's own writing, which put honesty of emotion
and truth-telling above all, even to the point of laying his charac-
ters' lives open at moments when they were most shamed and
overwhelmed. Ray's proclivity for scorning tricks in his writing,
his favoring simplicity over ornamentation, choosing economy
as the most telling sign of veracity—these seem present in ele-
ments of the Yakima landscape. The complement to this terrain
of exposure was perhaps the quiet intimacy Ray found near
streams and mountains in Port Angeles, where he lived a good
part of his final years.

Ray and I visited Yakima only twice—once in August in
1985 in search of film sites for his story "Tell the Women
We're Going,"* and also to attend his Davis High reunion. On
this last occasion we got together with Jerry King, a classmate

---

*Although the film was never made, it was a lovely pretext for the
trip. [T.G.]

who'd become a disc jockey, and he and Ray had laughed about what Ray had called their "bozo" days in his poem "The Projectile." Ray's high school times in Yakima—stealing hubcaps, hanging out with pals Jerry King, Dick Miller, King Cook Kryger, and Lyle Rousseau—are mutely present in Bob's photographs of the fairgrounds and of Playland, the shabby music hall where Ray danced to the music of Tommy and Jimmy Dorsey and on his first date got miserably drunk for that first time, and passed out so cold "people thought I had died."

Ray had received Ds in English and hadn't done much better in his other courses, so it was an amazement to him when his classmates at the reunion recognized him in the program as an "internationally known writer." When Ray was asked to stand and take their applause he was so happy just to be acknowledged that he fairly beamed.

When I was invited to Davis High after Ray's death, one of the English teachers we'd met at the reunion, Linda Brown, asked me which class I wanted to attend. "Bonehead English," I said, "because that's where Ray would have been." She happened to be teaching such a class, and we read aloud poems by Ray to the students, who put aside their baffled and dazed exteriors for the hour, and entered freshly the world they were living in, through the mediation of someone who had sat where they were sitting. I imagined Ray there in the mistakenly near-to-stupid zone, lagging and humiliated, with no bets on him to come out on top in anything.

It was extremely unlikely that a writer, growing up in a household where Zane Grey westerns and the newspaper were the only available reading materials, would come to affect world literature to the extent that Raymond Carver has. The fact that the stories seem to travel so easily would suggest that Carver Country finds its corresponding territory in the lives of people nearly everywhere. Although his characters were mostly blue-collar, especially in the early stories, the appeal of such lives seems not to have limited interest in his stories. Ray was as surprised as anyone to realize that by 1986 his stories had been translated into twenty-three languages, including Japanese, Hebrew, Portuguese, and Dutch. I remember when the first Japanese editions came into the house, how he turned the pages with a kind of bemused astonishment, starting at the back. "Can you beat this," he said. "Isn't this something."

In France, where the intellectual climate is such that its readers often look askance at writing which doesn't have some pervasive theoretical agenda, Ray's work became highly regarded for its clarity, and a fidelity to reality that quickened its inner strangeness—elements which hadn't been fashionable there since Maupassant, except perhaps in the Nouveau Roman.

After Ray's death an interviewer for the *Guardian*, James Wood, asked me what I thought had caused Ray's work to come to prominence both in America and around the world during the mid-1980s. In trying to answer I spoke mainly to what was happening in America during the Reagan era and what continues under the Bush administration. Ray's publication had happened to coincide with the fact of the poor having essentially been told to take care of themselves in the guise of the phrase "the private sector." The private sector was supposed to pick up humanitarian responsibilities the federal government had chosen to drop. It was mostly a verbal dance out of a costly arena for government. Already the hope, even for young middle-class people, of owning a home or of sending their children to college, had begun to slip from their grasp, while this reality for working-class people had hit earlier. If they were out of work and uninsured and fell ill, well it was just their tough luck.

A line from one of Ray's last poems, "His Bathrobe Pockets Stuffed with Notes," represents the embattled situation of many of his characters: "'We've sustained damage, but we're still able / to maneuver,' Spock to Captain Kirk." It's this attempt to maneuver, with and in spite of damage, which constitutes the heroic in Carver Country. There is also a phrase which I heard often in my childhood from the working people Ray and I grew up near: "I can't seem to win for losing." This verbal construction colloquially inscribes the two steps forward, three steps backward of life in Carver Country.

It was important to Ray that he give his characters full dignity, no matter how impoverished their circumstances, and I think this is certainly a part of their attraction for readers everywhere. Even when they seem on the verge of being overwhelmed by their struggles or by ruptures they feel with their surroundings or with their families or mates, they don't capitulate without an assessment of the damage. Ray's stories and poems are a personal record of individual lives lived with no safety net and no imagination of a safety net. The people who are out of work in his stories become more than statistics, for Ray had been one of these people. "I'm a paid-in-full member of the working poor," he'd told interviewers more than once.

When Ray and I first met and began to exchange histories he'd told me how, while he was nineteen and raising his young family, both his own parents and the parents of his first wife had taken turns appearing on their doorstep, asking to be taken in, and being taken in. There was the story in his childhood of having had to walk everywhere in the land of the car because his parents couldn't afford to own one. No wonder when, in 1982, we had finished the rewrite of a script on the life of Dostoevsky for Carlo Ponti, Ray took his share of the money and went down to the Mercedes-Benz dealership in Syracuse, New York.

He had never had a car that worked. He was wearing a brown V-necked sweater which he'd worn when I'd met him in Dallas in 1977, but the elbows had worn through. It was fall 1982 and just before the summer when he would receive the Mildred and Harold Strauss Living Award, which would allow him five years of writing time free from teaching. He'd told the Mercedes salesman he wanted to try out the latest model. Reluctantly the salesman took him out to the lot and, with the man riding impassively along, Ray was allowed to take the 1983 model for a spin. They drove past the rib take-out places, taverns and malls, out into the rolling countryside, then turned around and came back. When they pulled up near the showroom Ray noticed, with chagrin, that in his haste to get to the dealer's before closing time, he'd come out of the house in his bedroom slippers. No wonder the salesman had looked him over carefully.

"I like it," Ray said to the man. "I like it fine. When can you deliver it?"

"When would you like it?" the man had asked, rather stonily.

"Would tomorrow be too soon?" Ray said.

"I think we could arrange that," the salesman said, beginning to reappraise the situation. "How would you be paying for it, sir?"

"Is cash okay?" Ray asked.

"Cash is fine," the man said.

He might have pegged Ray as a drug dealer, or maybe he simply felt relieved not to have to substantiate the credit rating of the eager, but rather unlikely looking, customer at his elbow. Ray told me over the phone about buying the car, and he was such a storyteller that every nuance of how he'd made that purchase seems alive in my memory. While all this was taking place I had been nursing my father, who was in the last stages of lung cancer in Port Angeles. That Christmas, Ray drove the Mercedes across country to Washington and when he arrived we christened it "The Mercedes that Dostoyevsky bought."

What made any success sweet for Ray was that in his youth he had lived firsthand the sweat and toil of earning, of working for bosses, the snarl and rip of the green chain at the sawmill, Boise-Cascade, where his father and uncle had worked as saw-filers in Yakima, Washington, during the 1940s and early 1950s. At various periods in his life Ray had assembled bicycles at Sears, picked tulips and hops, run errands for a pharmacy, managed a motel, and swamped floors on the night shift at a hospital in Arcata. He never forgot the flat-out drudgery, the way these jobs used people up and tossed them aside with little respect for the energies and lives offered there.

Ray knew enough not to think such striving was romantic. Anton Chekhov, his Russian mentor in the short story, had seen it as "the prosaic struggle for existence which takes away the joy of life and drags one into apathy." Ray had experienced from the inside the vagaries of the spirit caused by poverty, too little education, and a kind of numbness as regards the future which resulted in futile attempts to wall off pain with alcohol. Chekhov wrote, "Peasant blood flows in my veins, and you cannot astound me with the virtues of the peasantry," and Ray was fond of quoting these lines when some naive student or reporter attempted to make him a spokesman for the glories of a working-class existence.

While Ray never forgot these early jobs, he didn't want to

go back to that kind of work, and he felt for anyone who didn't have a way out of such a life. What he could do was to communicate that such lives were not without consequence, that the suffering was real and not to be disregarded. He had some early inspirational teachers and friends in Dennis Schmitz, Richard Day, Jim Houston, and John Gardner, exceptional writers themselves who saw the importance of what Ray was writing, and who stayed by him and encouraged him at a time when few cared whether the people in his stories were ever heard from.

Ray was always alert when anyone was talking about the hardship of work. In his stories he used the jobs people told him about or that he witnessed—my hairdresser, Judy Martin, who stood on her feet from 8 A.M. to 7 P.M. most days and who had a black rose tattooed on her ankle; my brother Morris's work as a gyppo logger and a powder monkey, setting dynamite off to blast logging roads into the ridge line; the beautiful flight attendant who exclaims in desperation, "I only have two hands," somewhere "over the steaming Mato Grosso"; Ray's janitorial work in a hospital where "a pale and shapely leg" had been left out on a table in the autopsy room he'd been in charge of cleaning; the young fire-eaters we'd seen in Mexico City whose throats had been scorched raw until their voices were lost; the obsessive vacuum cleaner salesman in "Collectors"; harried waitresses and secretaries; women who sold everything from vitamins to the family car to themselves; even the strange tweezer-armed photographer in "Viewfinder" who makes his living convincing people to buy Polaroids of their houses.

It was as if the people in Carver Country would have perished without a future tense in the language itself. Carver's people were working or they were out of work. Any day now they "expected to hear from up north" or "people's luck had gone south on them was all. But things were bound to change soon. Things would pick up in the fall maybe." In his stories Ray had been able, in a likeness to the voices and perceptions of the people themselves, to reveal the spiritual tenacity by which these people survived in spite of their limited means, and his readers at all economic levels of the population had been moved toward new awareness.

Surely Carver Country includes those who have disappeared into the powerlessness of alcohol for long tortured periods, some of whom sadly never emerge into sobriety, because the disease, at its worst, seems to require a near-death capitulation before its sufferers will surrender and move toward recovery. In Ray's own case he was hospitalized twice, the last time near kidney and liver failure. He was told on this occasion that he would certainly die, and soon, if he continued to drink. Previous to his collapse, Ray had gone drunk to Alcoholics Anonymous meetings, and after his release from the hospital he'd gone to Duffy's, a treatment center in northern California within sight of Jack London's house. This became the setting for the title story of his last fiction collection, *Where I'm Calling From*.

After his stay at Duffy's, Ray "fell off the wagon," partying in San Francisco in the company of friends who missed his drunkenness as an extension of their own. Thankfully he pulled out of it, took himself away from friends and family to a borrowed place he called "Chef's House" in a story he wrote from this period. Alone there, he brought himself down on "hummers," little shot glasses of whiskey administered at lengthening intervals.

Gradually he realized it had been a week and he hadn't had a drink; then a month had passed; and by the time I met him for the first time in November of 1977 in Dallas, five months of sobriety had accumulated. He was extremely fragile and, I realize now, that coming to that Dallas writers' conference at Southern Methodist University represented a very big risk for him. Such occasions are always fortified with liquor as the accompaniment to socializing, and Ray braved the overindulgences of others in order to read his stories and to join the company of writers there.

Michael Ryan, a poet and a mutual friend of ours, had invited us to participate in the conference along with Richard Ford, whom Ray was also meeting for the first time, and the poet Philip Levine, among others. I had heard of Raymond Carver and his work from fiction-writing friends in Missoula, Montana, where I'd gone to teach after the breakup of my second marriage. But I had never read his work and we had not met before this time, although we discovered later we had both been in Iowa City where Ray was teaching briefly at the Writers' Workshop in 1972, and where I was a student. We had probably ridden up or down with each other in elevators. But as we joked later, it hadn't been time for us to meet.

Sitting with poet Jack Myers and other friends in Dallas, listening to Ray read "Fat" and "Why Don't You Dance?" I realized immediately that I was in the presence of a sensibility the likes of which I hadn't seen before. His humor, a much overlooked element of his work, combined with a rueful sense of compulsive necessity in "Fat." His gift for the domestically bizarre was also especially poignant for me that day as he read "Why Don't You Dance," in which a man's household goods, arranged roomlike for sale on his lawn, become an exposed metaphor of the man's vacated life and marriage.

When I recall Ray standing before us in Dallas, shifting nervously as if he was just able to keep from fleeing the scene, I add to it now what I didn't know then—that this was the first reading he'd given since he'd become sober and, as such, represented a true act of courage. I also add the knowledge, of course, that we would be spending the rest of his life together, and knowing this now, marvel that so little of that future was present for me then, except for admiration of his writing and an affection for the awkwardly gentle man who was so gratefully and humbly before us.

I remember encountering a description of something which had been said of Chekhov to the effect that in his presence people felt they had the ease in which to be themselves, and that even in their weaknesses they would not be judged. All pretense and falsity, all pettiness fell away in his company. This seems an uncannily accurate rendering of the effect Ray had on people as well. His passage through the near-death corridors of alcoholism had left him full of compassion and an ability to love. What was even more winning was that, unlike so many people one encounters, he also knew how to accept love. This somehow communicated itself immediately on sight in his slightly hunched posture and in the shy but attentive way he entered into conversation. He had seen it all and lived to tell it. He never underestimated anyone's pain or struggle. At the same time he never heaped credit upon himself for having overcome his illness. He knew it was a matter of grace, of having put his trust in what AA identifies as "a higher power," and of having miraculously been given the will to turn all temptation to drink aside.

Ray's sobriety was the single most empowering element of his life during our time together. Without that, nothing would have been possible. His state of grace included that the will to drink seemed to have been entirely lifted from him, as in the release from a curse. He was not like some recovering alcoholics we knew who were constantly balanced on the precipice of a possible plunge back into darkness.

There was only one time during our life together when I remember being afraid for Ray because of the possibility that he might drink again. This occurred in March of 1988. He'd strangely begun to feel a fearfulness about his sobriety and had started out for an AA meeting in Sequim, fifteen minutes from Port Angeles. Not too long after he'd left the house the telephone rang. It was Ray. He had been unable to locate the meeting and had ended up in a bar. "I've ordered a drink," he said, "but I haven't drunk any of it. It's still sitting on the bar." He was like a drowning man reaching out for a life raft. "Don't go back in there," I said, as evenly and as surely as I could. "Come home, Hon. Just get in the car and come home." When he arrived home safe and sober, I ran outside to meet him and we just stood there in the driveway a while and held onto each other. "You don't want to go back that way," I said. "Those demons are behind us."

Once the cause of the pressure in his head, the terrible headaches which caused him to lock his jaw, was discovered to be the result of a brain tumor associated with the lung cancer he had been fighting since October, we understood what had caused his brush with the old compulsion to drink. Ray had felt the shame and helplessness of his drinking days, but again he had been allowed an important escape, even during the terrible dilemma of the illness which would ultimately take his life. It meant that he could rightly sustain a vision of himself in his full mental and spiritual strength to the end.

Ray didn't romanticize what he called his "Bad Raymond" days. But he did maintain an affection for that fallible and wayward self he had preserved most indelibly in his fiction and in stories often recounted in the presence of friends. I can remember wonderful evenings with the painters Susan Lytle and Alfredo Arreguin in Seattle, during which Ray and Alfredo would be in tears with laughter while sharing some near-catastrophe tale of their separate drinking days.

It had been 1980 when Ray had first met Alfredo, who'd been a friend of mine since I had been seventeen and first in Seattle. Alfredo was still drinking when they met. But, inspired partly by his new friendship with Ray, Alfredo soon gained his sobriety. The two men were like companions who'd been tested in some unheralded but savage campaign, and each time they met there was an aura of the spiritual and physical carnage they had withstood and had miraculously survived. Ray saluted their friendship in the fictionalized character of Alfredo in his story "Menudo." Alfredo's gift to Ray was a painting he had done for us and presented as a wedding gift. It is called *The Hero's Journey* and became the jacket and end-paper art for *A New Path to the Waterfall*. The painting portrays salmon leaping toward a waterfall above patterned magenta waves. In the sky are what Ray called "the ghost fish," a stream of salmon floating in cloudlike serenity in the opposite direction. We hung the painting above our couch and meditated often in those last days on its pageantry of struggle and release, which was also, in a sense, a portrait of Ray's own life.

Through his sobriety Ray had been able to improve his own situation, but the fact that he couldn't secure this same release for his family's chronic troubles remained an ongoing heartache. Again and again Ray bent his energies toward consoling and helping his mother and other family members, even when it seemed no good news could come from those quarters.

No matter what stability Ray managed for his own life, it became a fact of life that he would be buffeted and unsettled by the dissatisfactions, demands, and pleas emanating from the direction of family—which included his mother, his ex-wife, his daughter, and his brother. His son, Vance, had joined us in Syracuse in 1981 to attend college and managed, for a time, to sidestep life in the desperate zone.

What one might call the tyranny of family would have to be

a main element in any characterization of Carver Country. It figured prominently in Ray's fiction. His characters, whether alone or within marriages or on the periphery of family, have compulsions which arise from the sheer need to be included or remembered. Often they are reduced to simply inventing usefulness for themselves. These compulsions take hold especially when they find themselves out of work. His characters sometimes serve these repetitive, desperate actions as faithfully as they might have worked jobs.

There is, for instance, the mother in "Boxes" who moves every few months, and who exemplifies the itinerant or gypsy nature of many of the characters in Ray's stories. Indeed, she represents a facet of American life in the way its people use up "place" and depend upon the idea and the possibility of a "next" or a "new" place as remedy and comfort. In AA shorthand, when an alcoholic does this it's called "taking a geographic," a sign that the drinker is trying to shake his or her troubles instead of dealing with them. But it is entirely possible that moving itself is now inscribed on the national psyche as something "normal" in situations of stress, loss, and despair.

"Boxes" was patterned on the peripatetic movements of Ray's mother, who came, on one of her many moves, to live in Port Angeles near us for a year. During the time I was with Ray he usually spent a couple of months a year in concern over his mother's next move. Her way of installing hopefulness was periodically to shed her surround. These relocations guaranteed that she would have the attention and resources of her two sons for a concentrated two-month period each year.

At times, the demands from all quarters by Ray's family for money reached such a pitch that he felt his connections with them had been reduced to this—the need and demand for cash. The constant din of these requests became the undertow he swam against, voicing his dismay in poems like "The Mail" and "The Schooldesk," in which he wrote, "And someone, someone is pleading with me. / Saying, 'For Christ's sake, don't / turn your back on me.'"

The fact that he had gone on with his life and his writing and had managed to achieve some financial security was, sadly, not a clear good in terms of his family. He balanced the rewards of his success against resentment, accusation, and the easily tapped guilt from the years when his drinking had held him in thrall and had made it impossible for him to give of either means or self.

Ray managed to preserve an attitude of forbearance and love which seemed, even so, to wave like a flag of surrender above what his family required of him. Almost like a litany he would say to me at times, "I don't have a heart anymore where they're concerned. That went a long time ago." Ray and his daughter had in common the specter of alcohol, and having broken free of it himself, he wished nothing less for his daughter and addressed his concern for her in "To My Daughter," a tough-love poem we've printed with Bob's photograph, and which called out to her not to make the same mistakes he had made. Sadly, he was never to see her free of the damage of alcohol.

In one of his last stories, "Elephant," he drew a portrait of a working-class character beset on all sides by the needs of family. The image of the father lifting the boy onto his shoulders and walking with him became central and seemed to ameliorate a conjoining sense of burden, duty, and fractured love presented in the story. As we worked through the drafts, it seemed that Ray and his character reached a kind of equanimity at the center of the unreasonable demands being made upon them. While it is true that the main character's burden is unyielding, he seems to have entered a state of spiritual strength by sheer virtue of his attitude of perseverance and benevolence.

This accommodation and spiritual progress was evident for Ray in relation to his own family, even when they themselves failed to be lifted free. It's never certain what it is that allows for growth in one's character and a tearing away of chaff toward clear vision, but Ray sought more than the petty and meager. He strove in his writing and life not to betray the true hardships of his experience. At the same time he didn't reserve enlightenment for the educated and the self-reliant. His characters might be ignominiously engaged in actions which belonged to the mire, to the partialities of their talents and the laxities of their wills, but he also allowed them their clear moments of recognition and communication, and he did so in their vernacular.

One story that was rather a breakthrough for Ray after *What We Talk about When We Talk about Love* was "Cathedral," which he began writing in the fall of 1982 on the train to New York City from Syracuse. My friend Jerry Carriveau had phoned from Maryland to say he wanted to visit us. His wife had recently died of cancer, and he'd come east to spend time with her relatives. Jerry had been blind since birth and in 1970 I'd taken a job working with him for the Seattle Police Department for a year. Our job in the Research and Development Department involved, among other tasks, devising a single-print retrieval file system for fingerprints. In preparation for Jerry's visit, I'd told Ray how I'd drawn fingerprint patterns out on a tablet for my friend in such a way that they formed a raised surface. Then I'd guided his hand over them, simultaneously giving him a verbal description which corresponded to what he was feeling under his fingertips. Ray was masterful in converting this detail when he fictionalized the visit of a blind man in "Cathedral." He caused the blind man's hand to rest on top of the narrator's, thereby placing the narrator in the position of making the recognitions—not the other way around as it had been in the actual instance—and also increasing the intimacy between the male characters.

Ray generally hand-drafted his stories in one or two sittings. He secluded himself in his room and appeared only for cups of coffee or to check the mail. But "Cathedral" was drafted on a train paralleling the Hudson River, the very train Jerry had taken earlier from New York City for our reunion in Syracuse. Ray and I had been given the loan of an apartment for our stay in the city by a friend who was to be away for a few days. This trip was to have been a vacation, a time to see films and plays, and to eat at some good restaurants. It was the first free time we'd had in a long while. But instead of going out on the town, we both fell with a vengeance to our work and didn't venture out except in the evenings.

The apartment was strangely encumbered by an enormous, sleek cat that could stand on its hind legs and knew how to turn doorknobs with its paws. When we attempted to shut it out it would yowl pitilessly and fling itself at the door, or we would hear the click of the latch and feel it pounce onto our bed in the middle of the night. Ray wasn't a cat lover, except for our Blue Persian (which he'd nicknamed "the Ground Owl"), and the insistent presence of this cat became more and more oppressive. When the cat perched on the sill near an open window one morning Ray began to look longingly out the seventh-floor window to the street below, no doubt imagining its death by accidental means. But in the end we simply wrote and coexisted with the animal, barricading ourselves into the bedroom at night with a chair Ray tilted against the door handle.

This cat comes back to me as emblematic of how, when I was with Ray, domestic acquiescence could shift subtly toward an unexpected malice, that benign menace so central to his writing.

While we worked together on "Cathedral" a phrase was coined that became a permanent part of our writing vocabulary. It eventually grew somewhat famous with our students and colleagues at Syracuse University. One day I had decided to take Ray to dinner at an Irish pub called Coleman's, across town in Syracuse. I'd been there for lunch with students, and the food had been a pleasant surprise after the pub-grub one got in Ireland. We'd started out a bit late and, since I hadn't driven there on my own, I began to hesitate about where I was going. Ray interpreted this as a sign that I was lost and began to despair about ever getting to Coleman's. Anxiety would begin to set in if we didn't get food into him at around 5 P.M. each day. Low-blood sugar was possibly a problem, though this was never diagnosed. As we passed a McDonald's or a Wendy's, Ray would say, "Let's just pull in here, Hon. We can go to Coleman's tomorrow." About the time I finally became genuinely lost, he spotted a pizza joint and again attempted to detour us. "Pizza. I'm just in the mood for pizza," he said. "Pizza's just what I had in mind." Ultimately we reached Coleman's and had a very fine meal, but the journey had left an impression.

Our habit of working was that once Ray had completed a

sufficiently clear, typed version, he would show it to me. When we'd gotten back to Syracuse from our stay in New York he was able to finish a typed draft of "Cathedral" and brought it down to the basement where I was writing one morning. We usually had our conferences in what we jokingly called the "Library," which was just a second-story room where a few of our shared books were kept. We'd sit on the couch side by side and move through each page of the story. But usually, as we began, I'd give a few weather signals about where I thought the story was at this particular stage. That morning I said, "Ray, this is going to be a completely amazing story, but you haven't gotten it to Coleman's yet. You've stopped at the hamburger stand." We both began to laugh because he knew exactly what I meant. The phrase "getting to Coleman's" became talismanic between us after that. When Ray eventually finished the present ending of "Cathedral," I said to him, "Well now, you have really gotten this story to Coleman's!"

It was a constant that those who had formerly been minor characters in the country's literature finally stepped fully into center stage in Ray's work. Their inarticulateness did not exempt them from pain and loss which had the ability to move us. I do still remember a certain cocktail party, however, at which a woman had approached Ray to complain that his characters just weren't intellectually stimulating enough to keep her attention. Then, as if that weren't enough she'd said, "I also find them just too depressing." We were so used to these stock responses that all we had to do was to look at each other a certain way when it happened in company, marking the spot so we could wash it out later alone. But patience had worn thin, maybe because she'd had her say under cover of alcohol, and this time I wanted to say mildly, "Hey, toots, why don't you just pop a Valium and get with the Wittgenstein."

I recall Chekhov's remark in a letter that "melancholy people always write gaily, while the work of those who are cheerful is always depressing." As a writer then, one couldn't have much control over whether the work would be depressing or uplifting since it was a factor of one's opposite nature. Ray's was a naturally buoyant nature and that meant he had the stamina to reflect the difficult terrain of the lives he portrayed. Ray also felt no writer should have to apologize for the stringency of his or her vision, nor did he ever feel obliged to be anyone's entertainment center. He understood instinctively that he was carrying the news about a people largely forgotten at the heart of the country. Their story was often grim and without recourse to the savvy bulwarks of the educated or of the financially secure.

Ray had been bankrupt himself twice by the time I met him. Our first disagreement was over whether or not he would take my credit card to a writer's conference in New Jersey where it might come to pass that he would have a sudden need for cash. He was sure he could convince people that there was a misprint on the card and that it should really read "Ted" instead of "Tess." He had the instincts of an outlaw with none of the finesse, though when trying to rent a car with him once at an airport I remember being astonished at how quickly, when questioned, he supplied the name of an expensive hotel we weren't staying at in the city, invented a job he didn't have, and slapped down my overextended Visa, which miraculously didn't register as such when they checked it.

On another occasion when he'd gotten himself in over his head by committing to go to a conference with me at a time when he flat out didn't want to travel, he'd called his prospective host and told him that his mother had had a stroke. Yes, he was sorry too, but well, it seemed it was out of the question to do anything but to stay by his phone. "Quick," he said to me after hanging up, "what are the symptoms of a stroke? I mean, what happens to you? They're going to call back to see how she's doing." I went to the conference alone, having to make daily health reports on Ray's mother who was meanwhile thriving in Sacramento.

The "cover-up," "side-step," "evasion," and "passing the buck" were all in Ray's bag of tricks when I met him. He'd needed these strategies during his long drinking career. In our early days, his habit of being on the run from bill collectors had caused him to avoid answering the telephone. I'd let him off at first, but after a while I made him take his turn. He'd told me about the police coming to his door in Cupertino,

California. They had shouted over a megaphone for all the neighborhood to hear that he should throw out his credit cards and come out with his hands up. "That's behind you," I told him. "We aren't going to live that way now."

I remember feeling afraid when I was first with Ray that living with him might turn out to be like stepping into one of his stories. It seemed that a very thin membrane might separate the world of chaos from that of order when Ray's perceptions came into play. Some events in our first months seemed to confirm my worst fears, but thankfully this period didn't last long.

My first week in the three-bedroom house he'd rented for us in El Paso in 1979, within sight of the racetrack on the New Mexico border, had begun in a very Carveresque fashion. I was fixing dinner, expecting Ray to come home any minute from his teaching job at the University of Texas, his first job sober. He'd been off booze a year and a half but he was still wobbly on a few essential corners. A knock came at the door and when I opened it a man in coveralls said he was there to turn off the gas. "But I'm cooking dinner," I'd said, appealing to some assumed sense of basic human decency. "I don't make the rules, lady," he said without so much as a flutter of sympathy. "The bill hasn't been paid and the gas, she goes off." Carver Country, it seemed, was a zone in which bills, for one reason or another, did not always get paid. Somehow I convinced the man that I would see to paying the bill, and that it wasn't good to make hardships for honest people. But from there on out I took over making sure the bills got paid.

There were times in those first six months together when Ray would get what he called "the willies." This is a state of unaccountable anxiety that is hard to quell and which recovering alcoholics recognize as a danger signal. These feelings will sometimes attach themselves with intensity to otherwise innocent occasions. The night before I was to leave alone on a trip to Ireland in our El Paso days, one of our new friends held a party for us and, much to Ray's consternation, brought out a tarot deck, intending to read everyone's fortune. If someone had produced a live tongue-flicking cobra and proposed we all handle it, I don't think Ray would have been any less terrified. He forbade our hostess to read my cards with a desperation that made you believe in fate, and before she knew what was happening we were into our coats and out the door.

Ray had a strange relationship to luck, to fate, which he loved to test with fishing, by a turn at the racetrack now and again, or at poker with friends. But let one bad sign rear its head in the rest of his life and he was away like a groom blundering into an undertakers' convention. No machine that let him down in those postdrinking days ever got a second chance. If the car sputtered or the dishwasher missed a cycle, out it went.

By the same token, "things" couldn't always rely on him in those days. It was as if objects eluded him in their placid pretence of doing nothing. One day he took a borrowed pickup to get some furniture that one of our friends had in storage and was loaning to us—it seemed there were many people in El Paso with two or three sets of everything. Ray arrived home with a chest of drawers which had one of the drawers missing. He'd heard of taping them shut but it just hadn't occurred to him. No way did he want to go back onto the freeway to see what had befallen that missing drawer. "But that belongs to someone else," I argued. "We have to go back." He didn't see it that way. But he reluctantly drove us to where we found the drawer on a curve, splintered in a place or two but mostly intact.

The following day I glued the drawer together and refinished it. It wasn't perfect, but at least we didn't have a chest of drawers with a gap. That day I sat Ray down for what he would have called "a serious talk." I hadn't planned what I would say, but somehow I knew this was a non-fooling-around matter. "Listen," I said. "I love you. I wouldn't be here if I didn't. But I did not come four thousand miles across this country to get bad luck. My luck is good," I said, "and I want it to stay that way. You'd better change your luck." I don't know what I thought I was doing—maybe trying to frighten him into a whole new way of life which had no room for the downward spirals he'd been caught in before. I hadn't the least intention of leaving, but I wasn't the daughter of a gambler for nothing, and I could throw a bluff in a way that could make a mouth run dry with certitude that I meant what I said.

It was a risk that seems in retrospect to have paid off. Ray did change his luck. Or it changed all on its own.

But the luck of people in Carver Country might be said to be indigenously and hopelessly bad. Their luck has always been bad, from the beginning of time and maybe even before time began, and it's easy to feel that no amount of threats or cajoling or solicitousness in their direction is ever going to bring it out of its nosedive. Still, people marooned in Carver Country are under the impression that ultimately they will be rewarded for their patience and suffering. They somehow have been spared the truth that luck settles like a dominion on the worthy and the unworthy, and that the only way it can be kept is by calling on it day and night with the insolence of the bottle for its genii. In the stories Ray wrote, their patience and longings are redeemed as they themselves may never manage in life.

Once Ray changed his luck all things did seem to come to him. During our first year he had thought he might never write again. Early in his sobriety he had even mistrusted his writing, had blamed it for his drinking, and had believed, mistakenly, that it was the cause of his misfortunes—the drinking, the bankruptcies, his poor employment record. Certainly his priorities were right: stay sober and everything else would take care of itself. Gradually he saw that I was writing and decided to try it again himself. By the time we'd moved from El Paso to Tucson in 1980, where I had a tenure track job at the University of Arizona, he'd begun to draft the stories which would become *What We Talk about When We Talk about Love*.

He was also feeling strong enough in his new sobriety by then that he volunteered to go to AA meetings with one of our friends who confessed he needed help. From time to time over the rest of his life Ray would help others by taking them to meetings, and there's no way to tell how many writers and readers who'd connected with his escape from alcoholism were helped by him through the mails or through just learning of his escape.

In our life together Ray gradually entered a sense of security and stability which had been denied him until then. By

1981 we had a house in Syracuse which we'd bought together, a car that wasn't breaking down every few days, teaching jobs at Syracuse University, and the stories Ray was writing, which would become *Cathedral,* the book which brought him nomination for the Pulitzer Prize and for the National Book Critics Circle Award. With this book, Ray's work took on a new richness and dimension, what he saw as a more generous tenor. The spiritual and stylistic growth in this work delivered his writing once and for all from the diminishment of the term "minimalist," which Ray had firmly rejected at the start. He preferred the more accurate identification of his style as that of a "precisionist." And indeed, critics looking at the entire body of work since have seen the earlier period of *What We Talk about When We Talk about Love,* heavily engineered by his then editor, Gordon Lish, as the most "uncharacteristic" and least representative period of Ray's writing.

As the years of sobriety and literary accomplishment accumulated, Ray's face lost the bloated vagueness it had carried when I'd first met him. The jawline firmed up and the muscled places, where humor and a sense of confident well-being had come together, seemed to restore a youthful mischief to his looks. He grew, if possible, even more handsome. His inner pride in himself made him enjoy looking his best. I became his barber early on and clipped away the fluffy sideburns of his drinking days, got him to wear clothes which fit, and for his forty-ninth birthday bought a leather jacket for a trip to Paris, because, I had joked, I wanted him to look like Camus. But in April of 1987 when we walked hand in hand through the streets of Paris on our way to visit Ray's French publisher, our new friend, Olivier Cohen, on the Boulevard St.-Germain, Ray looked like no one but himself—a man in full possession of his life who knew his work was respected. Our love and confidence in each other ran like a current through it all.

The idea to marry had been Ray's. The impetus was the heartbreaking news given by his doctor in Port Angeles that tumors had once again invaded his lungs. Coming as it did, two months after radiation treatments for a brain tumor, it demanded all of our spiritual resources. We had to face the fact that his life and our life together was ending, and yet find courage to live out of and beyond that certain loss. Ray was as brilliant about imaginatively dealing with what was happening to us as the doctor had been at Chekhov's death, in thinking to send down for a bottle of champagne when a less inspired sort would have persisted in sending for oxygen. "I'll be a corpse by the time it arrives," Chekhov had told his doctor, and the physician had then thought of the right gesture, bringing the celebration of the life forward at its moment of closure. This scene was given in Ray's last story, "Errand," but with a Carveresque shift of emphasis from the doctor to the waiter who brings the champagne.

So, after eleven years in which our loving had brought about a fusion of energies and spirit, while allowing for our own identities apart from each other, we decided to celebrate our relationship by marrying. We bought rings and picked up our plane tickets, told a few close friends, our literary agent in New York, and my family. We were married in Reno on June 17, 1988.

After the wedding at the Heart of Reno Chapel, across from the courthouse, we went to Harrah's to celebrate and I began a three-day winning streak at roulette. We threw ourselves into those days and, since there were no clocks to remind us, lost all track of time. I remember on the final morning, just before leaving Bally's (the hotel where we'd stayed), trying to convince Ray to come with me for a last throw of roulette. I had wanted Ray to be with me, as if that final casting of the dice were for him, and because, in some uncanny way, I had known the good fortune of the play before it happened. But Ray had already let go of his gambling days and would only halfheartedly play a few slots later at the airport. In some rightness of his own, he wouldn't go into the casino again. He preferred to stand with our luggage, his arms heaped with wedding flowers which had been wired to us by friends abroad. I hadn't been able to leave the flowers behind.

When Ray saw me running across the casino with my hands full of cash he began to brighten and to shout, "Did you do it, Hon? Did you win, Babe?" The flowers were crushed between us as he hugged me to him in his excitement. "We'll miss our bus," he said in the next breath. "Forget the bus," I said. "We're taking a taxi!"

Our friend Stanley Kunitz, the poet, told me after Ray's death that he couldn't recall any writer or artist during his lifetime who had been so genuinely mourned as Ray was. Besides the plain fact of Ray's genius being gone from the world, part of this outpouring was no doubt due to the fact that Ray was so young—barely fifty. We had all expected and hoped for many more years of his writing and company. It was a life cut short, and we suffered the loss as it was—an aberration, a blow, a chastisement to us all in our faulty assumptions about the future, about mortality and the turns of fate after long struggle.

But loss of Ray seemed to go beyond even the premature fact of it. He was beloved, and luckily he knew this, which somehow extends the benevolence of his presence more surely among us than if he had left in a state of self-banishment, as have some writers. Ray lived his last weeks and days in an urgency of creation, working against the shadows and haltings of his own body as it began to finally give way to the cancer, just managing to complete his final book, *A New Path to the Waterfall.*

On that last day of his life we played a videotape of the small, intimate wedding reception we'd held with family and friends in Port Angeles after our return from Reno. We laughed at some of the celebration antics during the party, including the escape of our Persian cat, Blue, into raccoon territory. My sister and mother had ended up under the deck on their knees trying to catch the cat and deliver him to safety. Then there was a moment on film where, reaffirming our commitment before friends, we bent to each other and kissed, as we had at our marriage in Reno, long and deeply, while everyone raised their glasses in a toast.

If I could add one element to Bob Adelman's portraits of Ray, it would be something impossible to show in photographs—his infectious laughter. In his years with me the house was full of this laughter, which came out of him as a stored-up gladness, a hilarity that ignited spontaneously while he talked on the phone to friends, or sat in his bathrobe reading aloud from a letter, or just in those domestic moments of companionship where histories have been so absorbed that the humors mix playfully into some heady, rare concoction of twin joyfulness. When I think "never again" of that beautiful sound that was most him for me, I have to be crushed, crushed and uplifted at once. Crushed because it is too beautiful. Uplifted because it is too beautiful to sacrifice to mourning, but must be treasured as that individual breath he was, entrusted to all who shared rooms and hearts with that laughter while he lived. And now again in the reflections and images which join us back to him here.

Unending

We did valiant battle the ten months before Ray died, but by May of 1988, we knew we weren't going to win. Ray died on August 2. So there was a period of time between May and August when we had to realize and deal with the fact that we weren't really going to get out of this. It was very, very hard. But it was also, strangely, a transcendent time. We were not as fully immersed in the agony of an ending as one might imagine. The closing down of our time seemed oddly and inexplicably to invigorate us and to make each moment more important than we'd ever believed it could be. It was as if, perhaps like hummingbirds, we'd suddenly discovered we could even fly upside down.

It's hard to communicate what those days were like, how we could, in fact, be happy. And we *were happy*, we had happiness the way the sun has the earth, in a continuous shining elsewhere, even when it's dark. Our elsewhere was Ray's poems. Even now it probably sounds like a blasphemy to say so, because we're supposed to be paying attention: Death is coming! But we didn't put our eye on death, we put our eye on *life*. And because we did—much got accomplished and was deeply felt.

Those were important times and we lived them intensely engaged, breath into breath, with time as precious and squandered to exactly our desires, a strange hybrid exhilaration, really. Which isn't to say that we didn't just weep together when we had first received the news, the actual and unavoidable news that the cancer had returned. No, we staggered

From "A Poetic Love: Tess Gallagher and Raymond Carver," in *The Heart of Marriage: Discovering the Secrets of Enduring Love,* by Cathleen Rountree (HarperCollins, 1996). Copyright © Tess Gallagher.

under that, and the shock of it drove us to our corners as our hearts scraped bottom. No, I'm not saying dire moments weren't there, but they weren't the *controlling* energies.

When actual death and physical separation came, it made me numb at first. I suppose I went into a kind of spiritual torpor, in order to preserve myself against the cold of it. I had been with Ray in such a state of fervent industry, trying to help him finish his book—the days were so full—and just to stay alive, of course, for as long as he could: our days were given over to those life-sustaining ministrations, hour by hour, moment to moment.

When, about a month after Ray had died, I saw pictures of myself in the funeral group, only then did I realize how my face was blunted with the immeasurable grief of losing him. Anyone who has lost a loved one has been where I was. That sudden bodily loneliness that is immense—to be alone in the house with all the personal effects suddenly made more than simple objects by the death of their owner—his shoes, toothbrushes, a stack of books he was meaning to read—all so plaintive and still.

Yet, we had been together so *well* it was hard to make the absence real to myself. I still felt his presence around me in quite a protecting, generous way, too. Beautiful and baffling.

A Nightshine beyond Memory

Ten More Years with Ray

In that quiet of quiets where we sometimes feel we speak with the dead, as one voice reaching into itself toward another, Ray has brought out the ghost in me. Maybe all our dead beloveds do this to a certain extent—bring out the ghosts in us, allow us to meet our dead-aliveness, that breathless presence made of our own anticipated absence, as we cross the life/death boundary in heart and deed, with our own mortality in mind.

I had experienced several important deaths prior to Ray's (my father's, my younger brother's accidental death at age fifteen, and a favorite uncle's murder). But it was Ray's death (August 2, 1988), because of its far-reaching impact on the totality of my life, that ultimately caused an osmotic flow of spirit to take place. Through my writing and my particular grieving and treasuring process, I came gradually to feel a world added to my world, whereas before, each death had left me robbed, divested. As I've said in my poem "Black Violets," "he's evergreen in me." The persistence of Ray's presence, the multifarious, even mysterious forms it has taken, are constantly surprising.

In my ongoing relation to Ray, I have reached beyond the simply "remembered." Perhaps this amplified state occurred with Ray because we were so melded to each other in every facet of our living. Certainly our writing life—that all-night diner of soul-making—always found us elbow-to-elbow, reading and writing in each other's margins. Ray still brightly informs all aspects of my living. I'm afraid I don't understand—

Published in *Philosophy and Literature* 22, no. 2 (October 1998). Copyright © Tess Gallagher.

except in the general disposition toward making-way-for-the-new—when I hear someone say: "Ten years had passed and I had to let my dead mate go."

I have no intention of letting Ray go. I can't conceive there would be any benefits, even if I could. Certainly there has been a "letting go" of physical presence. But one of my great blessings has been the emotional and spiritual penumbra of continuity I've come to experience—that blending of light with dark. What is for others perhaps a restriction of the beloved to the fringe of consciousness (the static memory of the beloved), has developed for me into a kinesthetic interplay of perfect shadow and full light. So any idea that I should divest myself, let go, move on, is, for me, against full aliveness. This will to repossess what at first was lost has been a blessedness. I've expressed the form of my reaching toward that unknown best in my poetry. Indeed, prose telling doesn't seem to have the vertical heft to carry what has occurred. Nor does it have sufficient silence.

Although I have experienced the absence of hand and brow, I have allowed and am allowed free passage to and from another reception, an opening, a conversation. My relationship to Ray in death has been an unexpected enlargement, accomplished through deeds of spirit and daily acts.

I still speak of Ray each day and am lucky to be able to do things for and even "with" him, as I feel his awareness within mine. I have courted his accompaniment, purposefully making an arena for fiction writing these past four years during the good fortune of the Lyndhurst Fellowship, which has allowed me to write my stories, *At the Owl Woman Saloon*. In this way I have also moved beyond those early stories Ray encouraged in *The Lover of Horses*. Ray also seems to have moved with me in the accomplishment of *At the Owl Woman Saloon,* for he is an important function of my self-witnessing—though one not confined to me alone, rather a beneficence shared and sustained with others.

In the introduction to my first poem after Ray's death, "Owl-Spirit Dwelling," I spoke of "a spiritual wideness I seemed to be sharing with Ray even in his absence." These few lines from Antonio Machado's "The Drab Brown Oak" give a sense of what I mean when I say "spiritual wideness":

Livid moon
Of an ancient afternoon
In the cold fields
More moon than earth.

I love the way the fields in this passage are so flooded by moonlight they cease being earth—are transformed by moonlight into a substance that belies what we *think* we know of earth. An exchange of the palpable with the impalpable takes place, an infusion, a conversion of matter into spirit. The dividend is a widening of the psychic, spiritual, emotional, and corporeal reach. Field becomes "more moon than earth."

It is no wonder the moon, in its metaphysical malleability, became the overvoice in *Moon Crossing Bridge,* the first stage in the reintegration of Ray into my inner life. The moon is the emblematic ghost-witness to earth. The cargo of those poems forged a word-bridge across which I felt I could move back and forth to Ray. Both the ritualized process of my grieving and the eventual writing of *Moon Crossing Bridge* had seemed to necessitate proximity to the grave. When, after six months, I'd at last been able to write poems again, I crossed the emptiness of having no one with whom to share them. I could see there would be an ongoing loss of the reciprocal nourishment, the almost intrapsychic way Ray and I had collaborated and inspired each other.

For two and a half years I visited his grave every day. Friends evidently feel I am safe enough now that they have told me they worried for me, that I looked "devastated" those first two years. And why wouldn't I have been? I was young really, forty-five, and—at the very center of my life, an extraordinary person, my deep love and heart's companion—was gone.

After writing *Moon Crossing Bridge,* I found I could carry and sustain Ray's presence, not as petals pressed into a book, but as a freshly grafted new form, an ongoing, forward-moving responsiveness. These poems, mistaken by some as simply artifacts of mourning, have been rather the replenishment of self, and of the beloved, to fertile inner ground. They *are* the new language, the persistence that language can be across absence, until the new thing is formed. The poems melded what had been parted; as the new form took hold, the distance between us dissolved.

Besides the alchemy of *Moon Crossing Bridge* there was *Portable Kisses,* which, though lighter in tone, nonetheless presented overlapping poems from the same period such as "Widow in Red Shoes," "Black Violets," and others. This book allowed me some respite from the pyschic intensities of *Moon Crossing Bridge.* It also restored the full spectrum of my humors. Ray's death, after all, was larger than grief, as *we* were larger than something that could simply be "taken away." He grew to represent for me, to *enact,* the infinite expansion of the heart, memory's capacity to swallow the "snow needle"* and then to stitch the spirit-presence into the creative fabric of daily life.

An inventory of all the important meetings and activities since Ray's death would be impossible. But let me tell some stories about the kinds of meetings which have enlarged my life and given signs of the large affection and simple devotion Ray's work generates in others.

Two weeks ago I serendipitously encountered three filmmakers at Ray's grave at Ocean View Cemetery. We weren't to have met until the following day when they were to film me for Italian television—a program on Ray financed by the Vatican, a fact Ray would have found amusing. I can hear him now: "My pal, the pope!"

Tommaso Avati and his director, Yozo Tokuda, along with their American cameraman from Chicago, Doug Clevenger, had driven from Chicago for three days in an Italian version of *On the Road*—their rented car having already collapsed once. Tommaso had contacted me from Rome by e-mail while he was completing his dissertation on Ray's stories. As a postgraduation adventure he had proposed to his father, a well-known director in Italy, that he make a TV documentary on Ray.

The meeting between these young filmmakers and myself was one of those times I felt Ray very much present. When I embraced Tommaso, this young man who'd come so far, out of love for Ray and his work, I could feel how moved he was to

---

*Paul Celan, "Snow-Part," *Last Poems.*

be there, close to where Ray rests. His genuine reverence for Ray held quiet stature on that seaside ledge. I had the sense that my arrival had unexpectedly thrown a door open to an infinite room. It was as if, because I had come, Ray was suddenly more present.

Before long all four of us set about cleaning Ray's grave, freshening it with flowers I'd brought and watering the huge potted plant my secretary, Dorothy Catlett, had left there before my recent homecoming from teaching at Bucknell University. The young men all seemed glad to be able to do something for Ray.

I pointed out the small black metal box at one end of the granite bench that flanks our gravesite and told them how it had been designed and made by prisoners in Oregon, Ray's birth state. Mary Beth Chenier, who was teaching both Ray's and my poetry at Shutter Creek Correctional Institution in North Bend, had asked me to deliver a poem of hers to the grave. It was raining when I had placed the poem under one of the stones left from my trips to the beach below the gravesite. I wrote Ms. Chenier that I was often sorry there wasn't a little box where one could leave poems and messages. She shared this remark with her students at the prison and they asked if they might construct such a box.

Their wish led Dick Catlett, my secretary's husband, to sketch the gravesite and take measurements. We suggested placement, the materials to be used, and Dick obtained permission from the cemetery officials to affix the box to the gravesite. Since February of 1996 it has received many poems, letters, business cards, photographs, and tokens of remembrance, the most recent being a sand dollar with a note responding to Ray's poem "Gravy," which is etched in granite on the small stone between our stones. The note read:

> 7–14–98,
> Me too, —gravy.
> And I'm grateful.
> Thanks again.
> J.K.

As these messages accumulate I periodically remove them to plastic casings in a binder stored at Ridge House where Ray and I lived until his death. My sister, Stephanie Barber, and I discussed whether the box ought to be equipped with a lock. The design had included the possibility of one. We decided against it, since that might possibly encourage someone to break into the box. Also, part of the visitors' pleasure, we guessed, would undoubtedly be in reading Ray's mail!

The gravesite itself, since the black granite stones were set in summer of 1990, has become a place of pilgrimage for writers and readers alike. Lovers go there informally to swear their vows; and Ray's poem "Late Fragment" has been requested for inscription on other graves, as well as for use at weddings. The editor of *Poetry Ireland* recently sought it for inclusion in an issue of *Most Loved Poems*. These few words seem to unite the living and the dead. I am always happy to learn how many people can quote the poem by heart:

> And did you get what
> You wanted from this life, even so?
> I did.
> And what did you want?
> To call myself beloved, to feel myself
> Beloved on the earth.

The following day, as filming began with my new Italian friends, Yozo asked, "When do you miss Ray most?" The question startled me. It seemed to assume an expression of grieving that no longer existed, as if I might be stopped in time back there in 1988. I realized that I had ceased to miss Ray as in those early soul-rending ways. While I thought how to speak to this question, I marked for myself how far I'd come from Ray's death, remembering how I'd been unable for months to sleep in Ray's and my bed, how I'd fallen asleep on the couch each night watching old movies in the room where he had died. Every article of clothing, every casual scrap of paper with his handwriting singed my consciousness.

Even as I sketched a few personal details for an Italian audience, I realized there was no way, except in my poetry perhaps, for anyone to know more than the surface of what I had experienced. Talking could only point, not touch. In respect for the entirety of that "missing," I had resigned my professorship at Syracuse in 1989 and come home to Port

Angeles so I could give a period of time fully over to discovering the radically changed circumstances of my life.

But at the time of Yozo's question, ten years after Ray's death, the nature of how I missed Ray had metamorphosed. He'd become a pervasive hum, a clarity of purpose throughout my days and nights—so those early javelins, of reaching for his actual presence and finding him gone, no longer startled me or gave pang—sensations I re-created in poems such as "Now That I'm Never Alone" from *Moon Crossing Bridge.*

I felt a bit guilty, acknowledging this on camera, realizing I could no longer claim present devastation—rather that I lived otherwise, in a calm nimbus of confident self-ghosting, yet also in some inexplicable, matter-of-fact radiance of accompaniment by Ray's presence.

Our culture awards respect to sad drama, not to the steady accomplishment of the self made whole. Yozo's question, so considerately asked, also made me see how stopped in time I must be for those who come now to Ray largely as myth, as the great dead American writer. There was nothing to do but set the record straight, to acknowledge that, although Ray claims an important part of my attention each day, my life has gone on. I must earn a living. I teach. I continue my writing on many levels—fiction, poetry, translations, essays, art criticism, nonfiction travel pieces, and film. For periods when I'm not teaching I'm even able for correspondence. I look after my eighty-four-year-old mother. I make new friends, visit some I've known for thirty years, as time allows.

Ray has said that he entered his second life when we met. But Ray was my third life, and since his death I have been living my fourth life. For the past three years my life has included the Irish painter Josie Gray from Sligo County, Ireland. This relationship means that I am no longer alone for the five to six months of each year when Josie can be with me. I share a vital joy in encouraging the making of his art and in having his expertise as a storyteller close at hand. Beyond that, there is the witnessing and exuberance again of yet another ongoing discovery of love embodied.

Because Josie and I met many years after each of our mates had died, there is a sense of our having absorbed a primary loss, of speaking the same language—one that values what *was,* carries forward what *is* and gives sure fresh ground to the new making. I feel fortunate in having had seven years alone, for this allowed me to establish a grounding in how I would continue to carry Ray and his work, while giving my own life a strong footing. It might now occur to those who see me simply as a mothballed extension of Ray that I have been alive and fervent all along in my own right.

The Italian filmmakers seemed to feel it was okay for me not to be the ever-yearning widow of Ray. They had a fluid *caméra vérité* willingness for the truth which put me at ease. They were interested in finding out how things really were with me. Certainly I had now lost all chance of being a tragic heroine, but perhaps something more true to Ray and to life was being put before them. For, just as Ray's death had brought out the ghost in me, it had also caused me to cleave to life, and I could feel their respect for that. Giuseppe Ungaretti in his poem "Deathwatch" says it:

> Never have I hugged
> Life
> So hard.

When Ray's *All of Us,* his collected poems, was published in England by Harvill Press in fall of 1996, it was a terribly lonely time for me. Yozo's question called up that occasion. I had imagined how exuberantly Ray would have welcomed the book. He was so proud to be a poet, and I had celebrated and contributed to that love. On his gravestone the word "poet" comes first: "Poet, Short Story Writer, Essayist." To be sure of complimenting Ray, all one had to do was admire his poetry—that won his heart.

Once our mutual friends began to call to say how much they loved his collected poems, Ray's absence was softened and acknowledged. My colleagues at Whitman College also made an occasion of the book and I gave a reading from it on campus.

It has been a happy, if overdue, occasion that Ray's former editor of *A New Path to the Waterfall,* Gary Fisketjon, recently published the *Collected Poems* in America. The first and favorable review of *All of Us* in the July 27, 1998, issue of *Publisher's*

Weekly makes mention of "a marked turn toward the hopeful," an aspect of Ray's writing being given more attention in the poems, as in commentary about the stories from *Cathedral* on.

This American publication of Ray's *Collected Poems* bears out something I predicted in my introduction to *A New Path to the Waterfall,* that Ray's poetry would finally earn its place alongside his fiction, instead of being regarded as a lesser venture. I feel certain now that it will achieve full critical appreciation and the readership it deserves. Strange that the book had to appear first in England, but perhaps it is indicative of the conglomerate publishing malaise in America that we need others, in Ray's case the British, the Japanese, and the Italians, to tell us what matters in our own literature!

As I write, for instance, the BBC is broadcasting seven of Ray's short stories to honor the tenth anniversary of his death. Irish Radio in Dublin is broadcasting a tribute with me reading two poems from *Portable Kisses.* Riccardo Duranti, Ray's and my Italian translator, and Marco Cassini, Ray's Italian publisher, write me from Rome: "the anniversary was announced by a flurry of phone calls from magazines here that are publishing articles to celebrate it."

Another incidental but lovely salute from the English is the development and naming of the Raymond Carver Rose by Peter Beales, initiated by Ray's Harvill publisher, Christopher MacLehose. It joins those Ray and I planted at Ridge House in the months before his death. It remains a mystery why the deer forage on all but these roses!

The Japanese have an awareness of Raymond Carver's writing—poetry and fiction—which outstrips any other nation's, including our own, thanks to Haruki Murakami, the esteemed Japanese novelist and story writer who is also Ray's translator. Ray is translated into more than twenty languages, but the Japanese have access to a handsomely boxed complete multi-volume set of Carver. He is even taught to schoolchildren as they learn English in hand-sized, big-print editions.

When our mutual publisher flew me first class to Tokyo upon the Japanese publication of my *The Lover of Horses,* I was surprised by the large audiences, by the enthusiasm of the media for both my work and Ray's. I was put up at the Imperial Hotel in a sumptuous room near the Imperial Palace. My editor, Norio Irie, escorted me by train to Kyoto to meet Jyakucho Setouchi, the Zen nun and novelist, who has established a temple on the Sagano side of the Togetsu Bridge for comforting and sustaining women bereft by love. She knew both Ray's work and mine, and our conversation, about life, art, and love, appeared in the leading women's magazine in Japan. Our conversation remains a hallowed event for me where another grief-gate opened wide and I walked through.

The visit to Japan was very rewarding for me, but, because Ray wasn't with me, the beautiful welcome I met was inevitably bittersweet. Our proposed trip together in 1987 had been canceled because of his lung operation. The long bed Haruki Murakami had had specially built for Ray's six-foot, two-inch frame would never be used by us. I think of that unused bed as a strange artifact of our forever-changed circumstances.

Haruki's gifts to Ray have continued in his translations, which have fostered an ardent Japanese readership of Ray's work. There has also been Haruki's and his wife Yoko's friendship, which is a continuing consolation. They have spent time in my Sky House and I have visited them during their sojourn in Princeton. Haruki and I have read and deeply received each other's work. I have valued his respect for my fiction, his sense that I have found my voice there since Ray's death.

Speaking of Ray's Japanese readers reminds me of an incident where Ray and I were crucially present for a young Japanese college professor. This woman had been contemplating suicide when she had a dream in which she stood on a chair with a rope around her neck. A knock came at the door. When she said nothing, the door swung slowly open and Ray stepped into the room. He grinned a shy grin she had seen in a picture of him on the back of a book, and said "Hi!" Needless to say she couldn't continue her dream-suicide after that, but had to lift the rope from her neck and climb down from the chair to greet her guest.

The young woman had previously written to me. At the time her letter arrived, I had fallen ill with pneumonia. Nonetheless,

I had sensed her turmoil, and had managed a reply from my sickbed. The day after her dream, my answer arrived in Nagoya. Its timing and message confirmed, along with Ray's appearance, her release from the depressed state that had been leading her toward suicide.

This is not the first time I'd felt, without surprise, and quite beyond any New Age monkey business, as if Ray and I were somehow linked, each side of the grave, to affect lives. Another memorable occasion began in 1992 just as an unexpectedly heavy snowfall began to descend on Port Angeles. I was staying alone at Sky House, watching the fluffy wads laze past the windows, then melt into the Strait of Juan de Fuca. I had just begun to relish the fact that I was freed of my nightly errands to the post office, to my secretary, and then to Mother's to cook dinner. It was a rare contemplative alcove arranged by the weather.

Suddenly, a loud brisk knock came at my door. Since I seldom receive guests at Sky House, I wondered who it could be, and under these conditions. When I opened the door I found two young Japanese men, one of whom extended a black binder rather shyly. He began immediately to apologize for his unannounced arrival, but explained that the pages I now held were about Ray, that he'd done his dissertation on him in Tokyo. The snow was falling thickly, making the encounter surreal. I understood that for the young man, this was something like the presentation of a holy grail!

"Come in," I said, taking possession of the grail, then gesturing for them to remove their snow-encrusted shoes. They had borrowed their father's car and had worried the entire way lest they have an accident. They were clearly exhausted and relieved I'd taken them in.

I served tea, then suggested we call their parents to let them know they were safe. I spoke to their mother and said they mustn't try to return that night, that I'd look after them. Their names were Kanta and Shingo Yoshiike. Kanta was the writer of the dissertation. Shingo, who volunteered that his name meant "keen sense of smell," was there to lend moral support to his older brother. I commented that, with a keen sense of smell, he would always be able to visit his childhood. After conversation about their lives attending school in Tokyo, I suggested we walk to Ridge House. There we would find sleeping quarters and also food for the evening meal.

We made the trek in knee-deep snow up the Morse Creek Valley, past a fresh clear-cut softened by the lush snowfall. I had the sensation of dream-walking. I kept thinking of Ray, of how astonished he would have been, had he been alive to receive these young men. "Can you believe that!" he'd have said—"All the way from Tokyo to see *me!*" In fact, I believe those were exactly his words on the occasion when Haruki Murakami and Yoko had visited us at Sky House in 1986. How astonished he would be to know how many, from how far, have come since then!

Although I was clearly a stand-in for Ray, as I had been many times before—others having arrived from as far away as the Czech Republic, New Zealand, and Australia—I felt very glad to be able to welcome the Yoshiike brothers on Ray's behalf. Their sudden arrival and the snow-deep scene were reminiscent of a Chekhov short story—hunters marooned in a hut during a snowstorm.

No sooner did we reach Ridge House than stories began to flow from my guests. We had moved into Ray's comfortable large study with its leather couch and chairs. Before long the conversation turned to love. Kanta confessed that he had lost his first love recently to another, and this led to my recounting my "first love" experience. Then I told the story of how Ray and I had met. It had been the *second* meeting, not the first, I said, which had joined us. Five months after that second encounter in August of 1978 we'd begun to make a life together on January 1, 1979. I think I was trying to suggest the unpredictable readiness of love to either fail or succeed. Kanta was suffering from the loss of his love as if there would never be another. He was both right and wrong. I could see that this dashingly handsome young man was destined to unintentionally break many hearts himself.

One of the gifts of these encounters with Ray's admirers has been the volunteering of confidences. People would always tell Ray their innermost feelings. Maybe I also have developed that quality of listening, to a greater degree than before, from standing where he might have stood.

Kanta's remarks in my guest book preserve the childlike delight of our encounter:

What we Did:

1. You opened the door for us.
2. You showed us your house.
3. You had trouble finding your shoes.
4. We walked in the snow and,
5. We talked a lot!
6. We ate pancakes, chicken, and vegetables
7. Snow, snow, snow!

Shingo wrote: "You were more than kind to both of us. We were just two strangers to you and didn't really deserve this much treatment. But talking with you and listening to your story enchanted me. It made me think about my living a little more than I used to. Well, I'll write you after we safely get to Seattle, so see you then."

I felt close to Ray's essential tenderness of heart, with those two young people, sitting in his study, the fireplace cozily ablaze, above the snow-laden valley. The next morning I invited Kanta to sit down at Ray's Smith Corona and type a note to Ray, as had several other visitors and friends, including Haruki Murakami. It was an offhanded way of allowing them to imagine Ray "knew" in some sense that they were there. What Kanta wrote seems to speak for so many young readers who have come to Ray's work after his death. It reads in part: "You may not know me, but I know you. . . . Thank you very much, Mr. Carver. You are my, believe it or not, you are my hero." It is dated December 28, 1992.

Ray *had* become a modern-day hero, someone to look up to, a survivor, companionable to his readers, someone upon whose doorstep they might appear in the middle of a snowstorm and be taken in.

I had seen to that reception, as I have seen to so many welcomes for journalists, filmmakers, photographers, translators, and readers alike. Each year of the past nine, Dorothy Catlett and I have answered over seven-thousand pieces of correspondence, much of it dealing with Ray's work. I keep a special binder for poems written to him. There is a shelf in his study, above the books he read as a child, where dissertations on his work are accumulating.

One of my great pleasures during the past two years has been to teach Ray's stories and poems. I had heard from our friend, the poet Henry Carlile, who teaches at Portland State University, what fun it was to teach Ray's work. As the Edward F. Arnold Chair at Whitman College in 1996, I decided to offer a course entitled "Behind the Scenes with Raymond Carver." The class, much to my surprise, drew a large enrollment— sixty-five students. This meant I had to do most of the talking.

A prime objective was to trounce the simpleminded epithet of "minimalist" which had mistakenly become affixed to Ray's style in universities around the country and indeed, the world. The term was a shorthand that sidestepped the deep, generous writer Ray had become. It gave teachers a buzzword, which just didn't do justice. I knew Henry Carlile, as well as other professors around America, such as Fred Moramarco in San Diego, William Stull at Hartford, and Robert Coles at Harvard, had been doing their share to debunk the term.

Pasternak writes in a letter to Marina Tsvetayeva that the value of a writer "is determined by a third dimension—depth; it is this that raises the text in a vertical line off the page, and, most important, separates the book from the author." It was this third dimension we began to explore in my course. I compared versions of stories so the students could see that Ray finalized his stories in *Where I'm Calling From* toward the ample versions—rejecting, for instance, "The Bath"—a Gordon Lish–edited version of "A Small Good Thing"; similarly he had rejected the facile and insupportable ending Lish had affixed to "So Much Water So Close to Home" in the version of *What We Talk about When We Talk about Love*. Ray had also restored this story's length in *Where I'm Calling From*.

I set the record straight, that although "The Bath" was *published* first, it *was not the initial version*. Rather, "A Small Good Thing" had been written first. I never allow "The Bath" to be published in anthologies of Ray's work at home or abroad, but only inside the book *What We Talk about When We Talk about Love*. Ray felt the book, even at the time of its publication, did not represent the main thrust of his writing, nor his true pulse and instinct in the work. He had, in fact, even begged Gordon Lish, to no avail, not to publish the book in this misbegotten version.

In order to help the students see how Ray thought of his writing, I read aloud passages from his letters. One, written during the crucial time just after he'd achieved sobriety and begun to write again while living with me in 1979, told how he considered his writing what he had of religion and soul-making. I spoke of the fact that he had not written for four years because of alcoholism and the chaos in his life prior to our life together. I made the class aware of his valiance, his comeback from alcoholism.

Rather than simply asking the students to write papers, I invited them to invent creative projects concerning Ray's work. The response was: handmade books, contrapuntal recitations, maps, original songs, dances, plays, and even the documentation of a student's pilgrimage to the gravesite during spring break. Tom Luce, a freshman at the time, put together a web site (http://www.WHITMAN.edu/offices_departments/english /carver/thispage.html). It is, at this writing, one of three sites on the Internet addressing Ray's work. Because of Tom's industry and imagination, his site is easily the most complete and authoritative. It was recently selected as one of the ten most educational sites on the Internet by the BBC. Besides providing a chronology of Ray's life, by William Stull, and a listing of Carver sites in Port Angeles and Yakima, it also gives informal photographs and a forum called "Why I Love Ray," where readers can say how Ray's work and his life affect them. There have been queries from Croatia, Japan, South America, Spain, Ireland, Canada, and India. Tom has had approximately twelve thousand visitors since the site's inception in spring 1997 to July 1998.

The frequency of the site's usage is one indication of the high level of interest Ray's work still maintains for readers around the world. He continues to be included in many university curriculums as one of America's foremost practitioners of the short story. His stories are continually anthologized internationally. The short-story form itself, which made a comeback in the mid-1980s, thanks to Ray's work and influence, thrives, despite much clamor about the difficulty of getting volumes of short stories published. Nearly a collection a week arrives in my mail! The short story is more than alive and well in America. It is vital and has a steady, enthusiastic readership.

It's staggering really to look back over these years and see how much has happened in regard to Ray's posthumous publications. My own part in this would have been plenty to keep me busy. When I met Valerie Eliot, T. S. Eliot's widow, in Sligo summer of 1997, I saw how it is possible, as a literary widow, to give oneself over entirely to the absent presence and probably be quite satisfied. Although I have taken care not to do this, I am proud to have devoted an important part of my energies to Ray.

I have written seven introductions to his work, which include two consequential volumes of poems. I introduced Ray's uncollected work *No Heroics, Please;* a book of photographs, *Carver Country;* and wrote a foreword to the Robert Altman–Frank Barhydt screenplay *Short Cuts,* based on nine of Ray's stories. I've also written introductions to two Japanese editions and a Slovenian edition of his stories. My essays, introductions, interviews, and letters concerning Ray's work have appeared variously. The letters I wrote to Robert Altman as we worked on the film *Short Cuts* are important in understanding how I related to that endeavor.

All of the above writing for Ray has been done *in addition* to my own writing: seven books, two reprints, three limited-edition books, and numerous interviews, which I carefully hand edit. Included in these publications were four books of poetry, a book of short fiction, and my collaboration with the poet Liliana Ursu and Adam Sorkin on a translation of this Rumanian poet's first book in English, *The Sky behind the Forest,* which won a translation award in England and was short-listed for another prize in Oxford.

My fiction and poetry have been translated during this period into German, French, Dutch, Swedish, Italian, Japanese, and Catalonian. In addition, I consulted gratis for three years with Robert Altman during the various phases of making *Short Cuts,* a film which rightly received high critical acclaim and which saw to it that Ray's readership entered a wider phase, not only in the American consciousness, but internationally. I also consulted on four theater productions. I participated and consulted on seven radio and television documentaries about Ray (listed on the Tom Luce web site). Presently I have been advising Vicki Lloid of Whitman College on a dance production. She directed Ray's and my jointly written one-act play entitled *The Favor*—published in full for the first time in *Philosophy and Literature*.

This is only the briefest sketch of my involvement with Ray's work. When I think that I've also continued to teach, either part or full time—some of that teaching on a boat cruising the San Juans!—I'm certain that the strength to carry it all has come in good part from the excellent help and companioning of my secretary, Dorothy, who recently retired after nine years.

Dorothy is responsible for helping me establish an extensive archive of voice and videotapes, photograph and copyright files. She also organized the cataloging of Ray's and my joint and separate libraries. All this she accomplished along with the daily coordination of meetings, interviews, travel, and the publicity for readings and book tours. Her patient reading, attentive editing and preparing of manuscripts, both for Ray's work and my own, her coordination of my translation work, and her sure judgment in all matters, personal and professional, have undoubtedly been an enormous factor in the accuracy and abundance of the accomplishments, not to mention the equanimity with which I could work. Because of Dorothy and her husband Dick's genuine love for Ray and me, life has remained more than livable. I think the fact that she knew and revered Ray was important to the evolution of his continuing place in my life. She also helped me keep my balance when concerns toward Ray's affairs became unwieldy at times. "Your work is important too," she often reminded me, and then she helped clear the space for it.

Not without considerable struggle, these ten years have become an extremely fertile time for my writing and teaching. I was honored this May to receive an Honorary Doctorate of Humane Letters from Whitman College for my teaching and writing. It reminded me of how lucky I am to have two extraordinarily satisfying vocations: writer and teacher. When I accepted the honorary doctorate, I remembered Ray receiving his honorary doctorate at Hartford University and how gratified and humbly blessed he'd been. It was a joy inside the joy, a resonance behind the gift I received.

In spring 1998 my teaching carried me to Lewisburg, Pennsylvania, where I was Poet-in-Residence for the Stadler Poetry Center at Bucknell University. I taught undergraduates poetry writing in the country's only center expressly devoted to undergraduates. I feel very grateful in having been able to have these important forums for my own ideas about poetry and writing.

While at Whitman and Bucknell, I carried Ray's presence and work forward in my stories about him and in course offerings. The students had the benefit of someone who'd seen Ray's work as it arrived, straight from the pen. I learned from their reactions to his work and enjoyed how they came to admire the man inside it.

On my right hand I still wear Ray's moss agate stone, mounted in silver, which I bought for him in Oregon. It is next to our wedding band. On my wrist is his watch, for which it is now hard to find batteries. I also wear a red garnet from Josie Gray. On the other hand is the lapis friendship ring from Ray and another friendship ring with bands of black onyx from Mihnea, Liliana Ursu's son. If these adornments are any indication— life is full. Both the dead and the living are represented. For fidelity's sake, my maternal grandmother's wedding band, with fifty years of marriage, is next to my own wedding band.

I know Ray would be very happy at how I've continued to honor and enlarge the reach of his work. There was a reason he left this pleasure and privilege entrusted fully to me. He'd also be glad I've managed to attend to his work while bringing my own writing into substantial fruition over these ten years, for he was my best protector and advocate.

I recall the phrase Willis Barnstone applied to Dino Campana, an Italian poet I admire: "a nightshine in the memory." Ray is a nightshine to my soul, as it enacts daily what is central to my very being. I look forward to a lifetime of discovering new ways to bring him with me personally, and also toward his readers, while pursuing my own writing and my life.

In the poems I am presently writing I am interested, partly because of my inner dialogue since Ray, in a riffling of surface, keeping the undercurrent dark and strong—reflecting that breaking off which is truth outside saying, and which extends its porch of silence. Because of Ray's death and the new life that flows from it, I need pain rightly cloaked, so its wrists are more bare. Joy is there too, aplenty. "How glad I am you got to be happy!" I say to him in the heart-chapel, where our speaking goes on, and goes on. No, I can't tell you how he speaks, except that I am as sure of it as moonlight is sure of itself, when it takes the field. There is no way, no way ever, to stop the conversation with Ray—my bluest shadow, my white star of belonging.

I Asked That a Prayer

be offered at his grave,
although many of us were awkward about prayer,
and it seemed exposed to do so, to pray
there on the cliffside above the Straits.
I remembered how he once asked friends to offer
prayer at a meal
because he knew they did it
when he wasn't there.

This was the tenth anniversary
of his death. I already had my eyes closed,
because that's how I learned to pray
as a child, and that's how
I pray. This made a voice of my friend and
of the world. It said: the prayer will be a moment
of silence in which we each
offer up a prayer.

Silence then.
And, while we were in the middle of it
wind from the Straits rushed
like a hand over the chimes above the stone.
I thought: "he's here," and so did
everyone else. We even spoke about it
afterwards. Let ourselves know.
That's how he came to be with us.
Through a moment that was its own
speaking. I heard all of him in that broken-open
eternity. The bright metal
of chimes fumbling the sea air. Then

the wild precipice of peace
in which the earth itself
seemed to fall away in the silence.
Then the silence
after the silence.

—Tess Gallagher

Major Works by Raymond Carver
and Tess Gallagher

Raymond Carver

Call If You Need Me: The Uncollected Fiction and Prose. With a foreword by Tess Gallagher. London: Harvill Press, 2000.

All of Us: The Collected Poems. With an introduction by Tess Gallagher. London: Harvill Press, 1996; New York: Alfred A. Knopf, 1998; New York: Vintage Contemporaries, 2000.

Short Cuts: Selected Stories. With an introduction by Robert Altman. New York: Vintage Contemporaries, 1993.

No Heroics, Please: Uncollected Writings. With a foreword by Tess Gallagher. London: Harvill Press, 1991; New York: Vintage Contemporaries, 1992.

Carver Country: The World of Raymond Carver. With an introduction by Tess Gallagher and photographs by Bob Adelman. New York: Scribner's, 1990; New York: Arcade Publishing, 1994.

A New Path to the Waterfall. With an introduction by Tess Gallagher. New York: Atlantic Monthly Press, 1989.

Where I'm Calling From: New and Selected Stories. New York: Atlantic Monthly Press, 1988; New York: Vintage Contemporaries, 1989.

Ultramarine. New York: Random House, 1986; New York: Vintage Books, 1987.

Where Water Comes Together with Other Water. New York: Random House, 1985; New York: Vintage Books, 1986.

This list of the major works of Raymond Carver and Tess Gallagher was compiled by William L. Stull and Maureen P. Carroll.

Cathedral. New York: Alfred A. Knopf, 1983; New York: Vintage Contemporaries, 1989.

Fires: Essays, Poems, Stories. Santa Barbara: Capra Press, 1983; expanded, New York: Vintage Contemporaries, 1989.

What We Talk about When We Talk about Love. New York: Alfred A. Knopf, 1981; New York: Vintage Contemporaries, 1989.

Furious Seasons and Other Stories. Santa Barbara: Capra Press, 1977. Out of print.

Will You Please Be Quiet, Please? New York: McGraw-Hill, 1976; New York: Vintage Contemporaries, 1992.

Tess Gallagher

Soul Barnacles: Ten More Years with Ray. Ann Arbor: University of Michigan Press, 2000.

At the Owl Woman Saloon. New York: Scribner, 1997; Scribner Paperback, 1998.

My Black Horse: New and Selected Poems. Newcastle upon Tyne, England: Bloodaxe Books, 1995. Distributed in the U.S. by Dufour Editions.

Portable Kisses. Seattle: Sea Pen Press, 1978; Santa Barbara: Capra Press, 1992, expanded 1994; Newcastle upon Tyne, England: Bloodaxe Books, 1996. Distributed in the U.S. by Dufour Editions.

Moon Crossing Bridge. Saint Paul: Graywolf Press, 1992.

Amplitude: New and Selected Poems. Saint Paul: Graywolf Press, 1987.

The Lover of Horses and Other Stories. New York: Harper & Row, 1986; Saint Paul: Graywolf Press, 1992.

A Concert of Tenses: Essays on Poetry. Ann Arbor: University of Michigan Press, 1986.

Willingly. Port Townsend, Wash.: Graywolf Press, 1984. Out of print.

Under Stars. Port Townsend, Wash.: Graywolf Press, 1978; Saint Paul: Graywolf Press, 1988.

Instructions to the Double. Port Townsend, Wash.: Graywolf
 Press, 1976; Pittsburgh: Carnegie-Mellon University
 Press, 1997.

Raymond Carver and Tess Gallagher

Dostoevsky: A Screenplay. Santa Barbara: Capra Press, 1985.
 Out of print.

UNDER DISCUSSION
David Lehman, General Editor
Donald Hall, Founding Editor

Volumes in the Under Discussion series collect reviews and essays about individual poets. The series is concerned with contemporary American and English poets about whom the consensus has not yet been formed and the final vote has not been taken. Titles in the series include: